COMPLETE
JAPANESE
EXPRESSION
GUIDE

THE
COMPLETE
JAPANESE
EXPRESSION
GUIDE

Mizue Sasaki

CHARLES E. TUTTLE COMPANY
Rutland, Vermont & Tokyo, Japan

Published by the Charles E. Tuttle Company, Inc.
of Rutland, Vermont, and Tokyo, Japan
with editorial offices at
2-6 Suido 1-chome, Bunkyo-ku, Tokyo 112

Library of Congress Catalog Card No. 92-61821
International Standard Book No. 0-8048-1689-1

First edition, 1993

Printed in Japan

CONTENTS

INTRODUCTION   7

A GUIDE TO JAPANESE EXPRESSIONS   9

A LIST OF ADDITIONAL EXPRESSIONS   311

INTRODUCTION

In the past decade, there has been a sharp increase in the number of foreigners studying Japanese, and consequently, good textbooks covering all levels of the language have begun to appear. However, these textbooks tend to avoid the use of idiomatic expressions, which is unfortunate because these expressions are used very frequently in daily language.

Studying Japanese without coming to terms with the use of idiomatic expressions is like preparing a dish but forgetting to add salt. Idiomatic expressions are used all the time in Japanese, perhaps more often than in English. They appear in newspaper and magazine headlines and of course play an important role in literature.

When I was requested by the *Asahi Evening News* to write a weekly column on learning the Japanese language, I knew immediately that I wanted to direct my attention to idioms. This column has proven very successful, and has now run for many years.

When I had written about three hundred articles for my column, the Charles E. Tuttle Company approached me with an offer to write a book on idiomatic expressions. So, I went about preparing a text that would both teach idiomatic expressions to foreigners as well as allow Japanese people to learn how idiomatic phrases in Japanese are rendered in English.

In this book, I have chosen three hundred commonly used expressions and devoted one page to each. Each expression is introduced in a situational dialogue so that the reader can understand the context in which the expression is used. Then a brief explanation of the expression's meaning, derivation, and related forms is given, followed by additional example sentences that give various usages of the expression.

I tried in this book to provide examples of the expressions using natural, everyday conversation. A difficult aspect of Japanese is the different styles of language used by different classes of people, such as superiors and subordinates or men and women. Furthermore, different situations demand different language. For instance, the formal atmosphere of a wedding reception requires different expressions and wording than the casual talk between friends at an informal get-together. I have introduced a number of situations in the text—for example, conversations between department chiefs and subordinates, husbands and wives, and friends—in the hope that readers will be able to appreciate the different styles of languages used in various situations.

Learning idiomatic expressions does not involve just the language but also the culture. It comes as no surprise that derivations of idioms draw from diverse areas, such as Buddhist sayings, plays, sumo, gambling, and the samurai tradition. Those who know about the origins of the expressions might therefore appreciate Japanese culture that much more.

I wish to thank the following people for their help with the publication of this book: the staff of the *Asahi Evening News* and the readers of my column, who drew my attention to the importance of idiomatic expressions in Japanese conversation; the people who helped me with the translation of this text: John Millen, Paul Gilson, Patrick Codd, Timothy Phelan, and James Spahn, whose kind cooperation and encouragement contributed to the compilation of this work; and to the staff of the Charles E. Tuttle Company.

A GUIDE TO
JAPANESE
EXPRESSIONS

abura o shiboru

油を絞る

reprimand, reproach

TOMODACHI 1:

Dō shimashita ka?

TOMODACHI 2:

Kaisha no kuruma o butsukete, buchō ni abura o shiboraremashita yo.

FRIEND 1:

What's the matter?

FRIEND 2:

I had an accident with the company car and the department chief really gave me hell.

Abura o shiboru, literally "to squeeze out oil," means to severely reproach a person. When extracting oil from sesame seeds, rapeseeds, or soybeans, they are crushed, squeezed, and thoroughly pulverized. This process is similar to that of severely scolding someone.

EXAMPLES

1. *Shukudai o wasurete, sensei ni abura o shiborareta.*
   I forgot my homework and was chewed out by the teacher.
2. *Kare wa saikin, namakete iru node, sukoshi abura o shibotte okō.*
   Lately he's become lazy, so let's have a little talk with him.
3. *Kaigi de okashi na hatsugen o shite, buchō ni abura o shiborareta.*
   The department chief gave me a sound scolding because I said something out-of-line in the meeting.
4. *Anata ga sensei ni abura o shiborareru no wa atarimae da.*
   The teacher has good reason to rake you over the coals.
5. *Suzuki Sensei, uchi no kodomo, sukoshi abura o shibotte yatte kudasai.*
   Professor Suzuki, please give our child a bit of a talking-to.

abura o uru

油を売る

idle away one's time

SENPAI:

Kaeri ga osokatta ne. Doko de abura o utte itan' da?

KŌHAI:

Abura nanka utte imasen. Chanto shigoto o shite imashita yo.

SENIOR:

You're late getting back. Where were you loafing off?

JUNIOR:

I wasn't loafing off! I've been busy working.

Abura o uru means either to pass the time by engaging in idle talk or to waste time while at work or while attending to something. During the Edo period, people bought lantern oil from wandering merchants. When the oil containers became low, the oil would become viscous and thus took longer to pour. When this happened, the merchants would engage the housewives in light conversation. From this came the meaning of idling away one's time.

EXAMPLES

1. *Doko de abura o utte ita no desu ka?*
   Where have you been loafing?
2. *Konna tokoro de abura o utte inaide, shigoto o shinasai.*
   Stop shooting the breeze—here, of all places—and get back to work!
3. *Kare wa doko de abura o utte iru no ka, mada kaeranai.*
   He's still not back. Where can he be loafing off?
4. *Anata ni wa, watashi ga abura o utte iru yō ni mierun' desu ka?*
   Does it look to you as if I'm loafing off?
5. *Kanojo wa shigoto-chū ni muda-banashi o shite, abura bakari utte iru.*
   She does nothing but gossip at work.

ago de tsukau
顎で使う
boss around

OTTO:

Oi, soko no shinbun, totte kurenai ka? Ā, megane mo.

TSUMA:

Hito no koto, ago de tsukawanaide, jibun de nasattara ii noni.

HUSBAND:

Hey, would you get me that newspaper over there? Oh, and my glasses too.

WIFE:

Instead of bossing other people around, you should do it yourself.

Ago de tsukau, literally "to use the chin," means to order someone around or to have someone at one's beck and call. This expression comes from the way people tend to stick out their chins when ordering others to do something. Another expression using *ago* is *ago o dasu,* which means to burn oneself out.

EXAMPLES

1. *Shachō wa itsumo, shain o ago de tsukatte iru.*
   The boss is always ordering the employees around.
2. *Hito o ago de tsukaeru tachiba de wa arimasen.*
   You are in no position to be ordering people around.
3. *Kare ni ago de tsukawareru yō de wa, o-shimai da.*
   It's all over once he starts ordering you around.
4. *Kare no ago de hito o tsukau taido ni wa, gaman dekinai.*
   I just can't put up with the way he orders people about.
5. *Kachō wa buka o ago de tsukatte iru.*
   The section chief orders his subordinates around relentlessly.

aiso ga tsukiru

愛想が尽きる

lose patience with, lose interest in

MUSUKO:

Otōsan, boku, arubaito-saki, kubi ni natta yo.

CHICHIOYA:

Chikoku bakari shita kara da. Shachō mo kitto omae ni aiso ga tsukitan' da yo.

SON:

Dad, I've been fired from my part-time job.

FATHER:

It's because you were always late. You must have tried your boss's patience to the limit.

Aiso (affability) is a shortened form of *aisō,* and together with *tsukiru* (use up) implies completely losing patience or interest. Other forms of this expression are *aiso o tsukasu* (be fed up), *aiso o tsukasareru* (be given up by someone), and *aiso-zukashi* (spiteful remarks).

EXAMPLES

1. *Uso bakari tsuku node, kare ni wa aiso ga tsukimashita.*
   He's such an habitual liar. I've had it with him.
2. *Kare wa, koibito ni aiso o tsukasareta yō desu yo.*
   It appears that his girlfriend has lost patience with him.
3. *Anna hito nara, kanojo ga aiso o tsukasu no mo tōzen desu.*
   It's only to be expected that she'd lose interest in someone like that.
4. *Shomin o wasureta seijika ni wa, sukkari aiso ga tsukite shimatta.*
   I'm tired of politicians who don't care about the public.
5. *Kanojo wa uwaki suru otto ni aiso ga tsuki, rikon suru koto ni shita.*
   She was fed up with her unfaithful husband, so she divorced him.

aizuchi o utsu

相槌を打つ

chime in

BUCHŌ:

Kono yō ni susumetai to omoun' da ga.

BUKA:

Ē, sore de iin' ja nai deshō ka?

BUCHŌ:

Sakki kara, kimi wa aizuchi o utsu dake de, jibun no iken o iwanai ne.

DEPARTMENT CHIEF:

This is the kind of direction I'd like to move in.

SUBORDINATE:

Yes, I guess that would be fine.

DEPARTMENT CHIEF:

You've just been echoing me and not giving me your own opinions on the matter.

Aizuchi o utsu, literally "a set of hammers striking," originally described when an apprentice blacksmith worked with the master and they would coordinate their hammer strokes, one striking after the other. Thus, the expression refers to tactful responses that keep a conversation moving, phrases like "I see" and "really?"

EXAMPLES

1. *Kare wa hito no hanashi ni aizuchi o utte bakari iru.*

   All he does when you talk to him is agree with what you say.

2. *Dōshite, aizuchi bakari utsun' desu ka?*

   Why do you only echo what I'm saying?

3. *Ē? Kare ga aizuchi o uttan' desu ka?*

   What? You mean you actually got a response out of him?

4. *Kare ni aizuchi o utaseru to wa, kimi mo sugoi ne.*

   It really is impressive how you are able to get him to respond.

akaji ni naru

赤字になる

be in the red

OTTO:

Kozukai, mō sukoshi agete kurenai ka?

TSUMA:

Ie no rōn ya kyōikuhi ga kasande, maitsuki akaji na no. Totemo muri yo.

HUSBAND:

Can't you give me a little more pocket money?

WIFE:

With the way the house loan and school expenses have been mounting up, we're in the red every month. There's just no way.

Akaji ni naru means to be in the red; in other words, when one's expenses are more than one's earnings. The expression comes from the practice of filling in the deficit column in account books with a red pen.

EXAMPLES

1. *Maitsuki akaji na node, tsuma mo pāto de hataraku koto ni shita.*
   Since we're in the red every month, my wife began a part-time job.
2. *Kono mama uriage ga ochikomu to, akaji ni naru.*
   If sales continue to go down like this, we'll end up in the red.
3. *Kono mise wa hanjō shite iru yō de mo, akaji o kakaete imasu.*
   This store may appear to be prospering, but actually it's in the red.
4. *Kokka yosan ga akaji no kuni ga ōi.*
   Many countries have a budget deficit.
5. *Hoikuen no akaji o bazā de oginau.*
   The day-care center holds bazaars to make up for its losses.

amaku miru

甘く見る

think little of, not take seriously

DŌRYŌ 1:

Ano kaisha no saikin no uriage, sugoi desu ne.

DŌRYŌ 2:

Sukoshi amaku mite ita kamo shiremasen ne. Uchi mo ganbaranai to . . .

COLLEAGUE 1:

That company's recent sales figures are impressive, aren't they?

COLLEAGUE 2:

Maybe we were underestimating them. We'd better get going ourselves.

Amai has many meanings, including sweet, romantic, indulgent, and optimistic. *Amaku miru* means to think lightly of or not to take something seriously. Other forms are *amaku mirareru* (be taken too lightly) and *amaku mite shimau* (underestimate).

EXAMPLES

1. *Kanojo o amari amaku mite wa ikenai.*

   You'd better not underestimate her.

2. *A-sha ni zuibun amaku miraremashita ne.*

   Company A doesn't think of us as serious competition at all.

3. *Onna da to omotte, amaku minaide kudasai.*

   Don't underestimate me because I'm a woman.

4. *Shiken o amaku mita no ga shippai no gen'in desu yo.*

   The reason you failed is that you didn't take the exam seriously.

asameshi-mae

朝飯前

a cinch, easy to do

TSUMA:

Kono nimotsu, suimasen kedo, todana ni shimatte. Anata nara, asameshi-mae deshō?

OTTO:

Ii yo. Shokuji no ato de, shimatte oku yo.

WIFE:

Could you put this luggage away in the closet, please? For you, its so easy.

HUSBAND:

Sure. I'll put them away right after I finish eating.

Asameshi-mae means something that is a cinch or a piece of cake. Literally "before breakfast," the phrase implies that something requires little energy and can be done with hardly any effort.

EXAMPLES

1. *Kare ni totte, Eibun no tegami o kaku no wa asameshi-mae da.*

   It's a cinch for him to write a letter in English.

2. *Otto ni wa, katei no daiku-shigoto nado, asameshi-mae da.*

   Taking care of the carpentry work around the house is a cinch for my husband.

3. *Kanojo ni totte, kyōshitsu no fun'iki o akaruku suru no wa asameshi-mae datta.*

   It was easy for her to brighten up the classroom atmosphere.

4. *Nihon no keizai-ryoku nara, ano kuni o enjo suru no wa asameshi-mae desu.*

   Providing support for that country is a simple matter considering Japan's economic might.

ato no matsuri

後の祭り

too late

SEITO:

Konna ni shiken ga muzukashiin' dattara, motto benkyō shite okeba yokatta.

SENSEI:

Ima kara itte mo, ato no matsuri da yo.   Kondo ganbarinasai.

STUDENT:

If I had known that the exam was going to be this difficult, I would have studied harder.

TEACHER:

It's too late to say that now. You'd better try harder next time.

Ato no matsuri, literally "after a festival," means being too late for something. This expression comes from going to the site of a festival after it's over and seeing the floats and stalls that have served their purpose and no longer have any use.

EXAMPLES

1. *Kare ni ima sara ayamatte mo, ato no matsuri deshō ne.*
   Even if I apologize to him now, probably the damage is already done.
2. *Ima goro, shōbōsha ga kite mo, ato no matsuri desu yo.*
   Even if the fire engines came now, it's too late for them to be of any help.
3. *Saishūkai ni niten ireta ga, ato no matsuri datta.*
   We scored two points in the last inning, but it was too late.
4. *Ima sugu ni, taisaku o kangaenai to, ato no matsuri ni narimasu yo.*
   If we don't think of a countermeasure right now, we'll have missed our chance to do anything.
5. *Kyanseru shita kippu o kai-modosō to shita ga, ato no matsuri datta.*
   I tried to repurchase the cancelled ticket, but it was too late.

atogama ni suwaru

後釜にすわる

succeed or replace someone

KAISHAIN 1:

Buchō wa konogoro, byōkigachi de, dōmo taishoku suru rashii desu yo.

KAISHAIN 2:

Sō naru to, kare no atogama ni suwaru no wa, dare deshō ne.

EMPLOYEE 1:

The department chief tends to get sick a lot these days. It looks like he's going to have to retire.

EMPLOYEE 2:

In that case, I wonder who will replace him.

Atogama, literally "the following pot," refers to a replacement or successor. It is also used to refer to a second wife. An *atogama* was a pot put on the hearth when there was still heat remaining from the previous cooking. The phrase implies that very little time has passed before a successor, or a new wife, comes along.

EXAMPLES

1. *Kachō ga mae no buchō no atogama ni suwatta.*
   The section chief replaced the department chief.
2. *Buchō no atogama ni suwatta hito wa, kare hodo yūnō de wa nakatta.*
   The person who succeeded the department chief was not as capable as the chief had been.
3. *Kare no atogama ni suwaritai hito wa ōzei iru.*
   Many people would like to step into his position.
4. *Kanojo ga senpai no atogama ni suwaru koto ni natta.*
   She ended up replacing one of her seniors.

ba-chigai

場違い

out of place

(kaisha no keieisha no kaigi de)
KAISHAIN 1:
Kono kaigi ni, zuibun ba-chigai na hito ga kite imasu ne.
KAISHAIN 2:
Ē, tashika kare wa, tenisu no senshu deshita yo ne.

(at a company management conference)
EMPLOYEE 1:
There are people at this conference who really look quite out of place.
EMPLOYEE 2:
Yes, take that fellow—he's a tennis player, isn't he?

Ba-chigai, which combines the *ba* from *basho* (place) and *chigai* (difference), indicates something that does not belong or is unsuitable for a particular place. Other expressions employing *chigai* are *ire-chigai* (pass a person at an entrance), *omoi-chigai* (misapprehension), *kan-chigai* (misunderstanding), *kiki-chigai* (mishearing), and *dan-chigai* (vast difference).

EXAMPLES

1. *Kare wa kekkon-shiki ni ba-chigai na fukusō de shusseki shita.*
   He attended the wedding reception wearing clothes inappropriate for the occasion.
2. *Ba-chigai na hito ga, kono kaigi ni dete imasu ne.*
   There are people at this conference who don't really belong.
3. *Koko ni kare ga iru no wa, ba-chigai ja arimasen ka?*
   This isn't the kind of place you would expect to find him, is it?
4. *Yahari, kaigi de no ano hatsugen wa ba-chigai datta deshō.*
   As I had thought, his comments in the meeting were out of place.

baka shōjiki
馬鹿正直
foolishly honest

TOMODACHI 1:
Dōshite koibito ni furareta no?

TOMODACHI 2:
Kanojo ni imōto no hō ga kirei da ne 'tte ittan' da.

TOMODACHI 1:
Kimi wa hontō ni baka shōjiki da ne.

FRIEND 1:
Why did your girlfriend dump you?

FRIEND 2:
I told her I thought her younger sister was better looking.

FRIEND 1:
You really are too honest for your own good.

Baka shōjiki means being honest to such an extreme that it becomes foolish. *Baka* (foolish) is written with the characters for horse and deer, but these are merely phonetic substitutes and offer no insight into the word's meaning. *Shōjiki* means honest. Another common expression using *baka* is *baka ni tsukeru kusuri wa nai,* literally "no medicine can cure a fool."

EXAMPLES

1. *Anata wa dōshite sonna ni baka shōjiki na no?*
   How can you be so naively honest?

2. *Kare ga anna ni baka shōjiki na hito da to wa omowanakatta.*
   I never thought of him as being so gullible.

3. *Kanojo ni hontō no koto o itte okoraseta no wa, baka shōjiki datta ka na?*
   I wonder if I was being too honest—telling her the truth and making her angry like that.

bakyaku o arawasu

馬脚を露わす

show one's true colors

DANSHI GAKUSEI:

Asu wa shigoto no mensetsu nan' da. Keiken ga nai kara, shinpai da yo.

JOSHI GAKUSEI:

Hen na koto o itte, bakyaku o arawasanai yō ni ne.

MALE STUDENT:

Tomorrow I have a job interview. I don't have much experience, so I'm worried.

FEMALE STUDENT:

Well, just be careful you don't say something strange and give yourself away.

Bakyaku o arawasu, literally "to reveal the horse's legs," means to reveal one's true character and thus give oneself away. In Japanese drama, when people played the part of a horse, one person would act as the forequarters and one as the hindquarters. If the actor's legs became exposed, the audience would know the truth. From this came the meaning of showing one's true feelings or thoughts.

EXAMPLES

1. *O-miai no seki de kanojo wa bakyaku o arawashita.*

   Upon meeting with her prospective husband, she showed her true self.

2. *Musuko ga mensetsu shiken de bakyaku o arawasanai ka to shinpai desu.*

   I worry that my son might show his true colors during the job interview.

3. *Sono jiken de, kare no bakyaku ga arawareta.*

   It was that incident that gave him away.

4. *Kare wa yopparatte bakyaku o arawashita.*

   He got drunk and showed himself for what he really was.

23

ban-kuruwase

番狂わせ

an upset, surprise

KISHA:

Kondo no senkyo no kekka wa igai deshita ne.

SEIJIKA:

Honto desu yo. K-shi ga shushō ni naru to wa, taihen na ban-kuruwase desu.

REPORTER:

The outcome of the recent election was quite a surprise.

POLITICIAN:

Indeed. It was a real surprise to see Mr. K become prime minister.

Ban-kuruwase comes from the world of sumo and refers to a surprise upset. Before each tournament, a list of the wrestlers *(banzuke)* is posted, ranking the wrestlers from lowest to highest. When a higher-ranked wrestler is beaten by someone of lower rank, the order of the *banzuke* is upset *(kuruwaseru)*.

EXAMPLES

1. *Kyō no sumō wa, yokozuna ga makeru to iu ban-kuruwase ga atta.*

   There was a surprise upset in today's sumo; one of the top wrestlers was defeated.

2. *Kare ga ichi-i ni naru to wa, tonda ban-kuruwase datta.*

   It was quite an upset for him to finish in first place.

3. *Kaigi de kanojo ga hantai shita no wa, ban-kuruwase datta.*

   It was quite a surprise to have her express her opposition at the meeting.

4. *Ban-kuruwase no kanojo no hatsugen ni, minna odoroita.*

   Everyone was shocked by her unexpected announcement.

5. *Ryokō-chū ni ressha jiko ni au to wa, tonda ban-kuruwase deshita.*

   It was a great shock to be in a train accident while we were on vacation.

bita ichimon

びた一文

a single penny

KYAKU:

Nē, ojisan, kore o-make shite.

TENSHU:

O-kyakusan, kore wa bita ichimon makerarenai yo.

CUSTOMER:

How about knocking a little off the price for me?

STORE OWNER:

Sorry, I can't cut the price a single cent.

Bita is an abbreviation for *bitasen,* a crude coin produced in the 16th century. At that time, a *mon* was the smallest unit of currency. Though these coins no longer exist today, their names live on in such expressions as *bita ichimon mo nai* (not have a cent) and *bita ichimon makerarenai* (not come down in price one cent).

EXAMPLES

1. *Ano mise wa takusan katte mo, bita ichimon makete kurenai.*
   No matter how much you buy in that shop, they won't give you any discount.
2. *Bita ichimon makete kurenain' nara, kono mise de wa kaimasen.*
   If you won't budge an inch on the price, I'll go elsewhere.
3. *Watashi wa kore de bita ichimon mōkeru tsumori wa arimasen.*
   At this price I don't expect to make a cent of profit.
4. *Kare wa isshō asonde kurashi, bita ichimon kaseida koto wa nai.*
   He has lived a life of leisure and never earned a penny.
5. *Jibun no chokin kara bita ichimon musuko ni yaru tsumori wa nai.*
   I have no intention of giving my son a single cent of my savings.

bō ni furu

棒に振る

spoil, ruin

KAISHAIN 1:

Kinō wa kachō no hikkoshi no tetsudai datta sō desu ne.

KAISHAIN 2:

Sō nan' desu. O-kage de nichiyōbi o ichinichi bō ni furimashita yo.

EMPLOYEE 1:

So you helped the section chief move house yesterday, didn't you?

EMPLOYEE 2:

That's right. It spoiled my whole Sunday.

Bō ni furu means to waste or ruin something. A *bō* is a long slender pole made of wood, metal, or bamboo. *Bō ni furu,* literally "to brandish a pole," is said to originate from the former practice of peddlers bearing poles on their shoulders when doing business. Until all their goods were sold, the peddlers would have to brandish that pole. If they didn't sell all their goods, they would be financially ruined.

EXAMPLES

1. *Kinō wa kimi no kichō na yasumi o maru ichinichi bō ni furasete, sumanakatta ne.*

   Sorry I ruined your holiday yesterday.

2. *Iie, bō ni futta wake de wa arimasen.*

   Not at all—it wasn't ruined.

3. *Kare wa mayaku ni te o dashite, isshō o bō ni furasareta.*

   He became involved with drugs, which ruined his life.

4. *Sonna koto de, kyaria o bō ni futte mo iin' desu ka?*

   Is that worth forfeiting your whole career for?

5. *Watashi wa sonna koto de, isshō o bō ni furu tsumori wa arimasen.*

   I have no intention of making a mess of my life because of that.

boro o dasu

ぼろを出す

expose one's faults

(miai no seki de)
MUSUME:
Okāsan, nani o o-hanashi shitara ii kashira.
HAHAOYA:
Hanasanai hō ga ii wa. Amari hanasu to boro ga demasu yo.

(at a meeting for an arranged marriage)
DAUGHTER:
What should I talk about, Mom?

MOTHER:
You'd be better off keeping as quiet as possible. If you talk too much, you'll reveal too many of your faults.

Boro refers to rags or tatters and with *dasu* (put out or show) means to expose one's faults and shortcomings. Other variations include *boro ga deru* (have one's faults revealed) and *boro o dasareru* (be made to show one's weaknesses).

EXAMPLES

1. *Ukkari suru to boro ga desō da.*
   If we're not on guard, we may reveal our weak points.
2. *O-miai de wa boro o dasanai yō ni ne.*
   When you meet your prospective spouse at a meeting for an arranged marriage, be careful not to show your bad side.
3. *Anata ga boro o dasun' ja nai ka to shinpai shite itan' desu yo.*
   I was worried that you might reveal your faults.
4. *Kaigi no seki de machigatta hōkoku o shite, boro o dashite shimatta.*
   I gave an incorrect report at the meeting and lost my credibility.
5. *Yokatta! Boro o dasanakute sumimashita.*
   Whew! I managed to keep up appearances until the end.

bu ga yoi / bu ga warui
分が良い／分が悪い
advantage /disadvantage

MUSUKO:
Otōsan, shōgi shiyō yo.
CHICHIOYA:
Omae to de wa, kochira no bu ga warusō da na.

SON:
Come on, Dad. Let's have a game of Japanese chess.
FATHER:
If I play with you, the odds are against me.

Bu ga yoi indicates that a person is in a favorable position in situations where competition is involved—for example, games, sports, or the corporate ladder. *Bu ga warui* has the opposite meaning; that one is not in a favorable position. Other forms include *kochira ni bu ga aru* (our side has a better chance of success) and *achira ni wa bu ga nai* (the odds are against them).

EXAMPLES

1. *Otōsan, shōgi nara boku ni bu ga arimasu yo.*
   Dad, I think I can go one better than you when it comes to Japanese chess.
2. *Dōmo, sochira no bu ga warusō desu ne.*
   It seems as if you are at a disadvantage.
3. *Hajime no uchi wa kochira ni bu ga attan' desu ga ne.*
   Well, in the beginning our side was doing better.
4. *Itsu no ma ni bu ga waruku nattan' desu ka?*
   How is it that our luck has turned against us?
5. *Shiai wa kore kara desu shi, mada mada kochira ni mo bu ga arimasu yo.*
   The match has just started and we still have every possibility of winning.

bunan

無難

acceptable, safe

TSUMA:

Ribingu rūmu ni kono e, dō kashira?

OTTO:

Chotto hade-sugi da to omou kedo.

TSUMA:

Ja, mō chotto bunan na mono ni shimashō ka?

WIFE:

What do you think of this painting for the living room?

HUSBAND:

I think it's a bit too gaudy.

WIFE:

Well then, shall we pick something a little more subdued?

Bunan describes something that is neither bad nor particularly good, but that is the safest. *Nan* means misfortune or difficulty, and the prefix *bu* negates the meaning of *nan*. Other uses of *bu* include *buji* (safely, without incident), *burei* (impoliteness), *buaisō* (brusqueness), and *bushō* (indolence, laziness).

EXAMPLES

1. *Kekkon suru nara, bunan na hito o erabinasai.*

   If you are going to marry, choose a conventional partner.

2. *Anmari bunan sugiru no mo, tsumarimasen ne.*

   Something too conservative becomes boring, doesn't it?

3. *Kimi wa bunan na hatsugen shika shinain' da ne.*

   Every comment you make is just so innocuous!

4. *Sore ni kimenasai. Sono hō ga bunan da.*

   Take that one. That would be safer.

cha o nigosu

茶を濁す

deceive, evade, save appearances

TOMODACHI 1:

Kinō wa dēto dattan' deshō. Oishii mono, gochisō shite kureta?

TOMODACHI 2:

Sore ga nē, hanbāgā de o-cha o nigosarechatta.

FRIEND 1:

You went on a date yesterday, right? Did he buy you a good meal?

FRIEND 2:

He led me to believe that but all I got was a hamburger.

Cha o nigosu, literally "to cloud the tea," means to make words, attitudes, or facial expressions vague and ambiguous so as to deceive someone. *Kotoba o nigosu* has the same meaning. Other idioms using *cha* are *chabara mo ittoki* (a cup of tea will satisfy one's hunger only for a short while) and *chaban geki* (slapstick comedy).

EXAMPLES

1. *Sonna mono de o-cha o nigosu tsumori desu ka?*

   Are you trying to evade the issue?

2. *Konna mono de, o-cha o nigosarechatta.*

   I was taken in with something like this.

3. *Kēki de o-cha o nigosō nante kangaenaide ne.*

   Don't think you can get out of it by buying me cake.

4. *Iya, o-cha o nigoshita wake ja arimasen yo.*

   No, I'm not trying to avoid the issue.

5. *Shain-ryokō, yasui hoteru de o-cha o nigosu hōhō wa arimasen ka?*

   Is there any way we can keep the company trip expenses down—like using a cheaper hotel?

chinpun-kanpun

チンプンカンプン

incomprehensible, not understandable

BUCHŌ:

Kimi, ashita shōgi o shi ni, uchi ni konai ka?

BUKA:

Zan'nen desu ga, watashi shōgi chinpun-kanpun nan' desu.

DEPARTMENT CHIEF:

Would you like to come to my place tomorrow for a game of Japanese chess?

SUBORDINATE:

I'm sorry but Japanese chess is all Greek to me.

Chinpun-kanpun describes a word or thing that one does not understand at all. It is said that this expression came about when a person teasingly used it after having failed to understand the meaning of a Chinese word. Another theory suggests this word was an attempt to mimic a foreigner speaking. The shortened form is *chinpunkan* and is chiefly used in conversation.

EXAMPLES

1. *Gaijin ni hanashi-kakerareta ga, chinpun-kanpun de wakaranakatta.*
   A foreigner spoke to me but I couldn't make head nor tail of what he said.
2. *Watashi wa kottō no koto wa, mattaku chinpun-kanpun desu.*
   I don't have an inkling when it comes to antiques.
3. *Kare no setsumei wa, watashi ni wa chinpun-kanpun da.*
   His explanation was just gibberish to me.
4. *Konpyūtā no setsumeisho o yonda ga, marude chinpun-kanpun datta.*
   I read the computer operating instructions, but it was all Greek to me.
5. *Watashi wa Supeingo wa chinpun-kanpun desu.*
   Spanish is unintelligible to me.

chōchin-mochi

提灯持ち

flatterer

DŌRYŌ 1:

Ano hito, shachō ni o-seji bakari itte iru.

DŌRYŌ 2:

Ā iu no o, chōchin-mochi 'tte iun' desu yo.

COLLEAGUE 1:

That person is always flattering the president.

COLLEAGUE 2:

You call that type of person a brownnoser.

Chōchin-mochi refers to an assistant who is always trying to flatter his boss. This phrase comes from long ago, when wedding processions, funeral processions, and processions for people of importance were led by lamp bearers *(chōchin-mochi)*.

EXAMPLES

1. *Anata wa, itsu kara shachō no chōchin-mochi ni natta no desu ka?*
   Since when are you the president's minion?

2. *Kare, tanomareta wake de mo nai noni, shachō no chōchin-mochi o shite iru.*
   He acts like the president's assistant even though he wasn't asked to.

3. *Shinbun ga seijika no chōchin-mochi o suru to wa, nasakenai.*
   For a newspaper to be a pawn of politicians is shameful.

4. *Kyōju, gakuchō no chōchin-mochi wa, yamete kudasai.*
   Professor, please stop playing up to the dean.

5. *Anata ga buchō no chōchin-mochi o suru to wa omowanakatta.*
   I didn't think you would be the department chief's toady.

chōshi o awaseru

調子を合わせる

adjust to, adapt to, get along with

KAISHAIN 1:

Ashita, yasumō to omoun' da. Kachō ni kikaretara, byōki to itte oite kurenai ka.

KAISHAIN 2:

Wakatta. Umaku chōshi o awasete oku kara, shinpai suru na yo.

EMPLOYEE 1:

I think I'll take tomorrow off. If the boss asks, tell him I'm sick.

EMPLOYEE 2:

OK. Don't worry, I'll cover for you.

Chōshi o awaseru means to adjust pitch or tempo, to adjust one's attitude in order to get along well with others, or to adjust or fine tune a machine. *Chōshi o awasareru* is the passive form and *chōshi o awasesaseru* is the causative form. Expressions using *chōshi* include *chōshi ga yoi* (be skilled at getting along with others), *chōshi ni noru* (get carried away), and *chōshi-hazure* (be out of tune).

EXAMPLES

1. *(ōkesutora de shikisha ga) Kimi, chōshi o awasete kuretamae.*
   (an orchestra conductor) You, get in tune with everyone else.
2. *Kare ni chōshi o awaseru no mo, taihen desu ne.*
   It's difficult to get along with him.
3. *Muri ni chōshi o awasenakute mo ii desu yo.*
   Just relax and be yourself.
4. *Hontō wa, chōshi o awasetakunain' desu.*
   I really don't like to deal with him.
5. *Onaji kurasu no hito-tachi to chōshi o awasō to doryoku shitan' desu ga.*
   I tried to get along with my classmates.

33

daikoku-bashira

大黒柱

mainstay, breadwinner

CHICHIOYA:

Watashi mo teinen-taishoku da. Kore kara wa omae ga kono ie no daikoku-bashira da yo.

MUSUKO:

Wakarimashita, Otōsan.

FATHER:

I've reached my retirement. From now on you are going to be the breadwinner in this family.

SON:

I understand, Dad.

Daikoku-bashira refers to the central figure that supports a household or a nation. When a wooden house is built, a thick pillar is erected in the center to support the whole building. This pillar is called the *daikoku-bashira* (central pillar). From this, the expression has come to describe a person who sustains a house or company.

EXAMPLES

1. *Boku ga uchi no daikoku-bashira ni natte, ganbarimasu.*
   I'll become the breadwinner in the house and try my best.
2. *Kare ga daikoku-bashira de wa, tayori ni narimasen ne.*
   He is unreliable as a breadwinner.
3. *Kare wa nagai aida, kono kaisha no daikoku-bashira datta.*
   For a long time, he was the pillar of this company.
4. *Ie no daikoku-bashira ga inaku natte, taihen da.*
   Things are difficult at our house since we lost our breadwinner.
5. *Daikoku-bashira no kare ni tayori-sugite wa kawaisō desu yo.*
   It's unfair that people depend on him so much as their mainstay.

daikon yakusha

大根役者

poor actor

TSUMA:

Kono haiyū, suteki da wa.

OTTO:

Mikake wa yokute mo, daikon yakusha de wa shiyō ga nai yo.

WIFE:

This actor is so handsome.

HUSBAND:

He may be good-looking but that's not much use when he's such a lousy actor.

Daikon yakusha describes an actor with no talent. There are a few theories as to why *daikon* (Japanese radish) is employed in this expression. One theory claims that since the roots of the Japanese radish are *shiroi* (white), there is a relation to the sound of the word *shirōto* (amateur, novice). Another claims no matter how radish is eaten, it does not upset *(ataranai)* the stomach. This is the same *ataranai* that refers to an actor not hitting it off well with an audience.

EXAMPLES

1. *Kare wa daikon yakusha desu ne.*
   He is a lousy actor, isn't he.
2. *Shuyaku ga daikon yakusha de wa, omoshiroku arimasen yo.*
   The play isn't interesting, what with the leading actor being such a ham!
3. *Kanojo ga anna ni daikon yakusha da to wa omowanakatta.*
   I didn't think that her acting would be so wooden.
4. *Kare wa daikon dakara, yamesasemashō.*
   Since he's a poor actor, let's dismiss him.

dairokkan

第六感

sixth sense, intuition.

TOMODACHI 1:

Kanojo, kimi no koto suki mitai da ne.

TOMODACHI 2:

Dōshite wakaru?

TOMODACHI 1:

Boku no dairokkan ga hatarakun' da.

FRIEND 1:

It seems that she likes you.

FRIEND 2:

How do you know?

FRIEND 1:

It's just a feeling.

Dairokkan is one's intuition or sixth sense. Human beings possess five senses, namely sight, hearing, taste, smell, and touch. Many people believe there is also a sixth sense *(dairokkan)* that enables one to intuitively recognize or know something. This sense is referred to as *kan* (intuition).

EXAMPLES

1. *Watashi no dairokkan' tte, yoku ataru no yo.*
   My sixth sense often proves to be right.
2. *Kimi no dairokkan nante ate ni naranai yo.*
   Your intuition cannot be depended upon.
3. *Dairokkan de, kono senshu ga marason ni katsu' tte pin to kitan' da.*
   I could feel it in my bones that this athlete would win the marathon.
4. *Dairokkan ni tayori-sugite wa ikenai yo.*
   You shouldn't rely too much on a hunch.

dame-oshi suru

駄目押しする

double-check

TOMODACHI 1:

Kare, hontō ni tenisu oshiete kururun' deshō ne?

TOMODACHI 2:

Daijōbu da to omou kedo, ichiō dame-oshi shite okimasu yo.

FRIEND 1:

Do you think he'll really teach us tennis?

FRIEND 2:

I think it'll be all right, but I'll double-check with him just to be sure.

Dame-oshi suru has two meanings: the first is to double-check something, and the second is to add up the points (in a game, for example) even when it is fairly clear who is winning and who is losing. This meaning derives originally from the game of *go,* where the word *dame* refers to a neutral square that is not controlled by either player. Moves that lead to the forming of such squares need to be very carefully calculated before they are played.

EXAMPLES

1. *Ashita no kaigi no ken, buchō ni dame-oshi shite okimashō.*
   Let's double-check with the boss about tomorrow's meeting.
2. *Watashi no an ga saiyō sareru ka, dame-oshi shite kudasai.*
   Could you make doubly sure that he's going to accept my proposals?
3. *Kare ni sonna ni dame-oshi suru hitsuyō wa arimasen.*
   There's no need to check more than once with him.
4. *Kare wa dame-oshi sareru to iya ni naru tachi desu.*
   He tends to get irritated when you keep checking everything with him.
5. *Kore dake katte ireba, dame-oshi suru hitsuyō wa nai.*
   With the way we're winning, there's no need to play it safe.

dan-chigai

段違い

vast difference in levels

TOMODACHI 1:
Saikin, Eikaiwa, narai-hajimetan' desu yo.

TOMODACHI 2:
Sore de, Eigo ga dan-chigai ni umaku nattan' desu ne.

FRIEND 1:
I've recently started to study English conversation.

FRIEND 2:
So that's why your English has gotten so much better.

Dan-chigai, refers to two things that cannot be compared because of extreme differences *(chigai)* in level *(dan).* This phrase comes from *go,* where players are ranked according to their ability. For example, someone with skill level eight would be no match for a person with skill level two; the lower the level, the greater the skill.

EXAMPLES

1. *Anata no ie, uchi to wa dan-chigai ni hirokute urayamashii desu.*
   Your place is so much bigger than mine, it makes me jealous.
2. *Sasuga, ichi-ryū no resutoran wa dan-chigai no umasa desu ne.*
   Indeed, the food at this first-rate restaurant outclasses others.
3. *Nichiyōbi no kanchōgai wa, heijitsu to wa dan-chigai ni shizuka da.*
   On Sundays the government district is much quieter than on weekdays.
4. *Anata no shūnyū to watashi no de wa, dan-chigai desu.*
   There is a big difference in our income levels.
5. *Futari no jitsu-ryoku wa dan-chigai de, shiai ni naranai.*
   Our levels are completely different so we wouldn't be a good match.

dandori ga yoi

段取りがよい

efficient arrangements

BUKA:

Kaigi-yō no shiryō o junbi shite okimashita.

BUCHŌ:

Kimi wa shigoto no dandori ga yoi node, tasukaru yo.

SUBORDINATE:

I've prepared the data for the conference.

DEPARTMENT CHIEF:

It's a great help that you're so well-organized.

Dandori ga yoi means that something is undertaken with much care and efficiency. This expression is originally a term from the construction industry. When building stairs, how the *dan* (steps) will be taken *(toru*, which becomes *dori)* or determined is a calculated procedure. This *dandori* (determination of the height of the step) was an important criterion for the safety standard of a building. From this practice, the expression has derived its present meaning. *Dandori* often appears on its own.

EXAMPLES

1. *Kyō no kaigi wa totemo dandori ga umaku itta.*

   The arrangements for today's conference went very smoothly.

2. *Shikai no dandori ga warukute, kaigi ga nagabiita.*

   The meeting dragged on because the chairperson hadn't prepared for it.

3. *Kekkon-shiki no dandori, kyō sōdan shimashō.*

   Let's discuss the plans today for the wedding.

4. *Niji kara kaikaishiki o okonau dandori ni natte imasu.*

   The opening ceremony is scheduled to begin at two o'clock.

5. *Hachigatsu wa kaigai-shutchō ni iku dandori ni natte imasu.*

   I have arranged to take an overseas business trip in August.

dashi ni suru

出しにする

use as a pretext

CHŌNAN:

Otōsan, Hiroshi ga sukiyaki ga tabetai'tte.

CHICHIOYA:

Otōto o dashi ni shite wa ikenai yo. Hontō wa jibun ga tabetain' darō?

ELDEST SON:

Dad, Hiroshi says he wants to eat sukiyaki.

FATHER:

You shouldn't use your brother as an excuse. The truth is that you want to eat sukiyaki, right?

Dashi ni suru means to use a person or a thing to suit one's own convenience. *Dashi* is the nominalized form of the verb *dasu* (bring out, produce). The expression *dashi ni tsukau* also has the same meaning as *dashi ni suru*.

EXAMPLES

1. *Shachō no tanjōbi o dashi ni shite, pātii o hiraita.*

   Using the company president's birthday as a pretext, we threw a party.

2. *Watashi o dashi ni tsukawanaide kudasai.*

   Please don't use me as an excuse.

3. *Kare wa dashi ni sareta koto o shirimasen.*

   He doesn't know that he has been taken advantage of.

4. *Imōto o dashi ni shite, kare to yūenchi ni itta.*

   I used to take my younger sister along as an excuse for going to the amusement park with my boyfriend.

debana o kujiku

出ばなを挫く

thwart at the outset

OTTO:

Musuko no nyūgaku-shiki da to iu noni, ame ga futte iru yo.

TSUMA:

Kawaisō ni, debana o kujikarete shimaimasu ne.

HUSBAND:

You say our son has his school entrance ceremony today—well, it's raining.

WIFE:

The poor boy—that will put a damper on things for him.

Debana indicates the very outset of something, and with *kujiku* (crash), describes a situation where a person is eager to begin an undertaking or conversation but is prevented from doing so. The phrase *debana o oru* (*oru* means break) has the same meaning as *debana o kujiku*. *Debana o tataku* (*tataku* means strike) means to thwart an opponent at an initial stage.

EXAMPLES

1. *Sekkaku no nyūgaku-shiki ni ame de, debana o kujikaremashita.*
   Their enthusiasm was dampened by the rain at the entrance ceremony.
2. *Shinkon-ryokō de jiko ni ai, debana o kujikarete shimatta.*
   They had an accident during their honeymoon, and that put a damper on things from the very outset.
3. *Mazu itten senshu shite, aite no debana o otte shimaimashō.*
   First of all, let's get one point and baffle our opponent at the start.
4. *Kenka de wa, saisho ni aite no debana o tataku no ga katsu kotsu desu.*
   The trick to winning a fight is to get the jump on your opponent.

dō ni iru

堂に入る

excel, be outstanding

KANKYAKU 1:

Kyō no konsāto wa hontō ni yokatta desu ne.

KANKYAKU 2:

Ē, pianisuto no ensō mo, dō ni itte imashita shi.

AUDIENCE MEMBER 1:

Today's concert was really excellent, wasn't it?

AUDIENCE MEMBER 2:

Yes, the pianist gave a highly polished performance.

Dō ni iru indicates that one has become highly proficient. Prior to the Meiji era, all education in Japan took place in temples. *Dō* (temple) *ni iru* (entering) referred to entering school to study and learn.

EXAMPLES

1. *Kare no supiichi wa dō ni itte ita.*

   His speech was masterful.

2. *Dō ni itta shikai-buri datta.*

   His way of chairing the meeting was excellent.

3. *Kare no kyōshi-buri mo dō ni itte kita.*

   His style of teaching has become that of a seasoned veteran.

4. *Anata no ocha no o-temae wa dō ni itte imashita yo.*

   You have great expertise in the art of tea serving.

5. *Kare no nenrei ni shite wa, dō ni itta aisatsu o shita.*

   Despite his youth, he delivered an excellent address.

dōdō-meguri

堂堂巡り

going round and round

RŌSŌ-GAWA:

Giron shite mo, zenzen matomarimasen ne.

KAISHA-GAWA:

Kore de wa, dōdō-meguri o kuri-kaesu dake desu yo.

UNION REPRESENTATIVE:

No matter how much we argue, we don't seem to be getting anywhere at all.

COMPANY REPRESENTATIVE:

We're just repeating ourselves and going round and round in circles.

Dōdō-meguri has three meanings: first, circling around a *dō* (a Buddhist temple or Shintō shrine) offering prayers or holding ceremonies; second, repeating the same thing endlessly with no progress being made; and third, voting whereby Diet members cast ballots in a box placed on the rostrum. In conversation, the second usage is the most common.

EXAMPLES

1. *Dōdō-meguri no giron wa mō yamemashō.*

   Let's stop discussing this same thing over and over again.

2. *Anata to wa, ikura hanashite mo dōdō-meguri suru dake desu.*

   No matter how much I talk with you, we just go round in circles.

3. *Hanashiai wa, itsumo no yō ni dōdō-meguri desu.*

   As always, the negotiations are getting nowhere.

4. *Kaigi wa dōdō-meguri shite owarisō mo nai.*

   It doesn't appear that the meeting will be ending for some time since the discussion is going round and round in circles.

dosakusa ni magireru

どさくさに紛れる

take advantage of confusion

IE NO HITO:

Yūbe, pātii o shite iru aida ni dorobō ni hairaremashite ne.

KEISATSU:

Ā, dosakusa ni magirete haittan' deshō ne.

HOMEOWNER:

A thief got into the house last night while we were having a party.

POLICE OFFICER:

Oh, I see. So he probably slipped in while everyone was distracted.

Dosakusa ni magireru is used to describe taking advantage of a chaotic situation. In the Edo period, people who were caught during raids on gambling dens were sent to Sado Island to do forced labor. Using an inversion of the word Sado, the gamblers coined the phrase *dosa o kū* (*kū* literally means to eat) to refer to these sudden, chaotic raids. Over time this changed to the noun *dosakusa* which is also often used on its own to describe a confused situation.

EXAMPLES

1. *Watashi wa dosakusa ni magirete, senjō o nigedashita.*
   Taking advantage of the confusion, I fled from the battlefield.
2. *Kono dosakusa ni magirete, futari de dokoka ni ikimashō.*
   Let's sneak out of here while everyone's distracted.
3. *Kare wa sekiyu-shokku no dosakusa ni magirete, ōmōke shita.*
   He made a lot of money during the disorder caused by the oil shock.
4. *Tsuma to kekkon shita no wa, sengo no dosakusa no naka deshita.*
   I married my wife in the midst of the postwar commotion.

dotanba

土壇場

the last moment

MUSUKO:
Okāsan, boku konban tetsuya de benkyō shinakutcha. Ashita, shiken nan' da.
HAHAOYA:
Anata wa dōshite dotanba ni natte awaterun' deshō ne.

SON:
Mom, I'll have to stay up all night studying tonight. I have an exam tomorrow.
MOTHER:
Why is it that you leave everything to the last minute and then go into a panic?

Dotan is made up of the kanji for earth *(do)* and platform *(dan)* and formerly referred to the place where decapitations were performed. From this *dotanba* has come to be used when describing a situation in which one has one's back to the wall—a time when something has to be taken care of.

EXAMPLES

1. *Dotanba ni kite hanashiai ga okonaware, sensō wa kaihi sareta.*
   Last-minute negotiations took place and war was averted.
2. *Jitai wa dō naru ka, dotanba ni naranai to wakarimasen.*
   We can't tell how things will turn out until the last moment.
3. *Iyoiyo dotanba desu.*
   The long-awaited moment has finally arrived.
4. *Dotanba ni natte, awatenaide kudasai.*
   When you reach that critical moment, don't lose your cool.
5. *Dōshite shiai mae no dotanba made, renshū shinakatta no desu ka?*
   Why didn't you do any training until the match was almost upon you?

en no shita no chikara-mochi

縁の下の力持ち

person whose work is not recognized

BUCHŌ:

Kimura-kun no shigoto-buri wa dō dai?

BUKA:

Yoku yatte kuremasu. Wareware no ka no en no shita no chikara-mochi desu yo.

DEPARTMENT CHIEF:

How is Kimura getting on with his work?

SUBORDINATE:

He's doing well. He does all the thankless tasks in our department.

En no shita is the space beneath the veranda or floor and the ground, and *chikara-mochi* refers to a strong person. As this space under the porch is hidden from sight, so is the work of an *en no shita no chikara-mochi,* a person who bears continuous hardship for the benefit of others, unnoticed by the outside world.

EXAMPLES

1. *Kare wa kono ka no en no shita no chikara-mochi da.*

   He does the unrewarded drudgery work in this department.

2. *Haha wa wagaya no en no shita no chikara-mochi da.*

   Mom is the one who carries out the thankless tasks in our house.

3. *Seijika no hisho wa itsumo en no shita no chikara-mochi desu.*

   Politicians' private secretaries always do the unappreciated jobs behind the scenes.

4. *Anata wa en no shita no chikara-mochi de mo ii no desu ka?*

   Are you content even though your efforts go unappreciated?

5. *En no shita no chikara-mochi de iru no wa totemo muzukashii.*

   It's very difficult to carry on when one's efforts go unrecognized.

engi ga ii/warui

縁起がいい／悪い

good/bad omen

TSUMA:

O-mikuji o hiitara, daikichi ga atattan' desu yo.

OTTO:

Sore wa engi ga ii ne. Kitto ii koto ga aru yo.

WIFE:

When I drew my fortune-telling lot, it said I would be very lucky.

HUSBAND:

That's a good omen. Something good is sure to happen.

Engi ga ii refers to something that foretells good fortune. An *engi* is an omen. The opposite of *engi ga ii* is *engi ga warui*.

EXAMPLES

1. *Kekkon-shiki wa engi no ii hi ni kimemashō.*

   Let's decide on a lucky day for our wedding.

2. *Engi o katsugu nante, furui desu yo.*

   You're so old-fashioned, believing in omens.

3. *O-iwai no supiichi de, engi no warui koto wa iwanaide ne.*

   Don't say anything about bad luck in your congratulatory speech.

4. *Obāsan wa engi o katsugi-sugi desu yo.*

   Grandma carries things too far with her superstitions.

5. *O-shōgatsu ga tanjōbi to wa, engi ga ii desu ne.*

   New Year's Day? What a lucky day to have your birthday.

etai ga shirenai

得体が知れない

mysterious-looking, unfamiliar

MUSUME:

Okāsan, kono o-ryōri tabete minai?

HAHAOYA:

Kore wa nan' na no? Etai no shirenai mono wa tabetakunai wa.

DAUGHTER:

Mother, will you taste what I've cooked?

MOTHER:

What is this? I don't want to eat anything that's unrecognizable.

Etai indicates the real nature or appearance of something. *Etai ga shirenai* means that the true appearance of something is not known. In Buddhism, the color of the robes determined the particular sect or status of the wearer. If the sect or status of a person could not be ascertained by giving a cursory look at the robes that person was wearing, then people would say *etai ga wakaranai* (of indeterminate appearance). From this expression came *etai ga shirenai*.

EXAMPLES

1. *Tonari no hito wa shokugyō mo naku, etai ga shirenai.*

   The person next door is unemployed, and rather suspicious looking.

2. *Etai ga shirenai hito to wa, kuchi o kikanai koto ni shite imasu.*

   I make it a rule not to talk to suspicious-looking people.

3. *Etai ga shirenai mono ga sora o tonde iru.*

   There's a mysterious-looking object flying across the sky.

4. *Doa no mukō ni, etai no shirenai dōbutsu ga imasu yo.*

   There's some kind of animal outside the door.

5. *Etai no shirenai hito to wa, tsukiatte wa ikemasen.*

   You shouldn't associate with dubious people.

48

fu ni ochinai

腑に落ちない

hard to swallow, not convincing, not clear

BUKA:

Chōsa no kekka ga demashita ga.

BUCHŌ:

Kono kekka wa fu ni ochinai ne. Mō ichido shirabete kurenai ka?

SUBORDINATE:

The results of the survey are available.

DEPARTMENT CHIEF:

These results don't seem quite right. Check them again for me, will
you?

In the past, it was thought that discretion and judgment resided in the
fu (internal organs). From this, *fu ni ochinai*, literally "not go down
to the internal organs," came to mean not convincing. Another
expression employing *fu* is *fu no nuketa yō,* which describes a
complete loss of vigor caused by fright or sorrow.

EXAMPLES

1. *Kono tesuto no kekka wa fu ni ochimasen.*

   This test result doesn't sit right with me.

2. *Supiido mo dashite inai noni, tsukamaru to wa fu ni ochinai.*

   I don't understand how I could be arrested when I wasn't even speeding.

3. *Kono mitsumorisho no kingaku ga fu ni ochinakattara, dōzo jibun de o-tashikamenasai.*

   If you find this estimate hard to believe, please verify it for yourself.

4. *Kanojo ga dōshite okotte iru no ka, fu ni ochinain' da.*

   It's not clear to me why she became angry.

5. *Chokin no zandaka ga zero to wa, fu ni ochinai.*

   I can't comprehend why my savings balance is zero.

fui o utsu

不意を打つ

take a person by surprise, catch a person napping

SENSEI:

Kimi-tachi, kyō wa kore kara tesuto o shimasu.

SEITO:

E, fui o utsu nante hidoi desu yo.

TEACHER:

OK, everyone, we're going to have a test today.

STUDENT:

What? That's not fair giving a surprise test like that.

Fui o utsu, which combines *fui* (unexpectedness) and *utsu* (hit, strike), implies doing something without warning, especially after having observed the other person's unpreparedness. *Fui-uchi* (surprise attack) is also used. The passive form is *fui o utareru* (be caught unaware), and *fui o kurau* has the same meaning.

EXAMPLES

1. *Nihon no Shinju-wan kōgeki wa fui-uchi datta.*
   The Japanese strike on Pearl Harbor was a surprise attack.
2. *Fui o utareru to wa, hidoi desu ne.*
   It feels terrible to be caught off-guard.
3. *Yonaka ni yūjin ga fui-uchi de yatte kita.*
   A friend dropped in unannounced in the middle of the night.
4. *Shachō no kōjō shisatsu wa fui-uchi de, nan no junbi mo dekinakatta.*
   We weren't given any warning about the president's factory inspection and hadn't made any preparations.
5. *Sekkaku hisashiburi ni au no nara, kondo kara fui-uchi wa yamete kudasai.*
   It's been so long since we've met, next time please give me some notice.

furi-dashi ni modoru

振り出しに戻る

go back to the starting point, return to square one

KAISHAIN 1:

Kono aida no kaigi, nanika shinten ga arimashita ka?

KAISHAIN 2:

Sore ga, shinten suru dokoro ka, furi-dashi ni modotte shimaimashita yo.

EMPLOYEE 1:

Was there any progress made in the meeting the other day?

EMPLOYEE 2:

Rather than making progress, we ended up right back where we had started.

Furi-dashi ni modoru means to return to an original state or condition. There is a board game played at New Year called *sugoroku,* in which dice are thrown and players advance the number of squares indicated by the number thrown. The first person to reach the end becomes the winner. The starting point of *sugoroku* is called the *furi-dashi.* During the game, if players happen to land on a square marked *furi-dashi ni modoru,* literally "return to the starting point," they must start all over.

EXAMPLES

1. *Kare no kyōko na hantai de, hanashi wa furi-dashi ni modotte shimatta.*
   Due to his strong opposition, the discussion ended up going back to square one.
2. *Furi-dashi ni modotte, kangae-naoshite mimashō.*
   Let's rethink things, starting right from scratch.
3. *Hanashi wa dōdō meguri de, kekkyoku furi-dashi ni modotte shimau.*
   The discussion is going round and round in circles and is eventually going to end up right back at the starting point.

furui ni kakeru

ふるいに掛ける

screen, select

BUKA:

Nyūsha shiken ni, saiyō yotei no nanabai no gakusei ga kimashita yo.

BUCHŌ:

Furui ni kakete, shōrai, yūbō na hito dake nokoshitai.

SUBORDINATE:

The number of students taking the company entrance exam is seven times the number we plan to employ.

DEPARTMENT CHIEF:

I'd like to screen the applicants so we are only left with the ones with the most potential.

Furui ni kakeru means to select from a larger group only those things or people that meet certain standards or requirements. A *furui* is a round net used to sift sand or dirt so that the coarse grain is separated from the fine grain. Some things put in the net and shaken *(furui ni kakerarete)* are filtered out; other things remain in the net.

EXAMPLES

1. *Nikai-me no shiken de, jukensha wa furui ni kakerareru.*

   The examinees are screened with a second test.

2. *Furui ni kakerarete, yūnō na mono dake ga nokotta.*

   After the screening, only the capable ones remained.

3. *Watashi-tachi o nankai furui ni kakeru tsumori desu ka?*

   How many times do you intend to screen us?

4. *Ano kaiga konkūru de mo, sakuhin wa mazu, shorui senkō de furui ni kakerareru.*

   Even at the painting contest, the first screening is done with portfolios.

futokoro ga sabishii

懐が寂しい

be short of money

DŌRYŌ 1:

Asoko no resutoran, oishisō desu yo. Itte mimasen ka?

DŌRYŌ 2:

Saikin futokoro ga sabishikute ne. Zan'nen dakedo, kondo ne.

COLLEAGUE 1:

That restaurant is supposed to be good. Shall we give it a try?

COLLEAGUE 2:

Sorry, but recently I've been so short of money. Let's go there some other time.

Futokoro ga sabishii means to be short of money. Originally, *futokoro* referred to the pocketlike space in a kimono that was used to hold one's money. From this, *futokoro* came to mean the amount of money that a person had at any one time. *Futokoro ga samui* also means to be short of money whereas *futokoro ga atatakai* means to be carrying lots of money.

EXAMPLES

1. *Anata, konban futokoro ga sabishisō ne. Ogorimashō ka?*

   You seem to be a bit hard up tonight. Why don't I treat you to this?

2. *Kare wa itsumo futokoro ga sabishisō da.*

   He never seems to have any money on him.

3. *Kyō wa kyūryō-bi de, futokoro ga atatakain' desu yo.*

   I'm in the money today—it's my payday.

4. *Konpyūtā o kattara, kyū ni futokoro ga samuku natta.*

   Since I bought the computer, I've suddenly become short of funds.

5. *Ryokō ni ikitai ga, futokoro ga samukute ikesō ni mo nai.*

   I want to go away on holiday, but I'm so short of money at the moment that it doesn't look like I'll be able to.

gaten ga iku

合点がいく

make sense, have things come into focus

DŌRYŌ 1:

Yasui kyūryō de yoku konna hiroi ie ga tateraremashita ne.

DŌRYŌ 2:

Jitsu wa, chichioya no isan nan' da.

DŌRYŌ 1:

Ā, sore de gaten ga ikimashita.

COLLEAGUE 1:

On your small salary you've managed to build a large house.

COLLEAGUE 2:

Well, actually, I inherited the house from my father.

COLLEAGUE 1:

Ah, now that explains it.

Long ago, when masters of *waka* poems evaluated works written by their students, they would put a dot next to passages that they felt were well written. This mark indicating the master's approval came to be known as a *gaten*. Today, *gaten ga iku* is used to indicate that something previously not clear is now understandable.

EXAMPLES

1. *Kare no setsumei o kiite, yatto gaten ga itta.*

   After listening to his explanation, it finally made sense.

2. *Kare ga kaisha o yameta to wa, gaten ga ikanai.*

   It doesn't make sense to me why he quit the company.

3. *Kanojo ga ryūgaku shite ita to kiite, gaten ga itta.*

   It all made sense after I learned that she had spent time studying abroad.

4. *Dō desu ka? Kore de gaten ga itta deshō.*

   Well, does that bring things into focus for you?

geta o azukeru

下駄を預ける

entrust a matter to a person

TOMODACHI 1:

Kono mondai wa, anata ni geta o azuketai to omoimasu ga.

TOMODACHI 2:

Wakarimashita. Doryoku shite mimashō.

FRIEND 1:

I'd like to pass this problem on to you.

FRIEND 2:

All right. I'll see what I can do.

Geta are wooden clogs and *azukeru* means to leave something for another person to do. *Geta o azukeru* is used when the speaker, anxious to have a particular matter attended to, entrusts someone else with the task. The passive form is *geta o azukerareru* (be left with a matter).

EXAMPLES

1. *Amerika-seifu wa, sono mondai ni kanshite, Nihon-seifu ni geta o azuketa.*

   The American government has left the handling of that question up to the Japanese government.

2. *Nihon-seifu wa geta o azukerareta kakkō to natta.*

   The Japanese government was entrusted with conducting the affair.

3. *Kare ni geta o azuketa tame ni, mondai ga kojireta.*

   The matter was left up to him and this aggravated the problem.

4. *Geta o azukerareru hō mo, meiwaku desu.*

   It is also an annoyance for the person who is delegated with the task.

5. *Kono ken ni tsuite wa, gichō ni geta o azuketai to omoimasu.*

   Regarding this issue, I'd like to pass the matter to the chairman.

giri-date

義理立て

decorum, something done to be polite

BUKA:

Ojōsan no go-kekkon, omedetō gozaimasu. Kore, o-iwai ni sashiagete kudasai.

JŌSHI:

Kimi, sonna ni giri-date shite kurenakute mo yokatta noni.

SUBORDINATE:

Congratulations on your daughter's wedding. Please give this present to her for me.

SUPERVISOR:

You didn't have to go to all this trouble just to be polite.

At one time *giri* referred to what was considered rational behavior, but now it means good manners or social decorum. If we don't do something that we are expected to do, it is attributed to a lack of *giri* (*giri o kaku*) or bad manners (*giri ga warui*). To do what is polite is *giri o tatsu* (*giri-date* is a contracted form of this), whereas doing something merely because it is required is *o-giri ni suru*.

EXAMPLES

1. *Ikura toshiue to itte mo, watashi ni giri-date nado shinaide kudasai.*

   No matter what the difference in our ages is, please don't feel you must be so polite with me.

2. *On no aru sensei o uragitte wa, giri ga tatanai.*

   It's wrong to betray a teacher who has been good to you.

3. *Jōshi ni giri o kaku yō na koto, shinaide ne.*

   Don't be inconsiderate to your supervisor.

4. *Buchō no eiten de, minna o-giri ni miokuri ni itta.*

   The boss was going to be promoted and transferred, so just to be polite everyone went to see him off.

gishin anki

疑心暗鬼

suspicion begets fear, paranoia, anxiousness

ŌKURA DAIJIN:

Sekaijū ga Nihon no yarikata ni fuman o motte iru yō de.

SŌRI DAIJIN:

Sekaijū nante sore wa, anata no gishin anki desu yo.

MINISTER OF FINANCE:

It seems that there is dissatisfaction throughout the entire international community with the way Japan is handling things.

PRIME MINISTER:

The *entire* international community? You're being paranoid.

According to Chinese folklore, when one is doubtful *(gishin)* about something, even though there's nothing to fear, one is apt to see monsters hiding in the dark *(anki)*. In both Japanese and Chinese mythology, the monster *(oni)* is an imaginary creature with human form, a frightening face, and horns, who symbolizes human fears.

EXAMPLES

1. *Itsu no ma ni ka, gishin anki ni ochiitte shimatta.*
   Suddenly I was feeling frightened and anxious about everything.
2. *Kare ga kigyō supai nante, gishin anki desu yo.*
   You're just being paranoid in thinking that he's an industrial spy.
3. *Kore ga gishin anki da to, wakatte wa iru no desu ga . . .*
   I realize that I'm probably just being paranoid about this, but . . .
4. *Minna ga anata no uwasa o shite iru? Sore wa gishin anki da.*
   Everyone has heard that rumor about you? Come on, you're being paranoid.
5. *Iie, gishin anki nado de wa arimasen.*
   No, I'm not being overly suspicious.

gojuppo-hyappo

五十歩百歩

the same difference

MUSUKO:

Dotchi no e o konkūru ni dasō ka na?

HAHAOYA:

Dotchi mo gojuppo-hyappo ne.

SON:

I wonder which picture I should enter in the competition?

MOTHER:

I don't think it matters really; it's the same difference.

Gojuppo-hyappo indicates that there is not much difference between two or more things, and that none of them are especially good. The original saying is *gojuppo o motte hyappo o warau* (the man who has fled from the battlefield by fifty paces is laughing at the man who has fled by a hundred paces). As far as cowardice goes, there is really little difference between them.

EXAMPLES

1. *Futari no tenisu no jitsuryoku wa gojuppo-hyappo da.*

   Neither of them is particularly good at tennis.

2. *Koko ni aru jisho wa dore mo gojuppo-hyappo de, yaku ni tatanai.*

   There's not a lot of difference between these dictionaries; neither of them is of much use.

3. *Ano garō ga motte iru sakuhin wa dore mo gojuppo-hyappo, ii mono ga nai.*

   The works in that gallery are all the same—none are very good.

4. *Kimi-tachi no repōto wa gojuppo-hyappo, toku ni yoi mono wa nai.*

   There's not much to choose from among your reports—none of them are particularly good.

gokuraku tonbo

極楽蜻蛉

a happy-go-lucky fellow, a layabout

DŌRYŌ:

Musuko-san, dochira ni o-tsutome desu ka?

CHICHIOYA:

Sore ga, gokuraku tonbo de mainichi burabura shite irun' desu yo.

OFFICE COLLEAGUE:

Where does your son work?

FATHER:

He's such a happy-go-lucky type that he's just idling his days away.

Gokuraku (Buddhist paradise), used in contrast to *jigoku* (hell), is a world free of worry. *Tonbo* (dragonfly) suggests something carefree. Combined *gokuraku tonbo* refers to either a son who has been constantly sheltered by his parents or an unemployed person who spends his time doing nothing.

EXAMPLES

1. *Aitsu wa itsu made tatte mo, gokuraku tonbo da ne.*
   He'll always be an easygoing fellow.
2. *Otto ga gokuraku tonbo no uwakimono de, kurō shite imasu.*
   I'm having a hard time, what with my husband being a happy-go-lucky womanizer.
3. *Anna gokuraku tonbo to kekkon suru no wa, yurushimasen.*
   I won't allow you to marry such an easygoing character.
4. *Hataraki-bachi ni naru yori, gokuraku tonbo de itai.*
   I'd rather be a happy-go-lucky type than become a workaholic.
5. *Anata no yō na gokuraku tonbo wa, mita koto ga arimasen.*
   I've never come across a person as carefree as you are.

goma o suru
胡麻をする
curry favor

GAKUSEI (JOSEI NO KYŌSHI NI):

Sensei, konogoro masumasu chāmingu ni nararemashita ne.

SENSEI:

Goma o sutte mo, yoi ten wa agemasen yo.

STUDENT (TO A FEMALE PROFESSOR):

You are becoming more and more attractive these days.

TEACHER:

Your flattery won't get you a good grade.

Goma o suru means to court a person's favor without any sense of principle. When grinding sesame seeds in a mortar, the sesame seeds stick to the sides of the mortar. From this, the phrase has come to refer to someone attaching himself to various people, trying to curry favor. The nominal form *goma-suri* (a flatterer, flattery) and passive form *goma o surareru* (be flattered) also are frequently used.

EXAMPLES

1. *Kare wa itsumo buchō ni goma o sutte iru.*

   He is always currying favor with the department chief.

2. *Anata ni goma o surarete mo, ureshiku wa arimasen yo.*

   Even if you try to butter me up, I won't be pleased.

3. *Watashi ni goma o suru hitsuyō wa arimasen.*

   There is no need to court my favor.

4. *Anata o homete irun' desu. Goma-suri de wa arimasen.*

   I am complimenting you. This is not bootlicking.

gongo-dōdan

言語道断

scandalous, perfectly outrageous

SHACHŌ:

Kaisha no kane o tsukai-komu to wa gongo-dōdan, kimi wa kubi da.

KAISHAIN:

Hontō ni mōshiwake arimasen deshita.

COMPANY PRESIDENT:

It's perfectly outrageous of you to have embezzled the company's money. You're fired.

EMPLOYEE:

I'm very sorry for what I've done.

Gongo-dōdan means being flabbergasted by something and unable to put one feelings into words; it can also be used to describe something that is wrong and reprehensible. The term originally meant a profound Buddhist truth that cannot be expressed in mere words.

EXAMPLES

1. *Kokkai-giin ga kaigi-chū ni inemuri o suru to wa gongo-dōdan da.*

   It's scandalous for a Diet member to doze off while a parliamentary debate is in progress.

2. *Watashi ni damatte, chokin o tsukai-hatasu to wa gongo-dōdan da.*

   To spend all of our savings without consulting me—that is utterly outrageous.

3. *Takushii no untenshu no kuse ni, inemuri-unten o suru to wa, gongo-dōdan desu yo.*

   Falling asleep at the wheel is an inexcusable offense, especially for a taxi driver.

4. *Masaka, kare ga sonna gongo-dōdan na koto, shita no desu ka?*

   You mean he actually committed such an unspeakable act?

gori-muchū

五里霧中

up in the air, no idea what to do

TOMODACHI 1:

Kimi no kaisha, tōsan shitan' datte?

TOMODACHI 2:

Sō nan' da. Kore kara saki dō naru no ka, gori-muchū sa.

FRIEND 1:

What's this I hear about your firm going under?

FRIEND 2:

That's right. I'm at a loss as to what will happen to me now.

Gori-muchū refers to a situation in which a person does not know what to do or how things will turn out. In China, there is a story about a well-known scholar who detested meeting people. In order to avoid them, he used sorcery to conjure up a fog which covered a radius of five *ri* (one *ri* is 2.44 miles). Originally, *gori-muchū* meant to conceal oneself, but this meaning has gradually altered to that of not knowing what has or will happen.

EXAMPLES

1. *Sono keikaku wa gori-muchū no jōtai desu.*

   I have no idea of what will become of that project.

2. *Kore kara kono kaisha ga dō naru ka wa, gori-muchū desu.*

   We haven't the foggiest idea of what is going to happen to this company.

3. *Shikin ga sutoppu shita node, sakiyuki wa gori-muchū da.*

   Since funding has been cut, we are quite in the dark about our future.

4. *Kaigai de no seikatsu ga dō naru ka wa, mattaku gori-muchū desu.*

   I have absolutely no idea what it will be like living abroad.

5. *Gori-muchū no naka o tesaguri de aruite iru yō na jōtai desu.*

   I'm quite at a loss—as if I were groping around in the midst of a thick fog.

guchi o kobosu

愚痴をこぼす

grumble, complain, gripe

TOMODACHI 1:

Mō, kaisha yametai desu yo. Kyūryō wa yasui shi, hitozukai wa arai shi.

TOMODACHI 2:

Sonna ni, guchi o kobosu no nara, kaisha o yametara dō desu ka?

FRIEND 1:

I really want to quit. The pay is poor and they work me like a slave.

FRIEND 2:

Well, since you're complaining so much, why don't you quit?

Guchi o kobosu, which combines *guchi* (complaint) and *kobosu* (spill), means to repeatedly talk about a problem without solving it. *Guchi* was originally a Buddhist word used to describe a person who is unable to appreciate the true meaning of existence and is therefore a fool; *gu* means witless and *chi* means foolish.

EXAMPLES

1. *Kare wa itsumo guchi o koboshite bakari iru.*

   He never does anything but complain.

2. *Anna ni atama no ii musume-san na noni, dōshite anata wa sonna ni ano ko no guchi o kobosun' desu ka?*

   Even though your daughter is so smart, why do you complain about her so much?

3. *Guchi bakari kobosanaide, doryoku shite goran nasai.*

   Instead of just complaining, put some more effort into it.

4. *Kare wa tsurakute mo kesshite guchi wa kobosanakatta.*

   Even though it was difficult, he never complained.

gyūjiru

牛耳る

control, run, dominate, be at the helm

DŌRYŌ 1:

Kare, itsu no ma ni ka shusse shimashita ne.

DŌRYŌ 2:

Saikin wa kaisha o gyūjiru hodo ni narimashita yo.

COLLEAGUE 1:

That guy was promoted quickly, wasn't he?

COLLEAGUE 2:

These days, he's practically running the company.

Gyūjiru means to control an assembly, group, or organization and derives from the rite of sealing a promise among feudal lords during the Warring States period in ancient China. At that time, the ears of an ox (*gyūji*) were cut off and then split so that both sides could sip the ox blood in recognition of a promise made. The correct expression is *gyūji o toru* (take the ears of an ox); however, in conversation, *gyūjiru* is commonly used.

EXAMPLES

1. *Kono kai o gyūjitte iru hito wa dare desu ka?*
   Who is in charge of this meeting?
2. *Kare ga kono kaisha o gyūjitte iru hito desu.*
   He is the one running this company.
3. *Shiranai aida ni, kare ga gakusei-kai o gyūjiru yō ni natta no desu.*
   Before he realized it, he was in charge of the student meeting.
4. *Dōshite, bugai-sha no kanojo ni gyūjirarete iru no desu ka?*
   Why are you dominated by an outsider like her?
5. *Anata ni, kono kaigi o gyūjiru shikaku wa arimasen.*
   You don't have the qualifications to run this meeting.

ha ni kinu o kisenai

歯に衣を着せない

not to mince words

TOMODACHI 1:

Kyō wa sukoshi ii-sugita deshō ka. Dō ka, ki ni shinaide kudasai ne.

TOMODACHI 2:

Iie. Ha ni kinu o kisezu itte moraete, kaette yokatta desu yo.

FRIEND 1:

I may have said too much today. Please don't take it to heart.

FRIEND 2:

Not at all. It was good of you to be frank with me.

Ha ni kinu o kisenai means to speak one's mind without considering other people's feelings. It was believed that if one didn't put *(kiseru)* a covering *(kinu)* over one's teeth *(ha)*, whatever one was thinking would automatically come out of the mouth. *Okuba ni mono ga hasamata yō na iikata* is a way of speaking which conceals something or is not entirely honest.

EXAMPLES

1. *Kokusai-kaigi nado de wa, ha ni kinu o kisenai de, jibun no iken o nobeta hō ga yoi.*

   At international conferences and the like, it is better not to mince your words when expressing your opinion.

2. *Kare no ha ni kinu kisenai iikata wa, aikawarazu shinratsu da.*

   When he laid it on the line, his comments were biting, as usual.

3. *Kanojo wa, jōshi no shigoto-buri o, ha ni kinu kisezu ni, hihan shita.*

   She bluntly criticized her superior's work style.

4. *Kare no ha ni kinu kisenai tsuikyū ni, aite wa tajitaji datta.*

   The subject wilted under the direct assault of his persistent questioning.

5. *Okuba ni mono no hasamatta yō na iikata wa yamete kudasai.*

   Stop beating around the bush.

haisui no jin

背水の陣

a desperate, final effort

JŌSHI:

Kondo no shinseihin ga urenai to, kaisha wa tōsan da.

BUKA:

Haisui no jin no kakugo de, ganbarimasu.

SUPERVISOR:

If our new product doesn't sell well, the company will go under.

SUBORDINATE:

I'm prepared to give my utmost in a last-ditch effort.

Haisui no jin originally referred to taking up a position *(jin)* from which there was no way to retreat *(haisui)*. From this, the expression has come to refer to being placed in a position where, in the event of failure, an opportunity will not present itself again. According to Chinese folklore, in the Han dynasty there was an outstanding military commander who by fighting with his back to the wall, successfully led his allies to victory.

EXAMPLES

1. *Kyōryoku na raibaru mo senkyo ni shutsuba shita node, kondo no senkyo wa, haisui no jin de tatakawanakereba naranai.*

   Because a powerful opponent will also run, we will have to fight a last-ditch battle in the next election.

2. *Keisatsu wa, haisui no jin de bōryokudan-tsuihō ni nori-dashita.*

   The police have launched an all-out effort to eradicate organized crime.

3. *Seitokai wa haisui no jin de, jugyōryō-neage ni kōgi shimasu.*

   The student council is fighting valiantly in a protest against the raising of tuition fees.

haji o kaku

恥をかく

be humiliated, be embarrassed

OTTO:

Kinō wa konsāto de inemuri shite, warukatta ne.

TSUMA:

Hontō desu yo. O-kage de watashi haji o kaita wa.

HUSBAND:

It was awful of me to fall asleep during yesterday's concert.

WIFE:

You're quite right. I was really embarrassed, thanks to you.

Haji (shame) *o kaku* (bear) means to be embarrassed in front of people. The causative form is *haji o kakaseru* and the causative passive form is *haji o kakasareru*. Other expressions employing *haji* include *haji no uwanuri* (one embarrassing experience is compounded with another) and *haji shirazu* (nonchalantly do embarrassing things).

EXAMPLES

1. *Supiichi no monku o wasurete, hitomae de haji o kaite shimatta.*

   I was embarrassed because I forgot the text for my speech in front of all those people.

2. *Otto no warukuchi o shinseki no atsumari de ii, tsuma wa otto ni haji o kakaseta.*

   That woman embarrassed her husband by speaking ill of him at a gathering of their relatives.

3. *Tsuma ni haji o kakaseru to wa omowanakatta.*

   I didn't expect to be humiliated by my own wife.

4. *Anata ni haji o kakaseru tsumori wa nakatta noni.*

   But I didn't intend to embarrass you . . .

hako-iri musume

箱入り娘

girl who's had a sheltered upbringing, naive girl

GĀRUFURENDO:

Watashi no uchi, mongen ga hachiji na no.

BŌIFURENDO:

Ā, hako-iri musume to tsukiau no wa taihen da na.

GIRLFRIEND:

I have to be home by eight o'clock.

BOYFRIEND:

Ah, it's hard seeing a girl who's watched so carefully by her parents.

Hako-iri musume refers to a daughter whose upbringing is so strict that she is hardly ever allowed to go out. Originally, *hako-iri* referred to things of value that were placed in boxes, carefully stored away, and rarely taken out. Precautions were taken to ensure that the box and its contents were not infested by insects. In modern usage, the threat is not insects but young men.

EXAMPLES

1. *Watashi wa hako-iri musume nanka ja arimasen.*

   I'm not a naive girl who knows nothing of the world.
2. *Uchi no hako-iri musume ni, te o dasu na yo.*

   Keep your hands off our precious daughter.
3. *Hako-iri musume ni sodateta no wa, mazukatta.*

   It was wrong to give our daughter such a cloistered upbringing.
4. *Hako-iri musume wa seken-shirazu ga ōi.*

   Many girls from respectable families who have had a sheltered upbringing know nothing of the world.
5. *Uchi no oyome-san wa, hako-iri musume datta.*

   Our daughter-in-law had a sheltered upbringing.

haku ga tsuku

箔が付く

gain prestige, have a feather added to one's cap

TOMODACHI 1:

Satō-san, kondo hakase-gō o totta sō desu yo.

TOMODACHI 2:

Kore de, kare ni mata haku ga tsukimashita ne.

FRIEND 1:

I hear that Satō recently obtained his doctorate.

FRIEND 2:

That will be yet another feather in his cap, won't it?

Haku ga tsuku means being recognized by society and gaining prestige. *Haku* is foil or leaf made of gold, silver, copper, or tin, and is produced by beating out the metals until they are paper-thin. It is then added to structures or craftwork, giving the surface an attractive finish and increasing the value of the object. It is the association with this idea that gives the expression its present-day meaning. *Haku o tsukeru* (build up one's reputation) is the corresponding transitive form.

EXAMPLES

1. *Kokku ga Furansu de shugyō shi, haku ga tsuita.*

   The chef added to his reputation by undergoing training in France.

2. *Furansu ni itta no wa, tan ni haku o tsukeru tame desu.*

   The reason I went to France was merely to build up my reputation.

3. *Haku ga tsuite mo, doryoku shinakatta sei de shigoto no jitsuryoku wa amari arimasen.*

   Even though he has gained in prestige, he isn't very competent.

4. *Piano-konkūru de yūshō shi, haku ga tsuita.*

   Winning the first prize in the piano competition added a feather to his cap.

hame o hazusu

羽目 を 外す

have a wild time, get out of control

BUCHŌ:

Konban wa ōi ni nomō. Tsukiatte kureru ne.

BUKA:

Jitsu wa kanai ga byōki de, hame o hazusu wake ni ikanain' desu.

DEPARTMENT CHIEF:

Let's go out and have a good time drinking tonight. You'll come along, won't you?

SUBORDINATE:

Actually, my wife's sick so I can't really do anything too wild.

Hame o hazusu means to let oneself go and have a wild time. There are two suggested explanations as to the origin of this idiom, the first of which claims that *hame* means the bit that a horse holds between its teeth. Once this is removed, the horse can no longer be restrained or controlled. The second explanation claims that *hame* comes from *hameita,* a board that covers a hole or trench. Removing this board could lead to disaster.

EXAMPLES

1. *Kimi, yūbe wa hame o hazushi-sugita yo.*

   You were way out of control last night, you know.

2. *Jibun de wa, sukoshi wa yotte ita kedo, kesshite hame o hazushita tsumori wa arimasen.*

   I was a little drunk, but I didn't think I was out of control.

3. *Gaikoku dakara to itte, hame o hazushite mo ii wake de wa nai.*

   Being abroad is no excuse for acting wild.

4. *Anata, hame o hazusu ni mo gendo ga arimasu.*

   It's all right to let yourself go up to a point, but there are limits.

hana ga takai

鼻が高い

proud, stuck up

GAKUSEI:

Sensei, o-kagesama de, Tōdai ni gōkaku shimashita.

SENSEI:

Sore wa omedetō. Watashi mo yūshū na seito o motte, hana ga takai yo.

STUDENT:

Thank you for all the support you've given me. I have been accepted into Tokyo University.

TEACHER:

Congratulations. I am proud of having an excellent student.

Hana ga takai, literally "high nose," means to feel proud; *hana o takaku suru* is another phrase with the same meaning. Other phrases using *hana* include *hana ni kakeru* (be conceited or vain) and *hana ni tsuku* (get tired of or be fed up with).

EXAMPLES

1. *Rippa na musuko-san o o-mochi de, sazo hana ga takai deshō.*
   You must be so proud to have such a wonderful son.
2. *Kanojo wa totemo hana ni tsuku hito da.*
   She is really stuck up.
3. *Boku wa kimi no yō na koibito ga ite, hana ga takai yo.*
   I'm so proud to have a girlfriend like you.
4. *Sensei wa anata no koto de, totemo hana o takaku shite imashita yo.*
   The teacher was very proud of you.

hana-mochi naranai

鼻持ちならない

detestable, disgusting

DŌRYŌ 1:

Suzuki-san no hanashi wa musuko-san no jiman bakari de, iya ni narimasu ne.

DŌRYŌ 2:

Hontō ni, are wa hana-mochi narimasen ne.

COLLEAGUE 1:

Doesn't it make you sick the way Suzuki constantly brags about his son?

COLLEAGUE 2:

Yes, it really is hard to take.

Hana-mochi naranai combines *hana* (nose), *mochi* (endure, stay long), and *naranai* (not become), and translates as "so foul smelling that one cannot bear the stench." Thus this expression describes anything detestable or disgusting.

EXAMPLES

1. *Kare no gōman na hanashikata wa hana-mochi naranai.*

   I cannot stand his stuck-up way of talking.

2. *Seijika no taido no ōkisa wa hana-mochi narimasen ne.*

   I find the overbearing attitudes of politicians to be obnoxious.

3. *Kimi no ima no ōhei na ukekotae wa, hana-mochi naranai ne.*

   I find your arrogant answer to that question really disgusting.

4. *Hontō ni, Satō-san 'tte, hana-mochi naranai hito ne.*

   Satō really is a horrible person, isn't he?

hana-muke no kotoba

餞の言葉

farewell remarks

SHIKAISHA:

Sore de wa, futari no kadode o iwatte, sensei ni hana-muke no kotoba o itadakimasu.

SENSEI:

Go-kekkon omedetō . . .

MASTER OF CEREMONIES:

I'll now call on the professor to extend a few words of farewell to the couple, wishing them good luck for their new life ahead.

PROFESSOR:

Congratulations on your marriage . . .

Hana-muke no kotoba, a combination of *hana* (nose) and *muke* (point or direct), refers to the heartfelt words one expresses to someone from whom one is parting. In the past, it was a common practice to point the nose of one's horse towards his or her destination and pray for safety. *Hana-muke ni* (as a farewell present) refers to money or other valuables that are given as a parting gift.

EXAMPLES

1. *Ryūgaku suru kimi ni, hana-muke no kotoba o okurō.*

   Let me extend some farewell wishes before you leave to study abroad.

2. *Subarashii hana-muke no kotoba, arigatō gozaimasu.*

   Thank you very much for your splendid farewell speech.

3. *Sotsugyō suru seito-tachi ni, hana-muke no kotoba o o-negai shimasu.*

   Would you mind saying a few words to the graduates to wish them good luck for the future?

4. *Kono hon, tenkin no hana-muke ni sashiagemasu.*

   Since you are going to be transferred, I'd like to give you this book as a farewell gift.

hanashi ga nitsumaru

話が煮詰る

discussion narrows down

TOMODACHI 1:

Shain-ryokō no keikaku, dō narimashita ka?

TOMODACHI 2:

Hanashi ga dandan nitsumatte kimashita yo.

FRIEND 1:

How are the plans for the company trip progressing?

FRIEND 2:

The discussion is gradually starting to get somewhere.

Nitsumaru, and its intransitive form, *nitsumeru,* means to boil a liquid until the excess moisture disappears. When combined with *hanashi* (talk), it indicates that negotiations have reached a final stage. Other expressions using *nitsumaru* include *giron ga nitsumaru* (the discussion seems like it will finally reach a conclusion), *mondai-ten ga nitsumaru* (the controversial point is close to resolution), and *keikaku ga nitsumaru* (the planning is in its final stage).

EXAMPLES

1. *Hanashi mo nitsumatta yō na node, ketsuron o dashimashō.*

   Since the talks seem to be winding down, let's make our conclusions.

2. *Mō sukoshi, hanashi o nitsumete kara ni shimashō.*

   Let's do it after the discussion has narrowed down a little more.

3. *Hanashi wa nakanaka nitsumarimasen ne.*

   The talks don't seem to be progressing at all.

4. *Hanashi ga nitsumatte kara, ato no keikaku o o-hanashi shimasu.*

   Once this matter is worked out, we can discuss the rest of the plans.

hane o nobasu

羽を伸ばす

kick up one's heels

KAISHAIN 1:

Buchō, ashita kara shutchō datte?

KAISHAIN 2:

Sore wa ureshii ne. Shibaraku no aida, hane o nobasesō da.

EMPLOYEE 1:

I hear the chief is going away tomorrow on business.

EMPLOYEE 2:

That's great. It looks like we'll be able to kick up our heels for a while.

Hane (wings) *o nobasu* (spread) refers to behaving in a relaxed, unrestrained fashion—just like a bird spreading its wings and flying freely in the sky. Another phrase with *hane* is *hane ga haete tobu yō* (as if it had grown wings and flown away), which describes goods selling like hot cakes.

EXAMPLES

1. *Ie ni chichioya ga iru to, nakanaka hane o nobasenai.*
   When my father's at home I can't unwind at all.
2. *Kaigai-ryokō ni ittara, omoikkiri hane o nobasō.*
   When we go overseas let's really have ourselves a good time.
3. *Buchō ga bā de hane o nobashite iru tokoro o mite shimatta.*
   I came across our department chief having a binge in a bar.
4. *Natsu-yasumi wa benkyō o wasurete, hane o nobashitai mono desu.*
   When the summer vacation comes I'd like to forget my studies and have a good time.
5. *Watashi ga ryokō ni ittara, anata wa kitto hane o nobasun' deshō?*
   When I go away on my trip, I'm sure that you'll start fooling around.

happō bijin
八方美人
everyone's friend

DŌRYŌ 1:

Kimura-san wa, kono kikaku o totemo homete kuremashita yo.

DŌRYŌ 2:

Amari, matomo ni toranai hō ga ii desu yo. Kare wa happō bijin dakara.

COLLEAGUE 1:

Kimura spoke very highly of this plan.

COLLEAGUE 2:

You'd be better off not trusting him too much. He always just tells people what they want to hear.

Happō bijin refers to people who try to make others believe that they are their friend. *Happō* describes the eight points of the compass— north, south, east, west as well as northeast, southeast, northwest and southwest; in other words, all directions. When *bijin* (beautiful girl) is added to this, it indicates that the person is a beauty, no matter what angle she is viewed from.

EXAMPLES

1. *Kare ga anna ni happō bijin to wa omowanakatta.*

   I didn't think that he would try to please everybody that much.

2. *Amari happō bijin da to shin'yō sarenaku naru.*

   If you try too hard to be everyone's friend, you'll lose people's trust.

3. *Nihon no gaikō wa happō bijin gaikō to iwareru.*

   Japan's foreign policy is referred to as the policy of trying to be every nation's friend.

4. *Kanojo no tachiba de wa, happō bijin ni narazaru o enai.*

   In her position, she cannot help but try to please everybody.

hara no mushi

腹の虫

one's mood, feelings

TOMODACHI 1:

Nani o okotte irun' desu ka?

TOMODACHI 2:

Kanojo no itta koto ga amari ni hidoi node, hara no mushi ga osamaranain' desu.

FRIEND 1:

What are you so upset about?

FRIEND 2:

I just can't get over what my girlfriend said.

Hara no mushi, literally "stomach bug," refers to an imaginary bug in one's stomach that is the source of one's mood and that growls when one is hungry. Expressions using *hara no mushi* include *hara no mushi ga osamaranai* and *hara no mushi ga shōchi shinai*, both meaning to be irritated beyond one's patience, and *hara no mushi no idokoro ga warui*, meaning to be in a bad mood.

EXAMPLES

1. *Shachō wa ima, hara no mushi no idokoro ga warui desu yo.*
   The company president is in a bad mood right now.
2. *Hara no mushi no idokoro ga warui toki ni wa, kare ni chikazukanai hō ga ii.*
   It's better not to be near him when he is in a bad mood.
3. *Kare no yarikata de wa, watashi no hara no mushi ga shōchi shinai.*
   I can't stand the way he does things.
4. *Onaka ga suite, hara no mushi ga naki-dashita.*
   Being hungry, my stomach began growling.
5. *Musume wa damasareta koto de, hara no mushi ga osamaranai desu.*
   My daughter is very angry because she was tricked.

hara o waru

腹を割る

show one's true feelings, open up to someone

BUKA:

Buchō, kono aida no koto de, chotto o-hanashi shitai no desu ga.

BUCHŌ:

Sō da ne. O-tagai ni, ichido, hara o watte hanashita hō ga ii ne.

SUBORDINATE:

Could we talk about that matter sometime?

DEPARTMENT CHIEF:

Now that you mention it, I think it would be good for us to have a heart-to-heart discussion.

Hara o waru means to show one's true feelings. In Japan it is believed that one's true feelings come from the *hara* (belly). *Waru* means to split and open. Expressions using *hara* include *hara ga kuroi* (a wicked person with evil thoughts), *hara o kimeru* (be resolved to do something), and *hara o saguru* (indirectly try to find out a person's intentions).

EXAMPLES

1. *Kare ga hara o watte, hanashite kureru to ii noni.*
   It would be nice if he would just open up.
2. *Kare wa nakanaka hara o watte, hanasō to shinai.*
   He is rather reluctant to open up and talk.
3. *Kyō wa, hara o watte, hanashi-aimashō.*
   Let's have a heart-to-heart talk today.
4. *Hara o watte, hon'ne o itte moraemasen ka?*
   Could you please open up and tell me your true intentions?
5. *Hara o watte, hanashi-aete, yokatta desu ne.*
   I'm glad we had this heart-to-heart talk.

hashi ni mo bō ni mo kakaranai

箸にも棒にも掛からない

no hope of success

SAKKA:

Watashi no tomodachi no genkō, zasshi ni nosete moraesō desu ka?

HENSHŪSHA:

Zan'nen dakedo, omoshirokunakute, hashi ni mo bō ni mo kakarimasen yo.

WRITER:

Do you think my friend's article will be printed in the magazine?

EDITOR:

I'm afraid that his article was so dull that there's no chance of it being published.

Hashi ni mo bō ni mo kakaranai, literally "not being able to pick up something with either chopsticks or a large pole," refers to the futility of even trying something. Other expressions using *hashi* include *hashi no ageoroshi* (finding fault with every little thing) and *hashi yori omoi mono wa motanai* (be raised in luxury without having had any experience working).

EXAMPLES

1. *Kimi ga Orinpikku nante, hashi ni mo bō ni mo kakaru wake arimasen.*
   There's no way you could ever make it to the Olympics.
2. *Hashi ni mo bō ni mo kakaranakute mo, gekidan no ōdishon, ganbatte mitai.*
   Even if it's a long shot, I want to try out for the play.
3. *Anata to chesu o shite mo, watashi de wa hashi ni mo bō ni mo kakarimasen.*
   I wouldn't have a chance against you in a game of chess.
4. *Hashi ni mo bō ni mo kakaranai koto wa wakatte imasu.*
   I know I don't have a chance.

hashi-watashi

橋渡し

intermediary

SEIJIKA 1:

Kono mama de wa, nichibei kankei ni mondai ga shōjimasu ne.

SEIJIKA 2:

Dareka, hashi-watashi dekiru ningen wa inai deshō ka?

POLITICIAN 1:

At this rate, problems between the U.S. and Japan are bound to develop.

POLITICIAN 2:

Isn't there anyone who can serve as an intermediary?

Hashi-watashi, literally "to lay *(watasu)* a bridge *(hashi)* between two things," combines with *suru* to mean to serve as an intermediary, to play a bridging role, to mediate, or to act as a go-between.

EXAMPLES

1. *Aite to no hashi-watashi o shite kureru hito ga inai.*

   There is no one who will act as an intermediary for us.

2. *Kare wa hashi-watashi suru no ga tokui da.*

   He is very good at bringing two sides together.

3. *Kare no hashi-watashi de, nantoka dakyō ga seiritsu shita.*

   Thanks to his mediation, we were somehow able to reach a compromise.

4. *Buchō to no hashi-watashi yaku wa, kanojo ni makaseyō.*

   Let's leave it to her to act as mediator between the department chief and us.

5. *Nihon ni, Ōbei to Ajia no hashi-watashi yaku ga tsutomaru darō ka?*

   Can Japan really serve as an intermediary between the West and Asia?

hata-iro ga warui

旗色が悪い

unfavorable outlook

BŌIFURENDO:

Mō tsukareta kara, tenisu, yameyō ka?

GĀRUFURENDO:

Jibun no hata-iro ga waruku naru to, sugu yametagaru no ne.

BOYFRIEND:

I'm so tired. Why don't we stop playing tennis?

GIRLFRIEND:

Whenever you're not doing well, you always want to quit.

Hata-iro ga warui, literally "color of flag is bad," has its origins in feudal Japan. During battles, a general could tell how his allies were faring by looking at flags displayed for the occasion. Other expressions using *hata* include *hata o miru* (watch the condition of affairs in order to profit from them) and *hata o ageru* (begin a project).

EXAMPLES

1. *Hajime wa katte ita noni, dondon hata-iro ga waruku natte kita.*
   At first, we were winning, but the situation quickly deteriorated.
2. *Mikata no hata-iro ga warui node, shinpai desu.*
   I'm worried because our teammates seem to be losing.
3. *Hata-iro ga warukute mo, gyakuten suru kamo shiremasen yo.*
   Even though the odds are against you, things may turn around.
4. *Sā, kondo wa kimi no hata-iro ga waruku natte kita yo.*
   Well, this time the tables are turned against you.
5. *Watashi, hata-iro no warui hō o ōen shimasu.*
   I'll support the side that is losing.

hattari o kikaseru

はったりをきかせる

bluff

CHICHIOYA:

Omae-tachi, katte na mane o suru to, kandō suru zo.

MUSUKO

Otōsan, sore de hattari o kikasete iru tsumori?

FATHER:

If you do that, I'll throw all of you out of the house.

SON:

Dad, is that your idea of a bluff?

Hattari o kikaseru refers to misleading or frightening others by exaggerating things. The origins of *hattari* are unclear, although many believe that it derived from the practice of dealers calling out to gamblers during a dice game, *sā, hatta, hatta,* meaning come on, stake your bets, stake your bets. *Hattari o kakeru* and *hattari o kiku* have the same meaning as *hattari o kikaseru*.

EXAMPLES

1. *Kodomo-tachi ni, hattari o kikasete oita yo.*
   I bluffed the children into believing me.
2. *Keisatsu de wa, hattari o kikasete mo shikata ga nai.*
   There is no point in trying to bluff the police.
3. *Watashi wa donna hattari o kakerarete mo, odorokimasen yo.*
   No matter how much they exaggerate, I won't act surprised.
4. *Anata wa zenzen hattari no kikanai hito ne.*
   Your bluff has no effect whatsoever.

herazu-guchi o kiku

減らず口をきく

say smart, sassy remarks

MUSUKO:

Benkyō nanka, dōse atama ga waruin' dakara, muda da yo.

HAHAOYA:

Anata wa, herazu-guchi shika kikenai no?

SON:

It's a waste to study since I'm not very smart.

MOTHER:

Don't give me any of your smart remarks.

Herazu-guchi o kiku combines *herazu-guchi* (useless retort) and *kiku* (say) to refer to making a smart remark. An expression with the same meaning is *herazu-guchi o tataku,* and a similar expression is *kuchi no heranai hito,* which refers to someone who always acts like a smart aleck.

EXAMPLES

1. *Konogoro, musuko wa herazu-guchi bakari tataite iru.*
   Recently, my son has become a real smart aleck.
2. *Anata no herazu-guchi nado, kikitaku arimasen.*
   I don't want to listen to your smart remarks.
3. *Otōsan ni herazu-guchi o kiite wa ikemasen yo.*
   Don't talk back to your father.
4. *Benkyō mo shinai kuse ni, herazu-guchi bakari umaku natta.*
   Even though you don't study, you've become skilled at making sassy remarks.

heso-kuri o tameru

へそくりを貯める

save up secretly

IMŌTO:

Mā, suteki na emerarudo no yubiwa ne.

ANE:

Heso-kuri o tamete, yatto katta no yo.

YOUNGER SISTER:

My, what a lovely emerald ring!

OLDER SISTER:

I've been secretly saving my money and finally had enough to buy it.

Heso-kuri o tameru most commonly refers to money that a wife has secretly saved up. *Heso* originally referred to yarn from which wives would spin *(kuru)* thread. Over time, *heso-kuri* came to refer to money, and with *tameru* (save) now means to save up secretly. *Heso-kuru* means to put money away secretly.

EXAMPLES

1. *Otto ni naisho de, heso-kuri o tamete iru.*

   I'm putting money aside without letting my husband know.

2. *Kimi ga heso-kuri o tamete iru no wa, wakatte iru yo.*

   I know you have been secretly stashing away money.

3. *Kore wa watashi no heso-kuri de katta mono desu.*

   I bought this with the money I've been secretly saving.

4. *Heso-kuri ga tamattara, Yōroppa ryokō ga shitai.*

   I'd like to visit Europe when I have enough money saved up.

5. *Sukunai kyūryō kara heso-kuru no wa totemo taihen datta.*

   It was very difficult to save up money with my meager salary.

heta no yokozuki

下手の横好き

crazy about something yet unskilled at it

BUKA:

Mata go desu ka?

BUCHŌ:

Heta no yokozuki de ne. Yamerarenain' da.

SUBORDINATE:

Are you playing *go* again?

DEPARTMENT CHIEF:

I'm crazy about it, even though I'm not very good. I just can't stop playing.

Heta no yokozuki refers to someone who has great interest in something, but is not skilled at it. When used in reference to oneself, this phrase expresses modesty, but when used in reference to others, it pokes fun at them. *Yokozuki* by itself refers to something one likes immensely but is no good at, and *heta* means unskillful.

EXAMPLES

1. *Otōsan no karaoke, heta no yokozuki nan' dakara.*

   My father likes karaoke even though he's not very good at it.

2. *Watashi no uta, heta no yokozuki da to iun' desu ka?*

   Are you saying that my singing is no good?

3. *Heta no yokozuki ni kōchi o suru no wa tsukaremasu.*

   It is tiring to coach someone who's enthusiastic but not very good.

4. *Heta no yokozuki nante, go-kenson deshō.*

   You're just being modest saying you're no good.

5. *Heta no yokozuki to omotte itara, jōzu ni narimashita ne.*

   I didn't think you were that good, but you've really improved.

hi no kuruma

火の車

suffering due to lack of money

TOMODACHI 1:

Go-rippa na o-sumai desu ne.

TOMODACHI 2:

Sore ga, rōn ga taihen de kakei wa hi no kuruma nan' desu.

FRIEND 1:

What a splendid house you have!

FRIEND 2:

To tell you the truth, the loan payments are really hurting us. We don't have much left for living expenses.

Hi no kuruma stems from the Buddhist belief that good people go to paradise and bad people go to hell. *Hi no kuruma,* literally "fire car," is the vehicle used to carry sinners to hell; the fires make the sinners suffer even before they reach hell. *Hi no kuruma* eventually came to refer to suffering due to lack of money.

EXAMPLES

1. *Eigyō ga fushin de, kaisha no keiei wa hi no kuruma da.*
   Since business is slow, our company is hard up for money.
2. *Kokka zaisei ga hi no kuruma desu.*
   The national budget is in a pinch.
3. *Kakei wa hi no kuruma de, ryokō suru yoyū nado arimasen.*
   Our family finances are so tight that we have nothing to spare for a trip.
4. *Nōkigu no kaisugi de, hi no kuruma ni natte iru nōka ga ōi.*
   Because they purchased too much farm equipment, many farmers are hard up for money.
5. *Nantoka, hi no kuruma no jōtai o nuke-dashita.*
   Somehow we were able to overcome our financial difficulties.

hidari-mae ni naru

左前になる

have financial difficulties, have things go badly

KYAKU:

O-mise, raigetsu kara heiten suru sō desu ne.

TEN'IN:

Hai. Kyonen gurai kara hidari-mae ni narimashite.

CUSTOMER:

I hear this shop is closing down next month.

SALESPERSON:

Yes. Things have been going badly since last year.

Hidari-mae ni naru is used to describe a situation, often business-related, in which things have not gone well. Originally, *hidari-mae* referred to the way a deceased person's kimono was folded for the funeral—the left side folded over the right side, instead of the usual right over left. *Hidari-mae* became associated with something bad, and then with bad luck, especially with regards to money. *Hidari-mae* can be used by itself.

EXAMPLES

1. *Shōbai ga hidari-mae ni naru to, ginkō wa kane o kashite kurenaku natta.*

   When business slowed down, the bank stopped lending me money.

2. *Kanojo wa watashi ga hidari-mae ni natta to shitte, tsumetaku shidashita.*

   When my girlfriend found out that I was in financial trouble, she gave me the cold shoulder.

3. *Itsu kara o-mise ga hidari-mae ni natta no desu ka?*

   When did your shop start having financial problems?

4. *Kare no kaisha, saikin hidari-mae rashii desu yo.*

   It looks as if his company has run into hard times lately.

hidari uchiwa

左うちわ

taking things easy and not working

TOMODACHI 1:

O-taku no hatake, ichiokuen de ureta sō desu ne.

TOMODACHI 2:

Kore de, mō hatake-shigoto o sezu ni, hidari uchiwa de kurasemasu yo.

FRIEND 1:

I heard that you sold your farm for 100 million yen.

FRIEND 2:

Now I'll be able to sit back and take things easy—no more working in the fields.

Hidari uchiwa means not working and living an easy life. A fan, *(uchiwa)*, is usually held in the right hand; thus, if a person has a fan on his left *(hidari)*, it means that someone else is fanning him. In short, he is enjoying life without having to raise a finger.

EXAMPLES

1. *Kare wa taishokukin o takusan moratte, hidari uchiwa no mibun da.*
   He received a large sum of money when he retired and is now living very comfortably.
2. *Itsuka, hidari uchiwa no kurashi ga shitai mono desu.*
   Someday, I'd like to have a life of luxury.
3. *Kanemochi no musume to kekkon shite, hidari uchiwa de kurashitai.*
   I'd like to marry a girl from a wealthy family and sit back and take it easy.
4. *Kanojo wa, rōgo, hidari uchiwa de kurashimashita.*
   She lived comfortably when she got older.

hike o toranai

引けを取らない

hold one's own, compare favorably with

DŌRYŌ 1:

Yamamoto-san, shōgi no ude ga agarimashita ne.

DŌRYŌ 2:

Kimi datte, kare ni hike o torimasen yo.

COLLEAGUE 1:

Yamamoto's skill at Japanese chess has improved, hasn't it?

COLLEAGUE 2:

You're just as good as he is.

Hike o toranai means not giving in to defeat. On the battlefield, *hike* referred to being defeated and forced to retreat. *Hike o toranai,* literally "to not give the signal for defeat," over time changed to mean to be just as good or skillful as someone else. Other expressions using *hike* are *hikime o kanjiru* (have an inferiority complex) and *hike o toru* (be defeated or be inferior).

EXAMPLES

1. *Tsuma no ryōri wa ichiryū kokku ni hike o toranai.*

   My wife's cooking is on par with that of a first-rate chef.

2. *Kare no Furansugo wa tsūyaku ni hike o toranai.*

   He can hold his own as a French interpreter.

3. *Kono sakuhin nara tenrankai ni dashite mo hike o toranai deshō.*

   This work would not look out of place if it were in an exhibition.

4. *Kono shinseihin nara, tasha ni hike o toranai desu yo.*

   This new product will prove itself equal to those of other companies.

5. *Kono konpe de wa, kare ni hike o toru wake ni wa ikanai.*

   I can't afford to be beaten by him in this golf tournament.

hima o tsubusu

暇を潰す

kill time, waste time

OTTO:

Chotto pachinko ni itte kuru yo.

TSUMA:

Sonna koto de, hima o tsubusu nante mottai nai wa.

HUSBAND:

I'm going out to play a little pachinko.

WIFE:

That's such a poor use of your free time.

Hima o tsubusu, literally "smashing free time," means to do something because one has some extra time. In particular, this expression refers to killing time by doing something one may not be that interested in. *Hima-tsubushi* refers to free time. Other phrases using *hima* include *hima ga aku* (have free time) and *hima ni akasu* (give ample time to do something).

EXAMPLES

1. *Kyō wa nani o shite, hima o tsubusō ka na?*
   How am I going to kill time today?
2. *Hima-tsubushi ni honya e de mo itte mimashō.*
   Let's go to a bookstore and kill some time.
3. *Isogashikute, sonna koto ni hima o tsubushite iraremasen.*
   I'm so busy that I can't waste time doing something like that.
4. *Hima tsubushi ni, toranpu de mo dō desu ka?*
   How about playing some cards to kill time?
5. *Hima o tsubusu no nara, toshokan ni iku no ga ichiban da.*
   Going to the library is the best way to kill time.

hinshuku o kau

ひんしゅくを買う

be frowned upon

SEIJIKA 1:

Nihon wa motto yushutsu o herasu hitsuyō ga arimasu.

SEIJIKA 2:

Sō shinai to, sekai kara hinshuku o katte shimaimasu kara.

POLITICIAN 1:

Japan needs to further reduce its exports.

POLITICIAN 2:

If this isn't done, the world will look disapprovingly at us.

Hinshuku o kau means to incur disfavor, especially to the point where it becomes difficult to have any dealings with others. *Hin* (scowl) and *shuku* (shrink) both refer to knitting one's brow while frowning, a gesture of displeasure or dissatisfaction. *Kau,* in this expression, means to invite upon oneself. Other expressions using this meaning of *kau* are *hankan o kau* (rouse a person's hostility) and *nikushimi o kau* (incur a person's hatred).

EXAMPLES

1. *Kare wa mai-asa chikoku shite, dōryō no hinshuku o katte iru.*
   His colleagues dislike him because he is tardy every morning.
2. *Ki o tsukenai to, minna no hinshuku o kaimasu yo.*
   If you aren't careful, everyone will take a disliking to you.
3. *Sonna ni hade na kakkō o suru to sensei kara hinshuku o kau yo.*
   The teacher will disapprove of your dressing in such a gaudy way.
4. *Kare wa jibun no iken ni koshitsu shite, yūjin kara hinshuku o katta.*
   He held fast to his own opinion and lost his friends.

hippari-dako

引っ張りだこ

a person much in demand

IRAININ:

Sumimasen. Raishū, sensei ni go-kōen o o-negai dekinai ka to omoimashite.

HISHO:

Totemo muri desu ne. Sensei wa atchi-kotchi hippari-dako na mono de. Raigetsu nara, nantoka dekimasu ga.

CLIENT:

Excuse me, I was wondering if the professor might be able to give a lecture next week.

SECRETARY:

I'm afraid it's quite impossible. The professor is very much in demand. However, next month might be possible.

Hippari-dako refers to a popular thing or person that is keenly sought after by many different people. *Hippari-dako,* combining *hipparu* (pull) and *dako* (kite), is used in connection with people, such as popular singers, teachers, doctors, and attorneys, and with things, such as a product that everybody wants.

EXAMPLES

1. *Ano bengoshi wa ude ga ii to, hippari-dako desu.*
   They say that attorney is very good and thus very much in demand.
2. *Kare wa sugoi ninki de, hippari-dako no sensei desu.*
   He is a very popular teacher and is much sought after.
3. *Shinshōhin ga konna ni hippari-dako ni natte, ureshii desu ne.*
   I'm delighted that our new product has taken off so well.
4. *Kanojo wa pātii de hippari-dako deshita.*
   She was the life of the party.

hito-hata ageru

一旗揚げる

attain success, seek one's fortune

BUCHŌ:

Kimi, chika-jika kaisha o yameru sō da ne.

BUKA:

Hai, yūjin to kaisha o setsuritsu shite, hito-hata ageyō to omoimashite.

DEPARTMENT CHIEF:

I hear you'll be leaving the company in the near future.

SUBORDINATE:

Yes, I've been thinking of setting up a company with a friend and making a name for myself.

Hito-hata ageru, meaning to launch into a new venture, originally described flags that were used on the battlefield in feudal Japan. After a victory, a special flag *(hito-hata)* would be raised *(ageru)* to signal that the enemy was defeated. Over time, *hito-hata ageru* became synonymous with any success in life, and then broadened in meaning to include the idea of undertaking a project.

EXAMPLES

1. *Kare wa itsuka hito-hata ageyō to omotte iru.*
   He's planning on making it big someday.
2. *Kare wa hito-hata ageru kikai o neratte iru.*
   He's on the lookout for a chance to succeed in the world.
3. *Anata mo, hito-hata agete mitai to omoimasen ka?*
   Don't you feel like trying to make a name for yourself too?
4. *Kare wa hito-hata agete, seikō shita.*
   He set out to seek his fortune and found success.
5. *Hito-hata ageru ni wa, shikin to jinzai ga hitsuyō da.*
   In order to make a name for yourself, funds and talent are necessary.

hitori-zumō

独り相撲

a futile effort

TOMODACHI 1:

Kanojo ni rabu retā kaita noni, henji ga konain' desu yo.

TOMODACHI 2:

Sore wa kitto, anata no hitori-zumō desu yo.

FRIEND 1:

Even though I wrote her a love letter, there's been no reply.

FRIEND 2:

Surely for you it's a completely futile effort.

Hitori-zumō, literally "one-person sumo," has two meanings. One refers to a single person imitating two people engaged in sumo wrestling. This can be observed at many shrines during Shinto ceremonies. The other refers to fighting despite the absence of an opponent, which is futile. This second usage is frequently used in colloquial Japanese.

EXAMPLES

1. *Don Kihōte wa fūsha o aite ni hitori-zumō o totte ita.*
   Don Quixote attacked a windmill to little avail.
2. *Shachō o aite ni shite mo, hitori-zumō ni naru dake desu.*
   If you oppose the company president, it will just be in vain.
3. *Kare to giron shite mo, hitori-zumō ni owatte shimau.*
   With him, you might as well be arguing with a wall.
4. *Konna ni doryoku shite mo, hitori-zumō ni narisō desu.*
   Even though I've put in this much effort, it seems to be futile.
5. *Fūfu-genka wa itsumo watashi no hitori-zumō desu.*
   Domestic quarrels for me always lead nowhere.

hiya-meshi o kū

冷飯を食う

be treated coldly, be kept in a low position

BUKA:

Buchō ni shōshin, omedetō gozaimasu.

KACHŌ:

Arigatō. Boku mo zuibun nagai aida, hiya-meshi o kutte kita kara ne.

SUBORDINATE:

Congratulations on your promotion to department chief.

SECTION CHIEF:

Thank you. It's about time. I've been kept in a low position for so long.

Hiya-meshi o kū derives from eating *(kū)* cold *(hiya)* rice *(meshi)*, and refers to being dependent upon another household for one's upkeep or, more colloquially, to being given a hard time or being treated coldly. *Hiya-meshi o kuwasu* means to treat someone coldly, and like *hiya-meshi o kū*, is frequently used to describe work-related situations.

EXAMPLES

1. *Aitsu wa namaiki dakara, shibaraku hiya-meshi o kuwasete okō.*
   Because he's so conceited, let's just ignore him for a while.
2. *Buchō ni hankō suru to, hiya-meshi o kuwasaremasu yo.*
   If you defy the chief, you'll be left out in the cold from then on.
3. *Kare wa sainō ga aru noni, hiya-meshi bakari kutte kita.*
   Even though he is talented, he has had nothing but harsh treatment.
4. *Shachō ni mo, hiya-meshi o kuwasareta jidai ga atta.*
   Even the company president had a period when he was treated indifferently by his superiors.

hongoshi o ireru

本腰を入れる

set about in earnest

TOMODACHI 1:

Tochi no nedan ga takai ne.

TOMODACHI 2:

Seifu mo tochi-taisaku ni hongoshi o ire-hajimeta yō desu yo.

FRIEND 1:

Land prices are high, aren't they?

FRIEND 2:

It appears that the government has begun to make serious efforts towards countering rising land prices.

Hongoshi o ireru means to do something in earnest. *Hongoshi* originally referred to a proper stance as in, for example, sumo, when a wrestler assumes a certain stance before engaging in the actual bout. Taking this stance indicated that the wrestler was prepared to fight. A similar expression is *koshi o ireru.*

EXAMPLES

1. *Juken-benkyō, kyō kara hongoshi o irete kakarō to omoun' da.*

   I think from today I'll get down and study hard for my exams.

2. *Shōgi de, kare ga hongoshi o iretara, totemo kanawanai.*

   In Japanese chess, nobody can match him when he gets down to business.

3. *Ikura tanonde mo, seifu wa hongoshi o ireyō to shinai.*

   Despite having been asked a number of times, the government has made no attempt to pursue this seriously.

4. *Itsu ni nattara, hongoshi o irete kureru no desu ka?*

   When are you going to take this up in earnest?

5. *Kare ni wa, hongoshi o ireru tsumori wa mattaku nai.*

   He has no intention whatsoever of putting everything he has got into it.

hora o fuku

ほらを吹く

talk big

ANI:

Kondo no tanjō-iwai ni, shinju no nekkuresu o katte ageyō.

IMŌTO:

Oniisan, mata hora o fuiteru. Katte kureta koto nai noni.

OLDER BROTHER:

How about I buy you a pearl necklace for your next birthday?

YOUNGER SISTER:

There you go talking big again. You've never even bought me anything before.

Hora o fuku, literally "to blow a conch shell," means to exaggerate and talk big. Originally, the military and mountain priests blew conch shells as a signal or warning. From this the meaning has changed to exaggerate. The nominal form is *horafuki,* which describes one who threatens or intimidates others or one who tells tall tales. *Hora* alone is also used to mean an exaggeration or tall tale.

EXAMPLES

1. *Hora nanka fuite imasen. Hontō desu.*
   I'm no braggart, really.
2. *Anata no koto, minna ga horafuki to itte imasu yo.*
   Everyone says that you are full of hot air.
3. *Ni-mētoru no sakana o tsukamaeta nado, kitto hora desu yo.*
   He caught a fish two meters long? I'll bet you it's a tall tale.
4. *Ano hito wa horafuki dakara, shinjite wa ikemasen yo.*
   You mustn't believe him—he's always talking big.
5. *Kanojo ga jukkakokugo hanaseru nante, hora deshō.*
   Saying she can speak ten languages—what a lot of talk.

hyōtan kara koma

ひょうたんから駒

an unexpected dividend

TOMODACHI 1:

Takarakuji o hirottan' desu yo. Sō shitara, sore ga issenman'en no atarikuji deshite ne.

TOMODACHI 2:

Sore wa hyōtan kara koma desu ne. Otoshinushi ga arawarenai to ii keredo.

FRIEND 1:

I found a lottery ticket. It turned out to be a winner, worth 10 million yen.

FRIEND 2:

That certainly must have been a surprise. I hope the guy who bought the ticket doesn't turn up.

Hyōtan kara koma, literally "a chess piece *(koma)* that comes out of a gourd *(hyōtan),*" refers to an unforeseen or unanticipated result. This expression is often used when something said in apparent jest turns out to be true.

EXAMPLES

1. *Hyōtan kara koma de, saisho no dēto kara sugu ni kekkon ni hanashi ga susunda.*

   What a surprise! On our first date he asked me to marry him.

2. *Chotto shita omoitsuki ga hyōtan kara koma de, daiseikō shita.*

   The small idea ended up producing an unexpected dividend and brought us great success.

3. *Jiken wa hyōtan kara koma no, omowanu tenkai o miseta.*

   The incident took a surprising turn.

4. *Kare no teian wa, hyōtan kara koma no hamon o yonda.*

   His suggestion created a totally unexpected stir.

98

hyōzan no ikkaku

氷山の一角

the tip of the iceberg

TOMODACHI 1:

Daijin ga datsuzei de tsukamarimashita ne.

TOMODACHI 2:

Kitto, are wa hyōzan no ikkaku de, hoka no seijika mo onaji da to omoimasu yo.

FRIEND 1:

The government minister was arrested for tax evasion.

FRIEND 2:

I feel sure that it's just the tip of the iceberg—other politicians are doing the same thing.

The part of an iceberg *(hyōzan)* visible above the surface of the water is only one-eighth or one-seventh its entire size. *Hyōzan no ikkaku* has the same meaning as the English expression "the tip *(ikkaku)* of the iceberg."

EXAMPLES

1. *Kono oshoku wa hyōzan no ikkaku ni sugimasen.*

   This corruption is merely the tip of the iceberg.

2. *Hyōzan no ikkaku to iu koto wa, mada hoka ni mo iru to iu koto desu.*

   When he says "this is the tip of the iceberg," he means that there are still others involved.

3. *Sanseiu wa taiki-osen to iu shinkoku na kankyō mondai no hyōzan no ikkaku desu.*

   Acid rain and air pollution are just the tip of the iceberg of a very serious environmental problem.

4. *Kare no taiho wa, hon no hyōzan no ikkaku desu.*

   His arrest is just the tip of the iceberg.

i no naka no kawazu

井の中の蛙

ignorant of worldly affairs, out of touch

TSUMA:

Watashi mo soto ni dete, shigoto ga shitai wa.

OTTO:

Dōshite? Kyūryō ga tarinai no?

TSUMA:

Iie, i no naka no kawazu ni narisō de, shinpai na no.

WIFE:

I want to get out of the house and get a job.

HUSBAND:

Why? Don't I make enough money?

WIFE:

No, it's that I'm worried I'm losing touch with the world.

I no naka no kawazu is a shortened version of *i no naka no kawazu, taikai o shirazu,* literally "a frog in the well knows nothing of the great ocean beyond." As the metaphor suggests, a frog that lives in a well doesn't know about things outside the well and believes that his little well is the entire world. The expression is used to describe people who have a very narrow outlook of things or who are ignorant of worldly affairs.

EXAMPLES

1. *Konna shigoto o shite iru no wa, i no naka no kawazu ga ōi desu yo.*
   In this line of work you'll find a lot of ignorant people.
2. *Daigaku no sensei ni wa, i no naka no kawazu ga ōi desu yo.*
   There are plenty of professors who are ignorant of worldly affairs.
3. *Watashi wa i no naka no kawazu de iru to omowanai.*
   I don't want to become ignorant of what's going on in the world.

ichika-bachika

一か八か

taking a chance

TSUMA:

Ima no jikan de wa, mō hikōki ni ma ni aimasen yo.

OTTO:

Ichika-bachika itte miyō. Moshika-shitara ma ni au kamo shirenai yo.

WIFE:

Look at the time! We won't make the plane.

HUSBAND:

Let's take a chance and go anyway. We might get there just in time.

Ichika-bachika means doing something even though one doesn't know whether it will succeed or not. There are two theories as to its origin, both related to gambling. One theory originates from *chōhan,* a dice game. The top part of the character for *chō* is read *ichi* and the top part of *han* is read *hachi,* together indicating odds or even. The other theory states that *ichika-bachika* is a corrupted form of *ichi ka batsu ka,* a dice game in which any roll other than a one constitutes a loss.

EXAMPLES

1. *Takarakuji, ichika-bachika katte miyō.*

   Let's try our luck and buy a lottery ticket.
2. *Sensei wa fuzai kamo shirenai ga, ichika-bachika itte miyō.*

   The profesor may not be in, but let's take our chances and go anyway.
3. *Ichika-bachika shūshoku-shiken o ukete miyō.*

   I'll chance it and take the employment examination.
4. *Naoranai to omou ga, ichika-bachika, kono kusuri o nonde miyō.*

   I don't think I'll get better, but I'll give this medicine a try. As they say, nothing ventured, nothing gained.

ichimoku-oku

一目置く

giving someone due respect

BUKA:

Kimura-kun, atama wa ii shi, handan-ryoku wa aru shi.

JŌSHI:

Kare wa minna ni ichimoku-okarete iru yō da ne.

SUBORDINATE:

Kimura's smart, and what's more he has good judgment.

SUPERVISOR:

Yes, it seems that he's respected by everyone.

Ichimoku-oku comes from the Japanese strategy game *go.* In *go,* the person recognized to be the weaker player is allowed to place *(oku)* his or her stone *(ichimoku)* on the playing board first. Consequently, *ichimoku-oku* has come to symbolize the act of recognizing another's superiority. The passive form of the verb, *ichimoku-okareru* (be respected), is also frequently used.

EXAMPLES

1. *Daremo ga kare ni ichimoku-oite iru.*

   He has the respect of everyone.

2. *Nihon no keizai-ryoku wa sekai ni ichimoku-okarete iru.*

   The superiority of Japan's economic power is recognized throughout the world.

3. *Kare wa kanojo no sainō ni ichimoku-oite iru.*

   He pays her due respect for her abilities.

4. *Kyōju wa uchū-ron de wa Tanaka-san ni ichimoku-oite iru yō da.*

   It would seem that the professor has acknowledged Mr. Tanaka's superiority in the discussion.

5. *Kimura-san ga ichimoku-okareru no mo wakarimasu.*

   I, too, can see why Mr. Kimura is respected.

ippai kuwaseru

一杯食わせる

be taken in

TSUMA:

A, anata, hebi yo!

OTTO:

Ippai kuwaseyō to shite mo muda da yo. Are tada no o-mocha deshō.

WIFE:

Look honey, it's a snake!

HUSBAND:

It's no use trying to put one over on me. It's just a toy.

Ippai kuwaseru, literally "to make someone eat a bowlful" or "to make someone drink a cupful," means to trick someone. *Kuwaseru* is the causative form of the verb *kū* (eat).

EXAMPLES

1. *Kare ni ippai kuwasete yarō to shita ga, shippai shita.*
   I tried to play a trick on him but I messed it up.
2. *Mō chotto de, kanojo no uso-naki ni ippai kuwasareru tokoro datta.*
   She almost put one over on me.
3. *Kanojo wa dokushin da to itte, kare ni ippai kuwaseta.*
   She deceived him by telling him that she was single.
4. *Kare wa, ippai kuwasareta to shitte okotte iru.*
   He is angry because he found out that he had been tricked.
5. *Daiya da to omotta noni. Kare ni ippai kuwasareta.*
   I thought it was a diamond. He took me for a ride.

ishi atama

石頭

hardheaded

GAKUSEI:

Chichi ga kitoku nan' desu. Shiken ukerarenain' desu ga.

KYŌJU:

Rakudai o shite mo ii no nara, sō shitamae.

GAKUSEI:

(kokoro no naka de) Nan to iu ishi atama da.

STUDENT:

My father is critically ill so I am afraid that I won't be able to take the examination.

PROFESSOR:

Well, suit yourself, if you don't mind failing.

STUDENT:

(to himself) What a hardheaded person.

Ishi atama, literally "rock head," is similar to the English word "hardheaded" and refers to someone who is inflexible, slow to understand, or obstinate.

EXAMPLES

1. *Buchō wa taihen na ishi atama desu.*

   The department chief is terribly hardheaded.

2. *Kare ga konna ni ishi atama to wa omowanakatta.*

   I hadn't realized he could be so inflexible.

3. *Hito wa toshi o toru hodo, ishi atama ni naru keikō ga aru.*

   The older people get, the more hardheaded they tend to become.

4. *Boku wa anata ga omou hodo ishi atama de wa nai yo.*

   I'm not as stubborn as you think I am.

isseki nichō

一石二鳥

killing two birds with one stone

OTTO:

Raishū, Hokkaidō ni shutchō suru koto ni natta yo.

TSUMA:

Ii wa ne. Kankō mo dekiru kara, isseki nichō ne.

HUSBAND:

I have to go to Hokkaido next week on business.

WIFE:

Lucky you. You'll be able to do some sightseeing as well, so you can kill two birds with one stone.

Isseki nichō is used when one action produces two profitable results. The expression means to be able to kill two birds *(nichō)* with one stone *(isseki)*, just like the expression in English.

EXAMPLES

1. *Shigoto no aima ni kankō mo dekite, isseki nichō da.*

   Between shifts, I can do some sightseeing and kill two birds with one stone.

2. *Sore wa isseki nichō no yoi kangae desu ne.*

   That's a good idea. That way we can kill two birds with one stone.

3. *Uriage mo kaisha no imēji mo agari, isseki nicho no aidia da.*

   Not only will sales increase, but it's good for our company's image. We'll be able to kill two birds with one stone with that idea.

4. *Sono shigoto wa shūnyū ni mo benkyō ni mo nari, isseki nichō.*

   That job serves a double purpose—you get to study and make money at the same time.

5. *Isseki nichō o neratta ga, ryōhō dame ni natte shimatta.*

   Although I wanted to kill two birds with one stone, both things fell through.

ita ni tsuku

板に付く

become natural or comfortable to one

BUCHŌ:

Kimi no sebiro-sugata ga yatto ita ni tsuite kita ne.

SHIN'NYŪ-SHAIN:

Hai. Dōmo arigatō gozaimasu.

DEPARTMENT CHIEF:

Your business suit finally looks like it belongs on you.

NEW EMPLOYEE:

Thank you very much.

Ita ni tsuku, which combines *ita* (board) and *tsuku* (attach) was originally used to indicate that an actor, having gained experience, was at last feeling comfortable about performing on stage. From this, the expression has come to refer to one's dress, action, or attitude being consistent with and entirely suited to one's position or profession. In short, *ita ni tsuku* suggests becoming accustomed to a certain set of circumstances.

EXAMPLES

1. *Kare wa zuibun ita ni tsuita shikai-buri desu.*

   Chairing the meeting comes quite naturally to him.

2. *Kare wa saikin shushō ga ita ni tsuite kita.*

   Lately he seems to be acting more like a real prime minister.

3. *Kanojo mo dandan hahaoya-yaku ga ita ni tsuite kimashita.*

   She has gradually adjusted to her role as a mother.

4. *Oku-sama, kimono-sugata ga ita ni tsuite irasshaimasu ne.*

   Ma'am, you look so natural wearing a kimono.

5. *Sono uchi, kitto ita ni tsuite kimasu yo.*

   I'm sure it will come naturally to her some day.

jibara o kiru

自腹を切る

dip into one's own pocket

KAISHAIN 1:

Kimura buchō 'tte, kimae ga iin' datte ne.

KAISHAIN 2:

Sō, yoku jibara o kitte, yūshoku o ogotte kurerun' da.

EMPLOYEE 1:

They say Mr. Kimura, the department chief, is generous with his own money.

EMPLOYEE 2:

Yes, he'll often dip into his own pocket and take you out to dinner.

Jibara o kiru, literally "to cut one's own belly," refers to using one's own money to pay for something that one isn't obligated to pay for. The original usage came from *seppuku* or *harakiri,* a ritualized form of suicide involving disembowelment using one's own sword. *Jibara* now refers to one's wallet.

EXAMPLES

1. *Shachō wa jibara o kitte, shain o yūshoku ni shōtai shita.*

   The company president dipped into his own pocket and invited the employees out for dinner.

2. *Kare wa jibara o kitte, kaisha no songai no anaume o shita.*

   He dipped into his own pocket to cover the company's losses.

3. *Musuko wa jibara o kitte, jibun-yō no denwa o hiita.*

   Our son put in a phone, paying for it out of his own pocket.

4. *Naze, kaisha no shutchō na noni, ōfuku no kōtsūhi wa anata ga jibara o kitta no desu ka?*

   Why did you use your own money for the round trip travel expenses on a business trip?

jigō-jitoku

自業自得

getting what one has coming

TOMODACHI 1:

Kaisha no okane o tsukaikomi shite, kubi ni natchatta.

TOMODACHI 2:

Sore wa kimi, jigō-jitoku da yo.

FRIEND 1:

I misappropriated the company's money and was fired.

FRIEND 2:

You have only yourself to blame.

Jigō-jitoku means paying the price for one's misdeed. The expression is made up of characters literally meaning "one's deeds, one's rewards."

EXAMPLES

1. *Supiido-ihan de tsukamatte mo jigō-jitoku desu yo.*

   It serves you right if you were caught speeding.

2. *Inu o kowagaru to shirinagara, tanjōbi ni koinu o purezento suru nante, kanojo ni kirawarete mo jigō-jitoku desu yo.*

   It serves you right if she hates you—giving her a puppy for her birthday when you knew she was afraid of dogs.

3. *Asobi-sugite rakudai shite mo jigō-jitoku to iu mono desu.*

   Failing the exam because you were playing around is an example of reaping what you sow.

4. *Sō natta no wa jigō-jitoku da to omoimasen ka?*

   Don't you feel that it serves you right the way things have turned out?

5. *Tashika ni jigō-jitoku kamo shiremasen.*

   I probably did ask for it.

jigoku mimi

地獄耳

sharp ears

TOMODACHI 1:

Ano kata wa yoku iroiro na hanashi o go-zonji desu ne.

TOMODACHI 2:

Ā iu kata no koto o jigoku mimi to iun' desu ne.

FRIEND 1:

She certainly does know a lot of different stories.

FRIEND 2:

That's what you call someone with big ears.

Jigoku mimi, which combines *jigoku* (hell) and *mimi* (ears), means either to be able to hear something once and never forget it, or to be quick to catch information and secrets about other people. Other expressions that use *jigoku* include *jigoku de hotoke* (to be in a predicament and meet someone who helps you) and *jigoku no sata mo kane shidai* (money talks).

EXAMPLES

1. *Sonna koto made shitte iru to wa, sasuga jigoku mimi da ne.*
   To know as much as you do; that's what I call having big ears.
2. *Kanojo wa jigoku mimi na node, ki o tsuketa hō ga ii.*
   You'd better be careful; she's got sharp ears and hears everything.
3. *Shinbun kisha wa jigoku mimi de nakereba tsutomaranai.*
   Without sharp ears, a newspaper reporter won't be very good.
4. *Jigoku mimi no kisha de mo, kono nyūsu wa shiranai darō.*
   Even a reporter with big ears wouldn't know about this news.

jūhachiban
十八番
one's specialty

SHIKAISHA:

Kekkon-shiki no hirōen de nanika utatte kudasai.

SHINRŌ NO YŪJIN:

Ja, watashi no jūhachiban o utawasete moraimasu.

MASTER OF CEREMONIES:

We'd like you to sing something at the wedding reception.

GROOM'S FRIEND:

OK, I hope you don't mind if I do my favorite old party piece then.

Jūhachiban, the eighteenth, refers to a favorite trick or performance—one's party piece. This expression comes from Kabuki, classical Japanese drama. At the end of the Edo period, a popular Kabuki actor, Danjūrō, selected eighteen plays he felt best displayed his family's theatrical talent. These became known as the *jūhachiban.*

EXAMPLES

1. *Kono uta wa anata no jūhachiban deshō.*

   I'll bet this song is your party piece, isn't it?

2. *Shushō no monomane wa kare no jūhachiban desu.*

   His favorite party trick is to impersonate the prime minister.

3. *Watashi ni wa jūhachiban to ieru hodo no gei nado arimasen.*

   I don't have anything in particular I can call a "party piece."

4. *Ā, kono kyoku wa kare no jūhachiban da.*

   Here we go, this song is his old favorite.

5. *Watashi ni mo jūhachiban to ieru mono ga areba yoi no desu ga.*

   I wish I knew some party tricks, too.

kabuto o nugu

兜を脱ぐ

admit defeat

TOMODACHI 1:

Tsukaretan' ja nai no? Sābu, zenzen ukerarenai ne.

TOMODACHI 2:

Kimi ga tsuyo-sugirun' da yo. Kono hen de kabuto o nuida hō ga yosasō da na.

FRIEND 1:

You must be tired. You can't return my serves at all.

FRIEND 2:

You're just too good for me. It looks as if I'd better admit defeat.

Kabuto are helmets worn by samurai warriors in battle. The removal of one's helmet was a declaration of one's intention to surrender. From this, *kabuto o nugu* (take off one's helmet) is used to indicate that one is admitting defeat, especially in sports matches and in disputes.

EXAMPLES

1. *Anata no make desu yo. Kabuto o nuidara dō desu ka?*
   You've lost. Why don't you admit you're beaten?
2. *Kantan ni kabuto o nugu wake ni wa ikimasen.*
   We can't simply give up.
3. *Mō sukoshi de, aite wa kabuto o nugimasu yo.*
   Your opponent is going to admit defeat any moment now.
4. *Fūfu-genka ni naru to, otto wa sugu kabuto o nuide shimau.*
   In an argument my husband throws in the towel right away.
5. *Konkai wa zettai ni kabuto o nugimasen yo.*
   There's no way I'm going to admit defeat this time.

kakiire-doki

書き入れ時

peak season

KYAKU:

O-mise, konde imasu ne.

TENSHU:

Kono kisetsu ga watashi-tachi no kakiire-doki nan' desu yo.

CUSTOMER:

The store is crowded, isn't it!

STOREOWNER:

This time of year is our busiest season.

In the past, storekeepers would write in registers to keep track of purchases made at their stores. When the store was doing good business, they would become busy recording the purchases in the register. From this practice, *kakiire-doki,* which was originally *kakiireru toki* (time for making entries in the register), came to mean the period with the largest sales and hence the largest profits.

EXAMPLES

1. *Denkiya wa fuyu ga kakiire-doki deshō.*

   The peak season for electrical appliance stores is probably winter.

2. *Depāto wa jūnigatsu ga kakiire-doki nan' desu yo. Bōnasu shiizun desu kara.*

   The busiest season for department stores is December, since this is the time when people receive their bonuses.

3. *Kakiire-doki wa isogashikute, yasumi mo toremasen.*

   During the peak season I am so busy I can't take a vacation.

4. *Kakiire-doki wa, kodomo mo mise no tetsudai desu.*

   In the busiest season, my children help out in the store, too.

5. *Yūgata ga uchi no mise no kakiire-doki nan' desu.*

   Evening is the busy time for our store.

kama o kakeru

鎌を掛ける

trick someone into confessing

OTTO:

Kimi, shigoto to kaji ikuji o ryōritsu saseru no wa taihen darō.

TSUMA:

Kama o kakete mo dame yo. Mada shigoto o yameru ki wa nai wa.

HUSBAND:

Honey, it's hard to keep a job, do the housework, and raise the kids, isn't it?

WIFE:

It's no use trying to trick me. I still have no intention of giving up my job.

Kama o kakeru, literally "to use a sickle," means to try to get someone to tell the truth, especially to skillfully question him and draw out the desired information. The expression derives its meaning from the use of a sickle *(kama)* to strike sparks from a flint.

EXAMPLES

1. *Kare ni kama o kakerarete, tsui hontō no koto o itte shimatta.*

   I was tricked by him and before I knew it had told him the truth.

2. *Kanojo wa kama o kakete, hanashi o hiki-dasu no ga umai.*

   She's good at tricking people into talking.

3. *Kama o kakerarete mo, kondo no jiko ni tsuite wa hon'ne o morashite wa dame desu yo.*

   Even if someone tries to trap you, you mustn't tell him what really happened at the accident.

4. *Hisho ni kama o kakete, shachō no sukejūru o kiki-dashita.*

   I pumped the president's schedule out of his private secretary.

kamo ni suru

鴨にする

make a sucker out of a person

OTTO:

Mata, mājan de makechatta yo.

TSUMA:

Mō, mājan suru no, yametara? Minna, anata o kamo ni shite iru no yo.

HUSBAND:

I lost playing mahjong again!

WIFE:

Why don't you give it up? Everyone just makes a sucker out of you!

Kamo ni suru combines *kamo* (wild duck) and *suru* (do, make), and means to take advantage of someone. This meaning arises from the fact that ducks are easy game for hunters. *Kamo ni naru* is the intransitive form, meaning be made a sucker or be a sitting duck.

EXAMPLES

1. *Sā, kondo wa dare o kamo ni shite yarō ka na.*

    Now, who will we make our next easy victim?

2. *Mājan de kamo ni sareru no wa mō iya desu.*

    I'm sick of being such a pushover at playing mahjong.

3. *Anata, shinseihin no muryō sanpuru ga moraeru kai ni haitta rashii kedo, kamo ni nariyasui kara ki o tsukete.*

    You're so easily taken advantage of! Be careful about joining that group, even if they offer you free samples of new products.

4. *Kawaisō ni, yowai rōjin ga kamo ni natte shimatta.*

    A frail, elderly person became an easy target for someone—poor guy!

5. *Tochi-baibai de wa, shiroto wa kamo ni sareyasui.*

    In land transactions, it is easy for inexperienced people to be taken for a ride.

kanban-daore

看板倒れ

not as good as it looks

CHICHIOYA:

Musuko no tegami wa goji darake da yo.

HAHAOYA:

Daigakuin made dete okinagara, kanban-daore yo ne.

FATHER:

Our son's letter is chock full of incorrect kanji.

MOTHER:

I guess having a graduate school degree isn't everything it's cracked up to be.

Kanban-daore describes something gorgeous in appearance but poor in substance, i.e., something which is not as good as it looks. *Kanban* are advertising signs set up outside theaters and shops, and *taore* means to push down. *Kanban-daore* means that something is not as good as it is advertised to be. Other expressions using *kanban* include *kanban ni itsuwarinashi* (be true to one's name) and *kanban o orosu* (close up shop).

EXAMPLES

1. *Konna mono o uru nante, ichiryūten mo sukkari kanban-daore da na.*
   To think that this shop is selling this kind of thing; even supposedly high-class shops are not what they used to be.

2. *Gakusei-yokozuna no kare mo, puro iri-go wa kanban-daore de chōshi ga denai.*
   Even though he was a sumo grand champion in college, he did not turn out to be as good as he looked once he turned pro.

3. *Konna aji de wa, kono resutoran mo kanban-daore da.*
   With food of such poor quality, this restaurant is no longer as good as it used to be.

kanko-dori ga naku

閑古鳥が鳴く

business is bad

OTTO:

Saikin, kinjo no eigakan ni wa ii eiga ga konai ne.

TSUMA:

Dakara, eigakan de wa kanko-dori ga naite iru wa.

HUSBAND:

Lately they haven't played any decent movies at our local theater.

WIFE:

That's why the movie theaters are deserted.

Kanko-dori ga naku means business is bad, i.e., that there are no customers and that things are deserted and lonely. *Kanko-dori* refers to a Japanese cuckoo and *naku* refers to its call.

EXAMPLES

1. *Saikin, chikaku ni yasui mise ga dekita node, ano resutoran wa kanko-dori ga naite imasu.*

   Because a cheap place recently opened nearby, that restaurant has been deserted.

2. *Rakugo no suki na hito ga hette, doko no yose mo kanko-dori ga naite iru.*

   The number of people who enjoy *rakugo* has decreased, and these kind of comic shows are deserted.

3. *Itsu kara kanko-dori ga naku yō ni natta no desu ka?*

   When did business become so slow?

4. *Sūpā no shinshutsu de, ko-uriten de wa kanko-dori ga naite iru.*

   After the big supermarkets moved into the area, business became really slow for the small retail shops.

5. *Fukeiki de, kankōchi de wa kanko-dori ga naite iru.*

   Because of the recession, the resort area is deserted.

kannin bukuro no o ga kireru

堪忍袋の緒が切れる

run out of patience

SEITO:

Okurete sumimasen. Nebō shita mono desu kara.

SENSEI:

Mata ka? Mō, kannin bukuro no o ga kireta.

STUDENT:

I'm sorry I'm late. I overslept.

TEACHER:

Not again! I just can't put up with this any longer.

Kannin means to endure hardship or to put up with another person's negligence or rudeness. Originally this capacity for forbearance *(kannin)* was metaphorically compared to a bag that was drawn together with a string or thread. When the bag was too full, the drawstring would break. Now, *kannin bukuro no o ga kireru,* literally "the drawstring of one's bag of forbearance breaks," has come to mean no longer being able to endure something.

EXAMPLES

1. *Kore ijō matasaretara, kannin bukuro no o ga kiresō da.*
   If I have to wait any longer, I'm going to lose my patience.
2. *Kare no kannin bukuro no o ga kiretara, kitto kowai desu yo.*
   It must be a fearful sight when he loses his temper.
3. *Watashi datte, kannin bukuro no o ga kireru koto mo arun' desu.*
   I have also been known to lose my patience.
4. *Chiisana koto ni, kannin bukuro no o o kirashite wa dame desu yo.*
   You shouldn't lose your temper over such a little thing.
5. *Mata uwaki desu ka? Mō kannin bukuro no o ga kiremashita.*
   You had another affair? I can't put up with this any longer.

kao ga kiku

顔が利く

have influence over people

CHICHIOYA:

Jidōsha jiko okoshitan' datte?

MUSUKO:

Otōsan, keisatsu ni kao ga kikun' deshō. Dō ni ka naranai ka na?

FATHER:

I hear you had car accident.

SON:

Dad, you have some influence with the police. Can't you do something?

Kao ga kiku refers to having a lot of influence. *Kao* (face) in this expression refers to a person's popularity and credibility. Other expressions using *kao* include *kao ga ureru* (become popular), *kao ga hiroi* (have many social contacts), *kao o uru* (try to become popular), *kao o kasu* (meet someone on request), and *kao o tsunagu* (meet someone in order to keep in touch).

EXAMPLES

1. *Kare wa Nihon-ginkō ni yoku kao ga kiku sō da.*

   He seems to have a lot of clout at the Bank of Japan.

2. *Ano kashu, saikin kao ga urete kita.*

   That singer has recently become popular.

3. *Kanojo wa kono machi de totemo kao ga hiroi.*

   She knows many people in this town.

4. *Sumimasen ga, ashita no kaigō ni kao o kashite moraemasen ka?*

   Would you be willing to attend the meeting tomorrow?

5. *Chijin to kao o tsunaide oku tame ni, ashita kaigō ni demasu.*

   I'll attend the meeting tomorrow to keep up my contacts.

kao ni doro o nuru

顔に泥を塗る

cause someone to lose face

BUCHŌ:

Kaigi de hatsugen suru toki wa, ki o tsukeru yō ni.

BUKA:

Go-shinpai naku. Buchō no kao ni doro o nuru yō na koto wa shimasen kara.

DEPARTMENT CHIEF:

Be careful about what you say at the conference.

SUBORDINATE:

There's no need for concern. I won't do anything that would reflect badly on you.

Kao ni doro o nuru, literally "to smear a person's face with mud," means to cause another person to lose face or become humiliated. *Kao* (face) refers to social honor. The passive form is *kao ni doro o nurareru* (being made to lose face). *Kanban ni doro o nuru* means to tarnish the reputation of one's company.

EXAMPLES

1. *Musuko wa manbiki o shite, oya no kao ni doro o nutta.*
   The boy shoplifted and disgraced his parents.
2. *O-negai dakara, oya no kao ni doro o nuru yō na koto wa shinaide kure.*
   I'm begging you—please don't do anything that might stain your parents' good name.
3. *Watashi nara kao ni doro o nuraretara, damatte wa imasen.*
   I wouldn't take it lying down if my name had been dragged in the mud.
4. *Kaisha no kanban ni doro o nuru yō na koto o shite, dōmo sumimasen deshita.*
   I'm profoundly sorry for having damaged the company's reputation in this way.

kata ni hameru

型にはめる

cast into a mold

HAHAOYA:

Kono gakkō no kyōiku hōshin wa nan desu ka?

KOCHŌ:

Seito o kata ni hamenaide, nobinobi sodateru koto desu.

MOTHER:

What is the teaching policy of this school?

PRINCIPAL:

To bring the students up in a relaxed fashion and not cast them into a mold.

Kata ni hameru means to do things in the traditional fashion or to force people to become the same. *Kata* can mean a system or an institution, the customary way of doing things, or a standard shape, size, or form. Expressions using *kata ni hamatta* include *kata ni hamatta hōhō* (a conventional method), *kata ni hamatta aisatsu* (a well-used greeting), and *kata ni hamatta kyōiku* (an orthodox education).

EXAMPLES

1. *Kodomo no uchi kara, kata ni hamete shimau no wa, yameta hō ga ii.*
   It's best not to cast someone into a mold from childhood.
2. *Kisoku ga kibishi-sugiru to, shain o kata ni hameru koto ni naru.*
   If the rules are too strict the employees will all be the same.
3. *Kare wa kata ni hamatta kangaekata o suru.*
   He thinks just like everyone else.
4. *Ano kachō, kata ni hamatta kotae shika dekinai no desu ka?*
   Doesn't the section chief have a mind of his own?
5. *Dōshite, kata ni hamatta kangaekata shika dekinai no desu ka?*
   Why can't you think for yourself?

kata no ni ga oriru

肩の荷が下りる

take a load off one's mind

TAISHIKAN'IN 1:

Gaikoku no shisatsudan, kaetta sō desu ne.

TAISHIKAN'IN 2:

Ē, buji ni yakume o oete, kata no ni ga orimashita.

EMBASSY STAFF MEMBER 1:

I hear the foreign observers have left.

EMBASSY STAFF MEMBER 2:

I'm relieved that nothing went wrong.

Kata no ni ga oriru means to be freed from worry or responsibility. *Kata* (shoulders) can carry baggage, an emotional burden, or responsibility. Other expressions using *kata* include *kata ni kakaru* (having responsibility or duty) and *kata o kasu* (help someone carry a burden). *Ni* refers to baggage and *oriru* means to take down. Another expression using *ni* is *nimotsu ga omoi,* which can mean that one's baggage is heavy or that one has a lot of responsibility.

EXAMPLES

1. *Kono shigoto o katazukete, hayaku kata no ni o oroshitai.*
   I want to finish this job quickly and get it off my back.
2. *Shigoto ga seikō de, kore de kata no ni ga orosemasu.*
   It's a load off my mind now that the job is successfully completed.
3. *Sue no musume mo totsugi, kore de kata no ni ga orimashita.*
   I'm so relieved that my last daughter is married.
4. *Taishoku suru made wa, kata no ni o orosesō mo nai.*
   It doesn't seem that I can relax until I retire.
5. *Yakume ga owatte, yatto kata no ni ga orita.*
   With the inspection over, the responsibility is finally off my shoulders.

kata-gawari suru

肩代りする

take over a person's responsibility, shoulder a person's debt

---

TOMODACHI 1:

Ii kuruma katta ne. Kondo kashite kurenai?

TOMODACHI 2:

Suki na toki, itsu de mo notte ii yo. Sono kawari, kuruma no rōn o ichibu, kata-gawari shite kurenai ka?

FRIEND 1:

You've bought yourself a nice car. How about lending it to me sometime?

FRIEND 2:

You can use it any time you like. In exchange, how about taking over and paying off a part of the loan for me?

Kata-gawari suru, which consists of *kata-gawari* (take over, transfer) plus *suru,* refers to a situation where a person hands over his obligations and liabilities to another party. In ancient times, a pole would be passed through a palanquin so that two men could carry it on their shoulders. When they became tired, the palanquin bearers would be replaced. Hence, this phrase developed from the image of a person substituting *(kawari/gawari)* his shoulders *(kata);* namely shouldering the other person's burden.

EXAMPLES

1. *Chichi ga shakkin o kata-gawari shite kurete, tasukarimashita.*
   My father helped me out by taking over the responsibility of my loan.
2. *Kata-gawari shite itadaita bun o henkyaku itashimasu.*
   I'm returning the portion of the payment you assumed on my behalf.
3. *Dareka PTA yakuin o kata-gawari shite kuremasen ka?*
   Won't someone please take over my responsibility as the chairperson of the PTA?

katte deru

買ってでる

take it upon oneself to do something, volunteer for a difficult job

MUSUME:

Otōsan, shujutsu shita hō ga iin' datte.

HAHAOYA:

Dare ka, zōki no teikyō o katte dete kurenai kashira?

DAUGHTER:

They say that father should have the operation.

MOTHER:

I wonder if anyone will volunteer to donate the organs necessary for the transplant?

Katte deru means to offer to help with or undertake a task without being asked to do so. *Deru* is used in many other expressions; for example, *todoke-deru* (submit something for official notice or approval) and *nanori-deru* (step forward and identify onself).

EXAMPLES

1. *Kanojo ga yakuin o katte dete kureta.*
   She took it upon herself to serve as an official.
2. *Kenka no chūsai o katte-deru hito wa inai no ka na?*
   I wonder if anyone will volunteer to arbitrate this dispute?
3. *Anata ga katte dete kurete, hontō ni yokatta.*
   I'm really glad that you volunteered to help out.
4. *Kyō, yakusho ni kekkon o todoke-dete kimashita.*
   We applied for a marriage license today.
5. *Kore o otoshita hito wa nanori-dete kudasai.*
   Would the person who dropped this please make himself known?

kemutagaru

煙たがる

want to avoid

OTTO:

Kodomo-tachi, chittomo boku to hanashitagaranai nē.

TSUMA:

Anata ga sugu shikaru kara, kemutagatte irun' desu yo.

HUSBAND:

The children don't want to talk to me at all.

WIFE:

You always scold them, so they try to avoid you.

Kemutagaru means to show that you are trying to avoid someone. *Kemutagaru* is the verb form of *kemutai,* an adjective meaning to be choked by smoke, to feel inferior, or to not want a close relationship with another.

EXAMPLES

1. *Kinō, o-sekkyō sareta kara to itte, itsu made mo otōsan o kemutagatte ite wa dame desu yo.*

    It's not good to avoid your father just because he lectured you yesterday.

2. *Atarashii shachō no koto o shain-tachi ga, kemutagatte iru.*

    The company employees are trying to avoid the new president.

3. *Kare ga minna ni kemutagarareru no mo tōzen da.*

    I can understand why everyone keeps their distance from him.

4. *Kare no doko ga, sonna ni kemutain' desu ka?*

    What don't you like about him?

5. *Anna ni ii hito dakara, kare ni wa kemutagarareru riyū nado, zenzen nai no desu.*

    Because he is such a nice person, there's no reason why people should want to avoid him.

ken mo hororo

けんもほろろ

curt, blunt, brusque

TOMODACHI 1:

Ie o tate-naosu no nara, ginkō de shakkin o shitara dō desu ka?

TOMODACHI 2:

Sore ga, atamakin ga nai node, ken mo hororo deshita.

FRIEND 1:

If you're planning to rebuild your house, why not take out a loan at the bank?

FRIEND 2:

Because I can't make a down payment, the bank was pretty curt in turning me down.

Ken mo hororo means to be rebuffed. In Japanese, the cry of the pheasant is *kenken-horohoro,* and *ken mo hororo* may have derived from this. One possible reason why *ken mo hororo* means curt or blunt is that the cry of the pheasant is a short, unpleasant-sounding call.

EXAMPLES

1. *Kanojo wa sukii ni ikō to sasotta noni, ken mo hororo ni kotowarareta.*
   When she asked him to go skiing, she was bluntly refused.
2. *Ken mo hororo ni kotowararete, hara ga tatta.*
   I got angry when I was flatly refused.
3. *Ken mo hororo na kotowarikata desu ne.*
   That's quite a nasty refusal, isn't it?
4. *Ken mo hororo ni kotowaru koto, nai deshō?*
   You don't have to be so caustic, do you?
5. *Dōshite, sonna ken mo hororo na taido o toru no desu ka?*
   Why are you being so brusque with me?

kenami ga yoi

毛並がよい

come of good stock

DŌRYŌ 1:

Kare wa mō kachō ni nattan' datte?

DŌRYŌ 2:

Kare no kenami no yosa ga uwayaku ni uketan' ja nai ka na?

COLLEAGUE 1:

So he's already become section chief?

COLLEAGUE 2:

I guess his good breeding must have impressed his superiors.

Kenami is the fur or coat of a dog or horse, and with *yoi* (good), it refers to good blood, a good family background, a good education, and a good upbringing.

EXAMPLES

1. *Kare wa kenami ga yoi kara, kono shigoto wa muri ja nai ka na?*

   For a person with such a good background, this job is probably not appropriate, is it?

2. *Ima no shakai de wa, kenami no yosa ga mono o iu.*

   In our society, coming from a good family goes a long way.

3. *Anna kenami no warui hito to wa, tsukiau no o yamenasai.*

   Stop associating with that person. She doesn't come from a good family.

4. *Watashi wa, kenami no yosa yori, jinbutsu no hō o taisetsu ni kangaeru.*

   For me, the quality of a person's character is more important than whether he comes from a good family.

5. *Kare wa kenami ga yoi no dake ga torie desu.*

   His only redeeming feature is his good family background.

keri o tsukeru

けりを付ける

settle a matter

TOMODACHI 1:

Sensō, itsu made tsuzukun' deshō?

TOMODACHI 2:

Kokuren ga chūkai shite, keri o tsukete hoshii desu ne.

FRIEND 1:

I wonder how long the war will continue.

FRIEND 2:

I wish the United Nations would intervene and settle this conflict.

Keri o tsukeru means to bring a matter to a conclusion, to wind up, or to bring something to a close. The intransitive form, *keri ga tsuku,* indicates that a matter is settled or that a solution has been reached. The expression's meaning of conclusion originates in classical Japanese, where *keri* was used as an auxiliary verb and was frequently placed at the end of a sentence.

EXAMPLES

1. *Hayaku repōto ni keri o tsukete, ryokō ni ikitai.*

   I want to quickly get my term paper over and done with, and then go traveling.

2. *Kono shiai wa, ato gofun de keri ga tsuku.*

   The outcome of this match will be decided in five minutes.

3. *Tenisu no shiai wa kare no sumasshu de keri ga tsuita.*

   The tennis match was decided by his smash.

4. *Kono jiken wa saiban de keri o tsukeru shika nai.*

   The only way to settle this affair is in court.

5. *Ā, yatto naganen no funsō ni mo keri ga tsuite, hotto shimashita.*

   Ah, I'm relieved to see this matter finally straightened out.

keta-chigai

けた違い

be in an entirely different class

ANE:

Otona ni nattara, sōri-daijin ni naru wa.

IMŌTO:

Onēsan no yume wa keta-chigai ni ōkii no ne.

OLDER SISTER:

When I grow up I'm going to become the prime minister.

YOUNGER SISTER:

Your dreams are certainly big, aren't they?

Keta refers to the vertical rods that pass through the beads in an abacus, and *chigai* means mistake. *Keta-chigai* can be used to describe a mistake made about a figure—such as mistaking 100 for 1,000—or to indicate that the value, grade, or degree of one thing is vastly different from another. Two similar expressions are *keta-hazure* and *dan-chigai*.

EXAMPLES

1. *Buchō wa buka-tachi to wa keta-chigai ni gorufu ga jōzu da.*

   When it comes to playing golf, the department chief is in a completely different class than his subordinates.

2. *Anata no kyūryō wa watashi to wa keta-chigai desu yo.*

   Your salary is in a different league from mine.

3. *Pikaso no e wa keta-chigai ni takakute, totemo kaenai.*

   Picasso's paintings are exorbitantly expensive, and I can't possibly afford one.

4. *Kare wa watashi-tachi to wa keta-chigai no ōkina ie ni sunde iru.*

   He lives in a house that is many times larger than ours.

5. *Kondo no bōifurendo wa keta-chigai ni yasashiin' desu.*

   My new boyfriend is much kinder than my former one.

128

kidō ni noru

軌道に乗る

get on track, get into the swing of things

TOMODACHI:

Atarashii jigyō no hō, ikaga desu ka?

JIGYŌNUSHI:

Ē, yatto kidō ni nori-hajimemashita.

FRIEND:

How is the new business?

ENTREPRENEUR:

It's just now getting on track.

Kidō ni noru means to adjust to a new routine. *Kidō* describes the movement of a body in a fixed orbit and *noru* means to ride. *Kidō ni noru* and *kidō ni noseru* are frequently used in reference to study, work, business, and training.

EXAMPLES

1. *Anata wa, itsu ni nattara kenkyū ga kidō ni norun' desu ka?*
   When are you going to start buckling down on your studies?
2. *Atarashii shigoto ga nakanaka kidō ni noranain' desu.*
   It's taking a while to get into the swing of things at work.
3. *Donna ni ima wa kurō shite mo, ichido kidō ni notte shimaeba, anshin desu.*
   No matter how tough it is now, once I get on track, everything will be fine.
4. *Jōba no shoshisha ga, renshū o kidō ni noseru no wa taihen desu.*
   It's hard for beginners at horseback riding to get on a regular practicing schedule.
5. *Shōbai ga kidō ni notte, yokatta desu ne.*
   It's good that your business is taking off.

kimo ni meizuru

肝に銘ずる

keep something in mind

BENGOSHI:

Ii desu ka? Ichido sain shitara, anata no make desu yo.

IRAININ:

Hai. Sono koto o kimo ni meijite okimasu.

LAWYER:

Once you put your signature to it, you've lost. Got it?

CLIENT:

Right. I'll bear it in mind.

Kimo ni meizuru means to bear something firmly in mind. In the past, it was believed that the *kimo* (liver) was where one's heart or mind was located. *Meizuru* means to inscribe or engrave.

EXAMPLES

1. *Kono koto wa kimo ni meijite oite kudasai.*

   Keep this in mind!

2. *Sono toki no chichi no oshie wa kimo ni meijite arimasu.*

   I was deeply impressed by what my father taught me back then.

3. *Kodomo no toki, hito o mikake de handan shite wa ikenai to kimo ni meijisaserareta.*

   As a child I had it branded into my mind that I shouldn't judge people by their appearance.

4. *Onaji shippai o kuri-kaesanu yō, kimo ni meijite okimasu.*

   I'll let it sink into my mind so that I don't repeat the same mistake.

kiri ga nai

切りがない

endless

BUKA:

Kyō wa zangyō shimashō ka?

BUCHŌ:

Shigoto wa ikura shite mo kiri ga nai kara, kono hen de kaette mo ii desu yo.

SUBORDINATE:

Shall I work overtime today?

DEPARTMENT CHIEF:

Since there is no end to this job in sight, you may as well go home now.

Kiri ga nai (knowing no bounds) is an extremely common expression. *Kiri,* from the verb *kiru* (cut), is used to express the idea of limitation; thus, with *nai* (no, none) it refers to something that is never-ending. Other expressions with *kiri* include *korekkiri* (just this one), *anatakkiri* (only you), and *hitorikkiri* (all alone).

EXAMPLES

1. *Anata to wa, ikura hanashite ite mo kiri ga nai.*
   No matter how much I talk with you, it seems we'll never get this settled.
2. *Sugoku onaka ga suite ite, tabete mo tabete mo kiri ga nai.*
   I'm so hungry that I don't think I'll be able to stop eating.
3. *Kanojo wa karaoke bā de utai-hajimetara, kiri ga nain' desu.*
   There's no stopping her once she starts singing in a karaoke bar.
4. *Sonna koto o ii-hajimetara, kiri ga nai deshō?*
   Once you bring that up, there'll be no end to the discussion.

kiri-kōjō

切り口上

stiff and formal way of speaking

KANGOFU:

Sensei, yakin o mō sukoshi herashite kudasai.

ISHA:

Sō kiri-kōjō de iwarete mo, watashi ni wa dō ni mo naranai yo.

NURSE:

Doctor, would you please reduce my amount of night duty a little?

DOCTOR:

Even if you ask in such a formal manner, there's nothing I can do.

Kiri-kōjō describes a formal, stiff way of speaking. In Kabuki, on special occasions such as the announcement of a new actor's first appearance on stage, the whole company lines up and each actor, in his own distinctive way, extends a word of greeting. This is referred to as *kōjō*. *Kiri-kōjō* is the address delivered by the leading actor, and is very stiff and formal.

EXAMPLES

1. *Zuibun, kiri-kōjō na hanshikata desu ne.*

   He speaks in quite a stiff, formal way, doesn't he?

2. *Konna derikēto na wadai o, sō kiri-kōjō de iwarete wa henji no shiyō ga nai.*

   When spoken to about such a delicate subject in such a formal fashion, I am at a loss as to how to reply.

3. *Iya ni kiri-kōjō desu ne. Dō ka shitan' desu ka?*

   That's a cold way of addressing someone. Is anything the matter?

4. *Ikura aite ga me-ue no ningen da to shite mo, sonna kiri-kōjō na tanomikata de wa, mazui desu yo.*

   Even if you're talking to a superior, it's unadvisable to make a request in such awkward formal language.

kiyū suru

杞憂する

worry needlessly, entertain groundless fears

GAKUSEI:

Sensei, nyūgaku-shiken ni ochitara, dō shimashō ka?

SENSEI:

Kimi, sore wa kiyū da yo. Kimi nara ukaru. Shinpai suru na.

STUDENT:

Teacher, what am I going to do if I don't pass the entrance exam?

TEACHER:

That's not something you need to worry about. You're going to pass. Don't worry about it.

According to Chinese folklore, there once was a man from a region called Ki who worried about everything. Believing that the sky would come falling down, he became so anxious that he could no longer sleep or eat. *Kiyū* is made up of that Ki and *yū* (distress). When used with *suru,* it means to entertain groundless fears.

EXAMPLES

1. *Watashi no shinpai wa kekkyoku kiyū deshita.*

   As it turned out, it was much ado about nothing.

2. *Kiyū da to wa wakatte ite mo, yahari shinpai desu.*

   I realize that I'm worrying unnecessarily, but I'm still worried.

3. *Masaka, tsuma ga jiko ni au nante. Kore ga kiyū de aru yō ni.*

   My wife wouldn't get into an accident. I hope this is just a groundless fear.

4. *Anata wa nan de mo warui hō e warui hō e kangaete, kiyū bakari shite imasu ne.*

   You do nothing but anticipate trouble, don't you?

kō itten

紅一点

the only female in a crowd of men, the only lady present

KYŌJU:

Kyōjukai wa dansei bakari de, josei wa watashi hitori nan' desu.

JO-KYŌJU:

Kō itten to iu tokoro desu ka? Kyōjukai wa dansei shakai desu ne.

PROFESSOR:

It seems that I'm the only woman attending this faculty party. All the other members are men.

ASSOCIATE PROFESSOR:

You're right. You are the only woman here, aren't you? Academia is certainly a male-dominated part of society.

Kō (crimson) *itten* (one) comes from a famous line in a Chinese poem that refers to a single crimson flower blossoming among a myriad of green leaves. Because of the association between the color red and the female sex, *kō itten* has come to mean one woman in a crowd of men. *Koku itten* (a single point of black) refers to a single man among a group of women.

EXAMPLES

1. *Wareware no shokuba de wa, kanojo ga kō itten da.*
   She's the only woman in our office.
2. *Kō itten dakara, dansei ni totemo moteru no yo.*
   I'm the only woman there so I'm really popular with the men.
3. *Shakaitō no tōshu wa kō itten de ganbatte iru.*
   She's putting in quite an effort working as the sole woman leader of the Socialist Party.
4. *Anata wa, kono kurabu no kō itten desu.*
   You are the sole female in this club.

134

kōin ya no gotoshi

光陰矢の如し

time flies like an arrow

GAKUSEI:

Ashita, daigaku sotsugyō shimasu. O-sewa ni narimashita.

SENSEI:

Mō sotsugyō desu ka? Kōin ya no gotoshi desu ne.

STUDENT:

I'm going to graduate tomorrow. Thank you for everything that you've done for me.

TEACHER:

You're graduating already? How time flies!

The proverb *kōin ya no gotoshi* is perhaps more common in written than in spoken Japanese. *Kō* (light) and *in* (dark) refer to the sun and moon, and combined they imply the passage of time. *Ya no gotoshi* literally means "like an arrow."

EXAMPLES

1. *Kono kaisha ni kite mō sanjūgonen, kōin ya no gotoshi desu.*

   I can't believe that thirty-five years have gone by since I started to work at this company.

2. *Taishoku ni saishite, kōin ya no gotoshi o jikkan shite imasu.*

   Now that I am about to retire, I realize how quickly time has gone by.

3. *Kōin ya no gotoshi, tanoshii sūjitsukan deshita.*

   I've had a good time. These last few days have gone by so quickly.

4. *Tanoshii toki wa kōin ya no gotoshi de, atto iu ma deshita.*

   Where did the time go? I've had so much fun that I can't believe it's time to go already.

5. *Tsuki-hi ga tatsu no wa hayai. Kōin ya no gotoshi da.*

   Time certainly has gone by quickly.

kōjitsu ni suru

口実にする

to plead something as an excuse; use as justification for

DŌRYŌ 1:

Ashita, gorufu ni ikimasen ka?

DŌRYŌ 2:

Zan'nen desu ga, kanai no guai ga warui mono desu kara . . .

DŌRYŌ 1:

Itsumo, sore o kōjitsu ni surun' desu ne.

COLLEAGUE 1:

Would you like to play golf tomorrow?

COLLEAGUE 2:

Well, unfortunately, my wife's not feeling well so really . . .

COLLEAGUE 1:

That's always your excuse isn't it?

Kōjitsu, which combines *kō* (speech) and *jitsu* (substance), originally meant the topic of conversation. When conversation turned to a subject that a speaker didn't feel comfortable discussing, he or she could turn to something else, a different *kōjitsu,* to talk about. The noun *kōjitsu* now means a justification or excuse.

EXAMPLES

1. *Isogashikute o kōjitsu ni shinaide kudasai.*

   Please don't give me the excuse that you're too busy.

2. *Anata wa sugu kyūryō ga yasui kara o kōjitsu ni suru.*

   Right away you give the excuse that "it's because my salary's low."

3. *Kaisha o yasumu ii kōjitsu, nai kashira?*

   I wonder if there's a good excuse I can use to take the day off from work?

4. *Ikura kōjitsu o itte mo, mō shinjimasen yo.*

   It doesn't matter how many justifications you give me, I don't believe you anymore.

136

koken ni kakawaru

沽券にかかわる

reflect badly on one's dignity

KŌCHŌ:

San'nen B-gumi no tan'nin wa, yoru pachinko-ya de arubaito o shite iru sō da ne.

KYŌSHI:

Ē, kono mama de wa, gakkō no koken ni kakawarimasu yo.

PRINCIPAL:

I hear that the teacher in charge of class 3B also has a part-time job at night at a pachinko parlor.

INSTRUCTOR:

Yes, and if the situation remains as it is, he could damage the school's reputation.

Koken ni kakawaru means to damage a person's reputation or dignity. *Koken* originally referred to the contract that a person selling land would hand over to the buyer. From this, *koken* described the process of determining the value of such a contact. Finally, *koken* came to refer to a person's reputation or dignity. This expression is generally used to take issue with a person when one's reputation is being compromised.

EXAMPLES

1. *Sore kurai de wa koken ni nado kakawarimasen yo.*
   Something as insignificant as that won't reflect badly on you!
2. *Satsujinhan o taiho shinakute wa, keisatsu no koken ni kakawaru.*
   If the police don't arrest the murderer, they will be discredited.
3. *Sonna ni koken ni kakawaru to o-kangae desu ka?*
   Do you think it will hurt your reputation all that much?
4. *Tsuma ni iede sareta no wa, otto no koken ni kakawaru.*
   Having his wife walk out on him will reflect badly on his dignity.

kokyō ni nishiki o kazaru

故郷に錦を飾る

make a grand homecoming

TOMODACHI 1:

Sumō-tori ni narun' datte ne.

TOMODACHI 2:

Ē, itsuka yūshō shite, kokyō ni nishiki o kazaru tsumori desu.

FRIEND 1:

I hear you are going to become a sumo wrestler.

FRIEND 2:

Yes, some day I'm going to win the championship and make a grand homecoming.

Kokyō ni nishiki o kazaru means to make a success of oneself in life and then return to one's hometown. *Nishiki* is a thick, silk brocade, woven in a complex pattern using gold, sliver, and various colored threads, and suggests something beautiful and splendid. *Kokyō* is a person's hometown and *kazaru* means to display. In the past, people always made a point of returning to their place of birth after having achieved success.

EXAMPLES

1. *Itsuka, jigyō ni seikō shite, kitto kokyō ni nishiki o kazatte misemasu.*

   I have no doubt that some day, having started my own company, I'll return home in glory—just you see!

2. *Kare ga anna ni shusse shite, kokyō ni nishiki o kazaru to wa omowanakatta.*

   I didn't believe that he would rise to such greatness and come home loaded with honors.

3. *Anata ga kokyō ni nishiki o kazaru no o matte imasu yo.*

   I'm waiting to see you make a triumphant homecoming!

kone o tsukeru

コネをつける

make connections, have an inside connection

GAKUSEI 1:

Shōsha ni shūshoku shitain' datte ne. Ukaru jishin aru no?

GAKUSEI 2:

Tabun ne. Senpai ni kone o tsukete oita kara.

STUDENT 1:

You said you wanted a job with a trading company, didn't you? Do you really think you'll be able to get such a position?

STUDENT 2:

Probably, because I'll get help from some of the guys I know who have already graduated and are working for trading companies.

In the 1950s, many companies made it a policy to refuse employing students with leftist backgrounds. As a result, it became common for students to rely on friends or acquaintances already working in the company where they were applying—their *kone* (inside connection)—to vouch for them. Since then, the expression has come to mean having or developing a relationship with people who can help in some way. Expressions using *kone ga aru* (have connections), *kone ga nai* (not have connections), and *kone ni tayoru* (rely on one's connections).

EXAMPLES

1. *Ima no uchi ni shachō to kone o tsukete oita hō ga ii yo.*
   You should network with the president of the company.

2. *Boku wa, kone ni nanka tayoritakunai.*
   I'm not the kind of person who likes relying on connections.

3. *Shachō to kone ga aru to wa, urayamashii na.*
   I envy your having connections with the president of the company.

koshi ga hikui

腰が低い

have humility

TOMODACHI 1:

Ano kata, yūmei na sakka desu 'tte.

TOMODACHI 2:

Sore ni shite wa, koshi no hikui kata desu ne.

FRIEND 1:

I hear that person is a famous writer.

FRIEND 2:

Even so, she's very humble.

Koshi ga hikui, literally "having a low waist," means to show humility toward others. The opposite is *koshi ga takai,* which means to be stuck up. Other phrases using *koshi* include *koshi ga omoi* (be reluctant to do anything), *koshi ga nukeru* (unable to move when in shock), and *koshi o sueru* (do things thoroughly and calmly).

EXAMPLES

1. *Kanojo wa, dare ni taishite mo, koshi no hikui hito desu.*

   She is humble to everyone, no matter what their status.

2. *Kondo kita buchō wa buka ni taishite, anmari koshi ga hikui node, odoroita.*

   I was very surprised that our new boss is so humble to his subordinates.

3. *Kimi, shin'nyū-shain wa, motto koshi o hikuku suru mono da yo.*

   You know, new company employees are supposed to be more humble.

4. *Kare wa, buka ni taishite, koshi ga taka-sugiru.*

   He is stuck up toward his subordinates.

5. *Ano senpai wa koshi ga hikukute, shinsetsu na hito da.*

   Even though he has seniority, he is a very humble and kind person.

140

kotsu ga aru

こつがある

have a knack or particular technique

TEN'IN:

Kono kagi dōshite mo akanain' desu yo.

TENSHU:

Kore wa, akekata ni kotsu ga atte ne. . .

SALESPERSON:

I just can't get this lock to open.

STORE OWNER:

Ah yes, there's a knack to opening this.

Kotsu ga aru is used to convey the idea that there is a particular technique or knack to doing something successfully. *Kotsu* was originally written using the character for bone but is now written in katakana. In the same way that bones form a core inside the human body, so *kotsu* has come to mean the main or central point that is the key to doing a difficult job well. *Kotsu* can be used alone or with verbs such as *wakaru* and *shiru*.

EXAMPLES

1. *Kono ryōri o oishiku tsukuru ni wa, nanika kotsu ga arimasu ka?*
   Is there any special trick that makes this cooking so tasty?

2. *Shigoto wa kotsu ga wakareba kantan desu yo.*
   Once you get the hang of this job it's easy.

3. *Kanji o oboeru kotsu, oshiete agemashō ka?*
   Shall I let you in on an easy way to remember kanji?

4. *Shigoto no kotsu ga yatto wakatte kimashita.*
   At last I'm getting the hang of this job.

5. *Kare to tsuki-au ni wa kotsu ga atte ne, oshiete agemasu yo.*
   Let me tell you a few things you should know if you want to get along with him.

kubi ni naru

首になる

be dismissed, be fired

KINJO NO HITO 1:

Kono goro, Kimura-san, itsumo ie ni imasu ne.

KINJO NO HITO 2:

Kaisha no okane o tsukai-konde, kubi ni natta sō desu yo.

NEIGHBOR 1:

Mr. Kimura is always at home these days, isn't he?

NEIGHBOR 2:

I hear that he misappropriated the company's money and was fired.

Kubi ni naru means to be dismissed from office. In Bunraku puppet theater, puppets that were no longer required were stored in such a way that only the neck *(kubi)* and head were exposed. It is believed that *kubi ni naru* derives from this practice. *Kubi ni suru* means to discharge or dismiss a person, as does the expression *kubi o kiru,* literally "cut off one's head." *Kubi ga tsunagaru* means that one gets in trouble but is allowed to remain in one's post.

EXAMPLES

1. *Kare wa, inshu-unten de jiko o okoshi, kaisha o kubi ni natta.*

   He lost his job with the company when he caused an accident while driving drunk.

2. *Hidoi fukeiki de, itsu kaisha o kubi ni naru ka wakaranai.*

   With the severe economic depression, I have no idea of when I might be laid off.

3. *Kanojo o kubi ni shitai no da ga, kumiai ga urusakute ne.*

   I'd like to give her the sack but the union would cause trouble.

4. *Kare o kubi ni suru nado, tondemo nai koto da.*

   The thought of him being fired is outrageous!

kuchibi o kiru

口火を切る

start, trigger

SEIJIKA:

Ryōkoku no daihyō wa dochira mo, jibun no kuni no rieki bakari kangaete, yuzurō to shinain' da yo.

KISHA:

Kō iu baai wa, Nihon ga hanashi-ai no kuchibi o kiru beki de wa arimasen ka?

POLITICIAN:

Delegates of both countries are thinking only of the advantages for their own country and are refusing to make any concessions.

REPORTER:

Don't you feel in this case that Japan should initiate negotiations?

Kuchibi o kiru means to be the first to start something. *Kuchibi* originally referred to explosives or to the flame of a musket, and *kiru* means to fire or ignite. From the idea of lighting the flame came the meaning of cause and beginning. In modern usage, *kuchibi* refers to the pilot light of a gas hot-water heater—the flame that ignites the gas.

EXAMPLES

1. *Kenka no kuchibi o kitta no wa, kochira-gawa datta.*
   We are the ones who started the fight!
2. *Iyoiyo nessen no kuchibi ga kirareta.*
   Finally a fierce fight broke out.
3. *De wa, watashi kara hanashi no kuchibi o kirasete moraimasu.*
   Well then, allow me to start the discussion off.
4. *Sono ronsō no kuchibi o kitta no wa kare no ronbun datta.*
   It was his thesis that triggered the controversy.

kugi o sasu

釘を刺す

call special attention to, make something clear

OYASAN:

Ii desu ka? Kondo, yachin o tainō shitara, sai-keiyaku shimasen yo.

SHAKUYA-NIN:

Sonna ni kugi o sasanakute mo daijōbu desu yo.

LANDLORD:

I'm warning you. If you don't pay your rent this time, I won't be renewing your contract.

TENANT:

You don't have to make it so painfully clear! I'll take care of it.

Kugi o sasu (driving in nails) means to call special attention to something so that the other person is unable to make excuses later on. The expression derived from carpentry, where nails *(kugi)* are used to make structures sturdier.

EXAMPLES

1. *Ōyasan ni kugi o sasarete shimatta.*

   My landlord nailed me down.

2. *Machigai no nai yō ni, kugi o sashite oita noni.*

   I even gave him a warning so that he wouldn't make a mistake.

3. *Isha ni shindenzu o miserarete, kin'en suru yō, kugi o sasareta.*

   The doctor made it perfectly clear that I should give up smoking by showing me my ECG.

4. *Kare ni wa kugi o sashite oita hō ga ii desu yo.*

   You'd better ask him very clearly about it.

kusai mono ni futa

臭い物に蓋

look the other way

TOMODACHI 1:

Minamata no kōishō wa, mada tsuzuite iru sō desu ne.

TOMODACHI 2:

Kaisha wa kusai mono ni futa de, hoshōkin o dasu koto de, owari ni suru tsumori rashii desu yo.

FRIEND 1:

I hear people are still experiencing the after effects of Minamata disease.

FRIEND 2:

It seems the company is trying to put a lid on the problem by just paying out compensation to the victims.

Kusai mono ni futa, literally "lid on a smelly thing," refers to covering up something one doesn't want others to see, to shut one's eyes to something, or to look the other way. This expression suggests that the best way to solve a problem is to cover it with a lid and pretend it doesn't exist.

EXAMPLES

1. *Kusai mono ni futa de wa, mondai wa kaiketsu shinai.*

   Ignoring a problem will never solve anything.

2. *Kusai mono ni futa de, hisan na shakai mondai kara, me o sorashite wa ikemasen.*

   One mustn't turn one's eyes away from the terrible social problems.

3. *Kusai mono ni futa de sumu hanashi de wa nai.*

   This is not a thing that is going to be settled by looking the other way.

4. *Tōji no kōgai taisaku wa, kusai mono ni futa to iu kanji datta.*

   At that time, it seemed the government's way of dealing with pollution was to look the other way.

145

ma ga nukeru

間が抜ける

be stupid, out of place

OTTO:

Dorobō ni hairaretan' desu ga, kinko wa akerarete inain' desu.

KEISATSU:

Ma ga nuketa hen na dorobō desu ne.

HUSBAND:

A thief broke into my house, but fortunately the safe was not opened.

POLICE OFFICER:

He's a strange thief, isn't he?

Ma ga nukeru can mean either to be disappointed when one's expectations are not fulfilled, or to look stupid after losing or forgetting something. *Ma* refers to the rhythm of music; when the rhythm is off, the music sounds strange. *Manuke,* a similar expression, refers to a dull person with poor manners who cannot carry on a conversation.

EXAMPLES

1. *Ie ni repōto o wasureta? Dōshite, kimi wa sō ma ga nuketerun' da?*
   You forgot your report at home? How can you be so stupid?
2. *Kare wa atama ga ii noni, tokidoki ma ga nuketa koto o suru.*
   Even though he's smart, he sometimes does stupid things.
3. *Anna ma no nuketa hito, mita koto ga nai.*
   I've never seen someone so out of place.
4. *Otto wa terebi o minagara, ma no nuketa henji o shite yokosu.*
   My husband gives mindless replies when he's watching television.
5. *Ano manuke, daiji na shorui o nakushite shimatta.*
   That idiot lost the important papers.

make-oshimi

負け惜しみ

unwilling to admit defeat

GAKUSEI:

Ano gakkō ni ochite yokatta. Ichido, rōnin shitakattan' da.

SENSEI:

Kimi wa aikawarazu, make-oshimi ga tsuyoi ne.

STUDENT:

I'm glad I wasn't admitted into that college. I wanted to take a year off before going to college anyway.

TEACHER:

As usual, you can't admit failure.

Make-oshimi combines *makeru* (lose) and *oshimi* (regret). This expression describes an unwillingness to admit failure. A person with this mind-set makes up excuses for all problems and denies losing in the face of defeat. Some common uses are *make-oshimi ga tsuyoi* (very unwilling to admit defeat), *make-oshimi no tsuyoi hito* (someone who can't admit defeat), and *make-oshimi o iu* (make excuses).

EXAMPLES

1. *Kanojo wa totemo make-oshimi no tsuyoi hito da.*
   She can't admit failure.
2. *Anata ga konna ni make-oshimi ga tsuyoi to wa omowanakatta.*
   I didn't think you were so unwilling to admit defeat.
3. *Make-oshimi o itte inaide, benkyō shinasai.*
   Stop making excuses and get back to your studies.
4. *Ano hito wa make-oshimi bakari itte iru.*
   That person is always making excuses.

mayu ni tsuba o nuru

眉に唾を塗る

take care not to be fooled

FUDŌSAN-YA:

O-kyakusan, kono tochi ga issenman'en nara, o-kaidoku desu yo.

KYAKU:

(kokoro no naka) Nandaka yasu-sugite, mayu ni tsuba o nuritaku naru na.

REAL ESTATE AGENT:

At ten million yen this land is a real bargain.

CUSTOMER:

(to himself) It seems too cheap. I'd better be on my guard.

Mayu ni tsuba o nuru, literally "to put saliva on eyebrows," means to take care not to be fooled or victimized. This phrase originated from the mythical belief that badgers were creatures that played tricks on people as they slept. The way one could prevent being fooled was to wet one's eyebrows with saliva. *Mayu ni tsuba o tsukeru* has the same meaning, and *mayu tsuba mono* is a thing that one should be wary of.

EXAMPLES

1. *Kare no hanashi, mayu ni tsuba o nutte, kiita hō ga ii yo.*
   Don't believe everything he says.
2. *Kare wa daiya to itte iru kedo, kau mae ni mayu ni tsuba o tsukete miyō.*
   He says this is a diamond, but we should be careful before buying it.
3. *Kare ga daigaisha no shachō to wa, mayu tsuba mono desu ne.*
   It's hard to believe that he is the president of a large company.
4. *Mayu ni tsuba o tsukete, damasarenai yō ni ne.*
   Be careful if he tries to sweet-talk you.
5. *Watakushi wa saisho kara, mayu tsuba mono da to utagatte itan' desu.*
   I was suspicious from the beginning.

me ga takai

目が高い

have a discerning eye

KYAKU:

Kono tsubo wa, minchō no mono desu ka?

KOTTŌYA NO SHUJIN:

O-kyakusama, sasuga ni, o-me ga takakute irasshaimasu ne.

CUSTOMER:

Does this pot date from the Ming dynasty?

ANTIQUE DEALER:

You certainly have a discerning eye, sir.

Me ga takai describes an ability to perceive the true nature of a person or thing—to have an excellent, discerning eye. Similar phrases with *me* include *me ga kiku* (be a good judge of) and *me ga koeru* (be a connoisseur). *Koeru* can mean to grow fat or to have a well-developed ability to discern. Other expressions using *koeru* include *mimi ga koeru* (have a discerning ear for music) and *shita ga koeru* (appreciate fine food).

EXAMPLES

1. *Kare wa, bijutsuhin ni kanshite wa, totemo me ga takai desu yo.*
   He has quite a discriminating eye for works of art.
2. *Okāsan no hō ga me ga takai kara, erande kudasai.*
   Since you're a better judge, mother, please choose.
3. *Kare wa me ga kiku kara, yoi mono o sashi-ageyō.*
   Since he has such refined tastes, let's give him something nice.
4. *Anata o erabu to wa, kanojo no me ga takai.*
   The fact that she chose you is proof of her fine judgement.
5. *Kimi mo, hito o miru me ga koete kimashita ne.*
   You've become quite a good judge of character yourself, haven't you?

me no ue no kobu

目の上の瘤

a stumbling block

KAISHAIN:

Kondo atarashii kachō ga irassharu sō desu ne.

BUCHŌ:

Kimi no me no ue no kobu ni naranai to ii kedo ne.

EMPLOYEE:

I hear that we're going to get a new section chief.

DEPARTMENT CHIEF:

I hope that he doesn't make work frustrating for you.

Me no ue no kobu, literally "a lump over one's eye," is used to refer to a person of higher rank or status who frustrates one's ability to function effectively. This phrase refers to a lump that grows over one's eye and impedes one's vision. A similar expression is *me no kataki,* which refers to a person or thing that is detestable and intolerable. *Kataki* refers to a person who one feels a deep hatred for and whom one wishes to destroy. This expression frequently appears as *me no kataki ni suru* (loathe the very sight of).

EXAMPLES

1. *Kare wa sono uchi me no ue no kobu ni narisō da.*

   It looks as if he may become a stumbling block for me in the future.

2. *Kachō ni totte, jitsuryoku no aru buchō wa kaette me no ue no kobu da.*

   For the section chief, having an efficient department chief is actually frustrating.

3. *Watashi wa ani kara itsumo me no kataki ni sarete iru.*

   My older brother always treats me as if I were an enemy.

4. *Kuruma wa, shizen hogo dantai kara me no kataki ni sarete iru.*

   Cars are detested by the conservationists.

me o shiro-kuro saseru

目を白黒させる

look bewildered

MUSUKO:

Okāsan, boku no Amerikajin no koibito ni atte kureru?

CHICHIOYA:

Omae, okāsan ga me o shiro-kuro saseterun' ja nai ka?

SON:

Mom, would you mind meeting my American girlfriend?

FATHER:

Can't you see your mother's bewildered at the very thought of it?

Me o shiro-kuro saseru, literally "to make one's eyes black and white," is used when one is surprised. Many expressions relate to the color of the eyes. *Me no kuroi uchi,* literally "as long as one's eyes are black," means as long as one is alive. *Me no iro o kaeru,* literally "change the color of one's eyes," is used to describe the look in one's eyes when one is angry, surprised, or completely absorbed in a task.

EXAMPLES

1. *Amerikajin ni Furansugo de hanashi-kaketara, kare wa me o shiro-kuro saseta.*

   The American looked bewildered when I spoke to him in French.

2. *Kanojo ni puropōzu shitara, kanojo wa me o shiro-kuro saseta.*

   She was quite stunned when I proposed to her.

3. *Chichioya no me no kuroi uchi ni, ōki na ie o tatete agetai.*

   While my father is still alive, I'd like to build him a large house.

4. *Kare wa, kuruma no koto ni naru to, me no iro o kaeru.*

   When the topic turns to cars, his face lights up.

me to hana no saki

目と鼻の先

a stone's throw away

TSŪKŌNIN:

Suimasen. Kabuki-za, doko desu ka?

TEN'IN:

Ā, sore nara, koko kara me to hana no saki desu yo.

PASSERBY:

Excuse me, can you tell me where the Kabuki Theater is?

SALESPERSON:

Ah, right—it's just a stone's throw from here.

Me to hana no saki means that the distance between two things is extremely close, like one's eyes and nose. *Me to hana no aida* has the same meaning. Another expression involving the use of eyes and nose is *me kara hana e nukeru* (be very sharp, intelligent), which indicates a high degree of intelligence with a keen sense of judgment.

EXAMPLES

1. *Kare wa, me to hana no saki no tokoro ni mo, kuruma de dekakeru.*
   He always uses the car, even to go just down the block.
2. *Tōkyō-eki nara, sugu me to hana no saki ni arimasu yo.*
   Tokyo Station? It's a stone's throw from here.
3. *Shachō no ie wa, watashi no ie no me to hana no saki ni aru.*
   My house is almost on the company president's doorstep.
4. *Kanojo wa me kara hana e nukeru yō na, atama no ii hito desu ne.*
   She's a very sharp person.
5. *Kare mo mukashi wa, me kara hana e nukeru yō na shōnen deshita yo.*
   When he was a boy, he too was quick-witted.

mentsu o tateru

面子を立てる

save face

TOMODACHI:

Kono aida wa seidai na kekkon-shiki deshita ne.

SHINRŌ:

Oya no mentsu o tateru tame ni, hiyō ga kakarimashita.

FRIEND:

Your wedding reception the other day was magnificent!

BRIDEGROOM:

It cost a good deal of money to keep up appearances for my parents' sake.

Mentsu o tateru, which combines *mentsu* (face, honor) and *tateru* (put up), means to ensure that honor and dignity are maintained. The intransitive form, *mentsu ga tatsu,* means that one's honor is upheld. *Mentsu o tsubusu* refers to making someone lose face and *mentsu ga maru-tsubure* means a complete loss of honor.

EXAMPLES

1. *Shachō no mentsu o tatete, supiichi o o-negai shiyō.*

   Let's ask our company president to make a speech to maintain appearances.

2. *Kimi ga kono shigoto o hiki-ukete kurete, watashi no mentsu ga tatta yo.*

   By taking over that job for me, you helped me save face.

3. *Sensei no mentsu o tsubusu yō na koto o shite, sumimasen.*

   I'm sorry for having done something that might tarnish your reputation, professor.

4. *Kimi no tame ni, watashi no mentsu wa maru-tsubure da.*

   Because of you I have suffered a complete loss of face.

5. *Otōsan no mentsu o tsubusu yō na koto wa shimasen.*

   I wouldn't do anything that might tarnish your good name, father.

mi kara deta sabi

身から出た錆

serve one right, suffer the consequences of one's own deeds

KOKUMIN 1:

Daijin no ninki wa sagaru bakari desu ne.

KOKUMIN 2:

Katte na gendō bakari desu kara, mi kara deta sabi desu yo.

CITIZEN 1:

The minister's popularity is rapidly disappearing, isn't it?

CITIZEN 2:

What with his selfish speech and behavior, he had it coming.

Mi kara deta sabi, literally "rust from the blade of a sword," means that one suffers because of a misdeed on one's part. The expression refers to a sword rusting in its sheath. Other expressions using *mi* are *mi ni oboe ga nai* (not realize one's guilt) and *mi ni amaru* (be more than one deserves).

EXAMPLES

1. *Kare ga zaisan o ushinatta no wa, mi kara deta sabi desu. Datte, pachinko bakari yatte chittomo hatarakanai no desu kara.*

   It serves him right that he lost his fortune. After all, he never works and just plays pachinko.

2. *Mi kara deta sabi to wa ie, kare mo ki no doku desu.*

   You may say that he asked for it, but I sympathize with him.

3. *Mi kara deta sabi to fukaku hansei shite orimasu.*

   I have no one to blame but myself—I am deeply sorry.

4. *Mi ni oboe no nai koto de tsuikyū o uketa.*

   I was accused of having done something of which I was totally innocent.

5. *Konkai no jushō wa, watashi ni totte, mi ni amaru kōei desu.*

   Being the recipient of this prize is a great honor for me.

154

michikusa o kū

道草を食う

fool around on the way, dawdle

MUSUKO:

Okāsan, itte kimasu.

HAHAOYA:

Yūgata, minna de shokuji ni ikimasu kara, michikusa o kuwanaide kaette irasshai.

SON:

I'm going now, Mom.

MOTHER:

We're all going out for dinner this evening, so come straight home.

Michikusa o kū refers to dawdling on the way to a particular place. Occasionally the verb *kū* (eat) is dropped. The phrase originates from the fact that horses, when grazing on the grass by the roadside, make little progress. In modern usage, this expression is used metaphorically, as in *jinsei no michikusa* (tarrying in life), to indicate that one deviated from one's purpose.

EXAMPLES

1. *Uchi no ko, itsumo gakkō kara no kaerimichi ni achikochi de michikusa o kuinagara kaette kuru.*

   My children never come straight home.

2. *Kaimono no kaeri ni, michikusa shinaide kaette ne.*

   Don't fool around on your way home from doing the shopping.

3. *Gakkō no kaeri ni hon'ya de michikusa o shita.*

   I spent some time browsing in the bookshop on the way home from school.

4. *Watashi no jinsei wa, michikusa mo sezu junchō ni kita.*

   Things for me have been progressing smoothly without a hitch.

mie o haru
見栄を張る
show off

OTTO:

Shachō no ie ni ikun' dakara, yoi kimono o kinasai.

TSUMA:

Anata, mie o haru koto nai wa. Kyūryō ga yasui koto, wakatterun' desu mono.

HUSBAND:

Since we're going to the company president's place, wear something nice.

WIFE:

There's no need to make a show, dear. He knows how little you earn.

Mie o haru describes being conscious of what other people think and making an outward show. *Mie* derives from *mieru* (be seen, visible). A related idiom is *mie o kiru* (assume a posture), which can refer to a Kabuki actor momentarily halting his action and assuming a striking pose, or mouthing off to someone in a self-confident way.

EXAMPLES

1. *Mie o hatte made, ōki na ie ni sumitaku arimasen.*

   I have no desire to live in a large house just for appearances' sake.

2. *O-tagai no koto wa nan' de mo shitte irun' dakara, boku no mae de, mie o haru hitsuyō wa nain' da yo.*

   Since I know you so well, don't feel that you have to show off just for me.

3. *Tonari no ie wa, mie o hatte kodomo o takai shiritsu no gakkō ni ikasete iru.*

   Our neighbors are putting up a good front by sending their children to an expensive private school.

migi-ude

右腕

right hand, right-hand man

JŌSHI:

Kimi, kore kara boku no migi-ude ni natte kurenai ka?

BUKA:

Hai, taihen kōei ni omoimasu.

SUPERVISOR:

From now on, I want you to be my right-hand man.

SUBORDINATE:

I would be honored.

Migi-ude can mean either a person's right hand or one's most dependable subordinate. This idiom originated in China, where people of higher rank were always seated on the right. Today in Japan, government employees are also seated from right to left according to rank. Other phrases using *migi* include *migi ni deru mono ga nai* (something or someone is the best) and *migi e narae* (line up and follow the person on your right).

EXAMPLES

1. *Migi-ude no buka ni yamerarete, komatte imasu.*
   I've been having a tough time since my right-hand man quit on me.
2. *Anata no migi-ude wa dare desu ka?*
   Who's your right-hand man?
3. *Shiizā wa migi-ude no Burūtasu ni uragirareta.*
   Caesar was betrayed by Brutus, his right-hand man.
4. *Kanojo wa, kore kara watashi no migi-ude ni natte kureru hito da.*
   From now on she will be my right hand.
5. *Watashi no migi-ude wa, totemo shinrai dekiru jinbutsu desu.*
   My right-hand man is a very reliable person.

157

mikake-daoshi

見掛け倒し

deceptive appearance, deceitful

BUCHŌ:

Shin'nyū-shain no shigoto buri, dō desu ka?

KACHŌ:

Gakureki bakari rippa de, mikake-daoshi desu yo.

DEPARTMENT CHIEF:

How are the new employees doing?

SECTION CHIEF:

They have good academic backgrounds but that's all.

Mikake-daoshi refers to having a deceptive appearance. *Mikake* refers to outer appearances, as in *mikake wa yoi ga, nakami wa wakaranai* (it looks good but there's no telling what the insides are like). *Daoshi,* which is a nominalized form of *taosu* (knock down), in this case is used to negate or devalue what precedes it.

EXAMPLES

1. *Kono hoteru, soto wa rippa na noni, mikake-daoshi desu ne.*
   This hotel only looks nice from the outside.
2. *Ano resurā, tsuyosō datta kedo, mikake-daoshi datta.*
   That wrestler only looked strong.
3. *Ano resutoran, aji ga warukute mikake-daoshi datta.*
   The restaurant looked nice but the food was terrible.
4. *Mikake-daoshi no tatemono da to jishin de sugu kowarete shimau.*
   A building that only looks strong will not survive an earthquake.
5. *Kare wa mikake-daoshi de, jitsuryoku wa zenzen nai.*
   He's all talk; in reality he has no ability.

mikka-bōzu
三日坊主

one who can't stick to anything

OTTO:

Akemashite omedetō. Kotoshi koso, nikki o tsukeru tsumori da.

TSUMA:

Mata, sonna koto itteru. Dōse, mikka-bōzu ni kimatte iru noni.

HUSBAND:

Happy New Year! This year I'm going to make a point of keeping a diary.

WIFE:

There you go again. You know that you can never keep your resolutions any longer than a day or two.

Mikka-bōzu describes one who quickly becomes tired of something, does not last long, or can't stick to things. This expression originally referred to men who became monks *(bōzu)* for three days *(mikka)* and then quit because they found the spartan religious life too difficult.

EXAMPLES

1. *Kanojo wa akippoi seikaku de, nani o shite mo mikka-bōzu da.*
   She's a quitter, no matter what she does.
2. *Otōsan no kin'en wa, itsumo mikka-bōzu nan' dakara.*
   My father can never stick to his frequent vows to give up smoking.
3. *Daietto mo, mikka-bōzu de wa, nan no yaku ni mo tatanai.*
   If you don't stick to your diet, it will be of no use whatsoever.
4. *Donna tsūshin kyōiku o ukete mo, itsumo mikka-bōzu de, nanimo mi ni tsukanai.*
   I can never stick to any correspondence course long enough to learn anything from it.

mizu no awa

水の泡

come to nothing

DŌRYŌ 1:

Kondo no purojekuto, chūshi ni natta sō desu yo.

DŌRYŌ 2:

Sore de wa, junbi ga zenbu mizu no awa ja nai desu ka?

COLLEAGUE 1:

I hear that our next project's been suspended.

COLLEAGUE 2:

Well, that means all of our preparations have come to nothing, doesn't it?

Mizu no awa can refer to foam or bubbles floating on water or it may be used as an idiom to describe an effort wasted by a blunder or mistake. *Suihō ni kisu* has the same meaning. *Suihō* is the Chinese reading of the characters for *mizu no awa*. Whereas *mizu no awa* is used colloquially, *suihō ni kisu* is more of a literary phrase.

EXAMPLES

1. *Koko de hara o tatete wa sekkaku no doryoku ga mizu no awa da.*
   If I lose my temper, all of my efforts will go down the drain.
2. *Ā, kore de wa nanimo ka mo, mizu no awa de wa arimasen ka?*
   Ah, does this mean that all this was for nothing?
3. *Anata wa, watashi-tachi no doryoku o mizu no awa ni shite shimau tsumori desu ka?*
   Do you intend to make all of our efforts go up in smoke?
4. *Kanojo ga kite kurenai to, shita junbi ga subete mizu no awa da.*
   If she doesn't come, all of our preparations will be in vain.
5. *Anata ga shitsurei na iikata no tame ni, subete ga mizu no awa da.*
   Because of your rude remark, everything has ended in failure.

160

mizu o sasu

水を差す

throw a wet blanket on

OTTO:

Daietto no tame ni ashita kara jogingu o hajimeru yo.

TSUMA:

Dōse, mikka bōzu ni kimatte iru wa.

OTTO:

Hajimeru mae kara, mizu o sasu yō na koto, iwanaide hoshii na.

HUSBAND:

In order to lose some weight I'm going to start jogging tomorrow.

WIFE:

Come on, you know you won't stick with it.

HUSBAND:

I'd appreciate it if you wouldn't throw a wet blanket on my plans before I've even begun.

Mizu o sasu refers to interfere or to sour someone's plans. The phrase derives from the idea of adding water to food in order to weaken a strong flavor or to paint in order to lighten a dark color.

EXAMPLES

1. *Sekkaku tsuri no dōgu o katta noni, tsuma ni mizu o sasarete, yaru ki o nakushite shimatta.*

   Even though he had bought fishing gear, his interest in the sport disappeared after his wife threw a wet blanket on his plans.

2. *Yatto kyanpu no sōdan ga matomatta to omotta noni, kare ga itsumo no yō ni mizu o sasu yō na koto o itta.*

   Even though I thought we had finally come to an agreement about our camping trip, as usual, he threw a wrench into our plans.

mizu to abura

水と油

like oil and water

TOMODACHI 1:

Gaikokujin rōdōsha no mondai ga funkyū shite imasu ne.

TOMODACHI 2:

Kono mondai de wa, gaimushō to rōdōshō ga mizu to abura no kankei desu kara ne.

FRIEND 1:

The problem of foreign workers has become quite a knotty issue.

FRIEND 2:

That's because the relationship between the Ministry of Foreign Affairs and the Ministry of Labor is like oil and water.

Mizu to abura, literally "water and fat" is used in the same way as the English expression "like oil and water." It is often used to describe two people or organizations that show a strong disapproval of each other. Both *mizu to abura* and *mizu ni abura* are used.

EXAMPLES

1. *Kare to kanojo de wa mizu to abura da.*

   He and she are like oil and water.

2. *Futari wa mizu to abura na node, kenka ga taenai.*

   Because they mix like oil and water, they never stop arguing.

3. *Ryōkoku no kankei wa, hajime kara mizu to abura datta.*

   From the start, the relationship between the two countries was like oil and water.

4. *Shachō to fuku-shachō wa izen kara mizu to abura no kankei datta.*

   The personality clash between the company's president and vice-president goes way back.

mizu-kake ron
水掛け論
an endless debate

TOMODACHI 1:

Nihon wa tokushu na shakai da to omoimasu yo.

TOMODACHI 2:

Sō wa omoimasen ne. Doko no kuni ni mo, tokushu na mono wa aru deshō.

TOMODACHI 1:

Kono mama de wa mizu-kake ron desu ne.

FRIEND 1:

I think Japanese society is unique.

FRIEND 2:

I disagree. All countries have some unique characteristics, right?

FRIEND 1:

I think we could go on arguing like this forever.

Mizu-kake ron refers to an argument or discussion in which both sides stick fast to their opinions and insist on their particular point of view. The expression originally referred to an interminable argument *(ron)* over bringing water *(mizu-kake)* to a rice paddy.

EXAMPLES

1. *Kare to wa ikura hanashite mo, mizu-kake ron ni naru dake da.*

   No matter how much you talk to him, it just ends up as a futile discussion.

2. *Kono mama de wa, mizu-kake ron ni naru bakari desu.*

   At this rate we'll just endlessly debate each other.

3. *Mizu-kake ron no kurikaeshi na node, kono mondai wa mata kondo hanashimashō.*

   We're just arguing around in circles again. Let's talk about this problem another time.

mizu-kusai

水臭い

standoffish, reserved, distant

TOMODACHI 1:

Shakkin no hensai ni komatte, sarakin kara karitan' da.

TOMODACHI 2:

Rishi ga taihen deshō. Mizu-kusai desu ne. Itte kurereba, watashi ga kashita noni.

FRIEND 1:

I was having trouble making my loan payments so I borrowed some money from a loan shark.

FRIEND 2:

The interest payments must be high. You shouldn't have been so reserved. If you'd asked, I would have lent you the money.

Mizu-kusai means to act in a reserved or formal manner with someone one is usually friendly with. The phrase originally referred to something having lost its flavor because it had been watered down. *Kusai* stresses a bad characteristic of something. Other expressions using *kusai* are *kabi-kusai* (musty, moldy), *sake-kusai* (smell of liquor), *doro-kusai* (crude), and *furu-kusai* (antiquated, out-of-date, old-fashioned).

EXAMPLES

1. *Sonna daiji na hanashi o watashi ni hitokoto mo sōdan shite kurenai nante, mizu-kusai.*

   Not consulting with me at all—that was so standoffish of you.

2. *Anata ga, sonna ni mizu-kusai hito to wa omowanakatta.*

   I didn't know you could be so standoffish.

3. *Mizu-kusai to wa omotta ga, meiwaku o kaketakunakatta.*

   I know I was being standoffish, but I just didn't want to cause any trouble.

mon-nashi

文無し

stone-broke

TOMODACHI 1:

Amerika o ryokōchū ni nimotsu o zenbu nusumaremashite ne. Mon-nashi ni natte shimatte.

TOMODACHI 2:

Sore wa kokoro-bosokatta deshō. Sore de, dō shimashita?

FRIEND 1:

While traveling in America I had all my bags stolen. I ended up flat broke. I didn't have a cent.

FRIEND 2:

You must have felt so helpless. What happened after that?

Mon-nashi refers to being without any money, i.e., being penniless and flat broke. A *mon* was a low denomination of currency used in Japan up until the Edo period, and *nashi* means none.

EXAMPLES

1. *Sofu wa zaisan o tsukai-kitte, mon-nashi ni natte shimatta.*
   My grandfather used up all his fortune, finally ending up penniless.

2. *Ano hito, hasan shite, mon-nashi da sō desu yo.*
   I heard that he went bankrupt and is now flat broke.

3. *Tatoe, anata ga mon-nashi de mo, watashi wa anata ga suki desu.*
   Even if you have no money at all, I'll still love you.

4. *Kare wa mon-nashi ni naru made, gyanburu ni okane o tsukai-tsuzuketa.*
   He continued gambling his money away until he was stone-broke.

5. *Kādo o tsukai-sugiru to, shiranai uchi ni mon-nashi ni natte shimau.*
   If you use your credit cards so often, before you know it you'll be stone-broke.

mono ni suru

物にする

make a success of something

KAGAKUSHA 1:
Kore wa, kon'nan na kenkyū ni narisō da.
KAGAKUSHA 2:
Kitto, mono ni shite misemasu yo.

SCIENTIST 1:
This research promises to be difficult.
SCIENTIST 2:
I'm sure we'll make a success of it. You'll see.

Mono ni suru means to make a success of something, and *mono ni naru* indicates achieving one's aim. The word *mono* has an extremely broad meaning—apart from referring to articles or goods, it can describe intangible things.

EXAMPLES

1. *Naganen kakatte, kenkyū o mono ni shita.*
   After many years, they brought the research to a successful conclusion.
2. *Furansugo o sankagetsu de mono ni suru no wa, taihen datta deshō?*
   It must have been difficult to master French in three months.
3. *Kono kikai wa sōsa ga muzukashikute, nakanaka mono ni naranai.*
   The operation of this machine is so difficult. I'm just getting nowhere at all with it.
4. *Ē, kare ga anata no koibito? Itsu mono ni shita no?*
   What? He's your boyfriend? When did you manage to hook him?
5. *Kare wa kokku to shite wa, mono ni narisō mo nai ne.*
   There's not much chance of him making the grade as a chef.

mono tarinai

物足りない

lack something

HISHO:

Kon'ya no pātii-kaijō, kore de yoroshii desu ka?

BUCHŌ:

Totemo yoi keredo, nanika mono tarinai ne.

SECRETARY:

Will this place be suitable for this evening's party?

DEPARTMENT CHIEF:

It's quite good but there's just something lacking.

Mono tarinai means that something is lacking, leaving one with a sense of dissatisfaction. *Tarinai* by itself means insufficient, while *mono tarinai* refers to something lacking from a psychological point of view. Compounds with *mono* include *mono osoroshii* (frightening, horrible), *mono sabishii* (lonesome, dreary), *mono sawagashii* (noisy, boisterous), and *mono shizuka* (quiet, tranquil).

EXAMPLES

1. *Yūshoku, oishikatta kedo, nanika mono tarinai desu ne.*

   Dinner was delicious; however, something was wanting.

2. *Kare wa majime da ga, seikaku-teki ni nanika mono tarinai tokoro ga aru.*

   He is an earnest type of person but there's something missing in his character.

3. *Kono kikakusho, aidea wa yoi ga, dokoka mono tarinai ne.*

   This plan has some good ideas but it leaves something to be desired.

4. *Kimi no doresu, suteki da ga, nanika ga mono tarinai ne.*

   Your dress is lovely but there's something lacking.

5. *Kyō no ensō wa, chotto mono tarinakatta.*

   Today's performance was not quite what it should have been.

mono wa tameshi

物は試し

giving something a try

OTTO:

Shinsha no kyanpēn ga aru yo.

TSUMA:

Mono wa tameshi, itte mimashō yo.

HUSBAND:

There's a sales promotion for some new cars.

WIFE:

Let's go and have a look.

Mono wa tameshi describes a situation in which one is unable to assess the merit of something until one has tried it. Other expressions beginning with *mono wa* include *mono wa kangaeyō* (it depends on how you look at it), *mono wa iiyō* (it depends on how you say it), and *mono wa sōdan* (two heads are better than one).

EXAMPLES

1. *Kaeru datte, mono wa tameshi, tabete miyō.*

   Well, it may be frog, but let's have a shot at eating it anyway.

2. *Hari de kega ga naoru sō da, mono wa tameshi, yatte miyō.*

   Acupuncture is said to be good for injuries, so I'm willing to give it a try.

3. *Mono wa iiyō de, yoku mo waruku mo naru.*

   It's not what one says but how one says it.

4. *Mono wa kangaeyō de, shippai mo yoi keiken ni naru.*

   Since everything depends upon your way of thinking, even failure can be a worthwhile experience.

5. *Mono wa sōdan desu ga, raishū atari, kaigi o hirakimasen ka?*

   We should talk the matter over and try to come to some agreement, so how about having a meeting some time next week?

mōten o tsuku

盲点をつく

find a vulnerable spot, notice a blind spot

KISHA:

Nichi-bei kōshō no kekka wa dō narimashita ka?

NIHON NO SEIJIKA:

Amerika wa migoto ni Nihon no mōten o tsuite kimashita yo.

REPORTER:

What are the results of the U.S.-Japan negotiations?

JAPANESE POLITICIAN:

Surprisingly, America pointed out something that we missed.

Mōten, a medical term referring to a blind or dark spot in the field of vision, refers to something that goes unnoticed. *Mō,* by itself means blindness, and combined with other words, can mean color blindness *(shiki mō)* or illiteracy *(mon mō). Tsuku* means to hit.

EXAMPLES

1. *Hōsekiten ga, keibi no mōten o tsukarete, dorobō ni hairareta.*
   The jewelry shop was robbed because of a weak spot in its security.

2. *Konna tokoro ni, jōhō-shisutemu no mōten ga aru to wa omowanakatta.*
   I never thought there would be a weak spot in the information system here.

3. *Dōryō ni kikakusho no mōten o tsukarete, awateta.*
   I panicked when a co-worker pointed out a point we overlooked in the project plan.

4. *Atama no yoi gakusei wa, yoku kyōshi no mōten o tsuita shitsumon o suru.*
   A clever student often asks about things the professor misses.

5. *Kare no seiji ni kansuru kiji wa mōten o tsuita mono ga ōi.*
   Many of his articles on politics point out things people usually don't notice.

moto mo ko mo nai

元も子も無い

lose everything

BUKA:

Chōsa ga taihen na node, kono atari de uchi-kirō to omoimasu ga.

JŌSHI:

Kimi, koko de yamete wa, moto mo ko mo nai yo.

SUBORDINATE:

I was thinking of ending the investigation.

SUPERVISOR:

If you give up now, all of our work will be wasted.

Moto mo ko mo nai combines *moto* (capital) and *ko* (interest) and refers to losing both the principal and interest of an investment. This phrase is used to warn someone about losing an investment, as in the example above. *Moto mo ko mo nakusu* also means to lose an investment or to have one's work wasted.

EXAMPLES

1. *Kaze de shiken ga ukerarenakute wa, moto mo ko mo nai.*

   It would be such a waste if I missed the test because of a cold.

2. *Dēta o nakushite shimatte, anna ni kurō shita noni, moto mo ko mo naku natta.*

   Because I lost the data, all of my hard work was wasted.

3. *Sore ja, moto mo ko mo naku natte shimatta wa ne.*

   I guess we lost our entire investment.

4. *Ie ga yakete, moto mo ko mo nakushite shimatta.*

   I lost everything when the house burned down.

5. *Kabu de moto mo ko mo nakushite shimaimashita.*

   I lost everything I had in stocks.

muda-ashi o hakobu

無駄足を運ぶ

go on a wild-goose chase

TOMODACHI 1:

Toshokan ni ittara, kyō wa yasumi dattan' desu.

TOMODACHI 2:

Sore wa, muda-ashi o hakonde shimaimashita ne.

FRIEND 1:

I went to the library today but it was closed.

FRIEND 2:

That was a wasted trip, wasn't it?

Muda-ashi o hakobu means to try to accomplish something without success. *Muda-ashi ni naru* and *muda-ashi o hakobu* can be used interchangeably. Expressions using *muda* include *muda-banashi* (idle talk), *muda-zukai* (wasting money), *muda-meshi* (unproductive, getting little work done), and *muda-jini* (a pointless death).

1. *Sakujitsu wa teikyū-bi na noni toko-ya ni itte shimai, muda-ashi o hakonde shimatta.*

   I went to the barber yesterday, but because it was a holiday, it turned out to be a wild-goose chase.

2. *Muda-ashi ni naru kamo shirenai ga, machi-awase no basho ni itte miyō.*

   We might be wasting our time, but let's go to the meeting place anyway.

3. *Sekkaku irashita noni, go-kibō no shina ga urikire de, muda-ashi ni natte, sumimasen.*

   I'm sorry that I can't be of any help, especially since you've come all this way, but the things you wanted are sold out.

4. *Muda-banashi shinaide, shigoto shinasai.*

   Stop chatting and get to work.

muga-muchū

無我夢中

completely preoccupied

SHIN'NYŪ-SHAIN:

Myōnichi yasumasete kudasai.

KACHŌ:

Mata ka ne. Watashi no wakai koro wa, yasumi nado torazu ni, muga-muchū de hataraita mono da yo.

NEW EMPLOYEE:

Please let me have the day off tomorrow.

SECTION CHIEF:

What again? When I was a young man I never took a holiday and was totally devoted to my work.

Muga-muchū means being engrossed by something, and not thinking about anything else. *Muga* (selflessness) is a Buddhist term that, when added to *muchū*, means to be so preoccupied with something that one forgets the existence of oneself.

EXAMPLES

1. *Kyonen no kono koro wa, muga-muchū de juken-benkyō shite ita.*
   This time last year I was completely preoccupied with studying for my university entrance exams.
2. *Kaji ni nari, watashi wa muga-muchū de nige-dashita.*
   A fire started and I fled in a wild panic.
3. *Kodomo-tachi ga muga-muchū de famikon-gēmu o shite iru.*
   The children are completely absorbed in playing computer games.
4. *Gorufu wa muga-muchū de suru hodo no supōtsu de wa nai.*
   Golf isn't the kind of sport that you would become totally wrapped up in.

mujun suru

矢盾する

contradictory

TOMODACHI 1:

Kane-mochi ni wa naritai kedo, kane-mōke wa shitakunai na.

TOMODACHI 2:

Anata no iu koto wa totemo mujun shite imasu ne.

FRIEND 1:

I want to be rich, but I don't want to have to make money.

FRIEND 2:

You're full of contradictions, aren't you?

Mujun suru describes something that is self-contradictory. The origin of this meaning is found in the two characters *mu* (halberd) and *jun* (shield). The story goes that there was a craftsman in China who used to sell halberds and shields. Every time he sold a halberd he would say, "This is the best. No shield is of any use against this." But every time he sold a shield, he would say, "This is the best. No halberd is of any use against this." From this contradiction came the present-day use of the word *mujun*.

EXAMPLES

1. *Kare wa jibun no itte iru koto ga mujun shite iru no ga wakaranai.*
   He's not aware of the contradictions in what he's saying.

2. *Chichi wa iu koto to suru koto ga itsumo mujun shite iru.*
   What my father says and what he actually does are always different.

3. *Anata no iken wa mujun shite iru to omoimasen ka?*
   Don't you think your point of view is somewhat self-contradictory?

4. *Kono kaisha no kisoku wa mujun ga ō-sugiru.*
   There are too many contradictions in this company's rules and regulations.

mune ga ippai ni naru

胸が一杯になる

be overcome with emotion

OTTO:

Dō shitan' dai?

TSUMA:

Musume kara no tegami ni, omowazu mune ga ippai ni natte . . .

HUSBAND:

What's wrong? Why are you crying?

WIFE:

When I read our daughter's letter, I couldn't help but get sentimental.

Mune ga ippai ni naru, literally "the chest becomes full," refers to one's chest filling up with feelings of sorrow, regret, or happiness. Other expressions using *mune* include *mune ga itamu* (be consumed with worry or grief), *mune ga sawagu* (one's heart pounds in apprehension or expectation), and *mune o utsu* (be moved emotionally).

EXAMPLES

1. *Anata no yasashii kotoba ni mune ga ippai ni narimashita.*
   I was very touched by your kind words.
2. *Kare ni aeru to omou to, mune ga ippai ni naru.*
   The thought of being able to see him fills me with emotion.
3. *Sensō de naku natta hito no koto o kangaeru to, mune ga itamu.*
   My heart grieves when I think of those who died in the war.
4. *Kodomo no kaeri ga osoi node, jiko de wa nai ka to mune ga sawagu.*
   The children are late getting home. I wonder if they had an accident.
5. *Eiga no kandō-teki na bamen ni, mune o utareta.*
   I was touched by the moving scene in the movie.

174

musha-burui

武者震い

trembling with excitement

SENPAI:

Nani o furuete irun' da? Sakkā no shiai ni deru no ga sonna ni kowai no?

KŌHAI:

Chigaimasu yo. Kore wa musha-burui desu.

SENIOR:

Why are you shaking? Are you that afraid of playing in the soccer match?

JUNIOR:

No. I'm quivering with excitement to get on with it.

Musha-burui refers to one's body trembling with excitement in anticipation of an important occasion. *Musha* is a samurai warrior, clad in armor and helmet. *Burui* comes from *furui* (shaking, trembling)—the shivering of the body due to cold or fear. Thus *musha-burui* originates from the fact that when warriors headed for the battlefield, they would be in a state of nervous tension and their bodies would tremble.

EXAMPLES

1. *Iyoiyo supiichi o suru ban da to omou to, musha-burui ga suru.*
   Whenever I think of it finally being my turn to make a speech, my body trembles in anticipation.
2. *Kowakute furuete iru no de wa arimasen. Musha-burui desu yo.*
   I'm not quivering in fear. I'm trembling in eagerness to get on with it!
3. *Hatsu-kōen no honban o mukaete, musha-burui ga tomaranakatta.*
   On the occasion of my first public performance, my body wouldn't stop shivering in anticipation.

mushi ga ii

虫がいい

taking a lot for granted

DŌRYŌ 1:

Kondo no Amerika-shutchō wa, boku ga iku yo.

DŌRYŌ 2:

Kimi wa, zuibun mushi ga iin' da ne. Hoka ni ikitai hito ga iru noni.

COLLEAGUE 1:

I'll go on the next business trip to the United States.

COLLEAGUE 2:

You certainly take a lot for granted. There are others who would like to go, you know.

Mushi ga ii means that one only selfishly considers whether something suits one's own convenience. *Mushi* refers to insects or worms, and in Japan there is a popular belief that a *mushi* dwells within a person's heart, influencing one's feelings. Phrases employing *mushi* include *mushi ga sukanai* (having a dislike for), *mushi ga shiraseru* (have a premonition), and *mushi no idokoro ga warui* (be in a bad mood).

EXAMPLES

1. *Sore wa jibun-katte de, mushi ga yo-sugimasu ne.*
   That's selfish—you're asking too much.
2. *Kondo no buchō wa, nan to naku mushi ga sukanai.*
   There's something about the new department chief that I just don't like.
3. *Kare ga kaette kuru 'tte, mushi ga shiraseta no. Yahari, kaette kita wa.*
   I had a hunch he would come home and, surely enough, he did.
4. *Chichi wa, kesa wa mushi no idokoro ga warukute, okotte bakari iru.*
   Dad got up on the wrong side of the bed and has been in a bad mood.

mu-teppō

無鉄砲

reckless, thoughtless

TOMODACHI 1:
Kanojo wa, baiku de Yūrashia-tairiku o ōdan suru rashii yo.
TOMODACHI 2:
Sore wa chotto mu-teppō nan' ja nai ka na?

FRIEND 1:
It seems that she's going to cross Eurasia on a motorbike.
FRIEND 2:
That's probably a bit foolhardy, I think.

Mu-teppō, literally "without a gun," means to do something without giving due consideration to the consequences. Since the idea of fighting without a gun was thought to be absurd, *mu-teppō* came to mean recklessness. A synonymous expression is *mukō-mizu.*

EXAMPLES

1. *Sonna mu-teppō na keikaku ga seikō suru hazu wa nai.*
   Such a rash scheme can't succeed.
2. *Shokuryō mo motazu ni, fuyu yama ni noboru no wa mu-teppō da.*
   It's mad to go mountain climbing in winter without taking provisions.
3. *Dōshite oyogenai noni uindo-sāfin o suru nante, sonna mu-teppō na koto o shita no desu ka?*
   Going windsurfing even though you can't swim! How could you be so reckless?
4. *Wakai koro wa dare de mo sukoshi wa mu-teppō na mono da.*
   Everyone acts a little rashly when they are young.
5. *Zuibun mu-teppō na unten o shimasu ne.*
   You really do drive quite recklessly, don't you?

namida o nomu

涙を呑む

endure a disappointment, swallow one's tears

TOMODACHI 1:

Shingaku suru no, yamerun' datte ne.

TOMODACHI 2:

Chichi ga byōki de ne. Namida o nonde, akirameru koto ni shita yo.

FRIEND 1:

I hear that you've given up on the idea of going on to university.

FRIEND 2:

My father's in poor health, so I've decided to accept my lot and give up the idea.

Namida o nomu, literally "to drink one's tears," means to endure the pain and regret of something that didn't work out as planned. *Namida o shiboru,* literally "to wring out tears," means to weep copiously as if the tears were being squeezed out of one.

EXAMPLES

1. *Kare to kōron ni nari, namida o nonde hiki-sagatta.*

   I got into an argument with him and reluctantly had to back down.

2. *Sensō ni makete, namida o nonde, aite no jōken o uke-ireta.*

   They lost the war and, swallowing back their tears, accepted the other side's conditions.

3. *Binbō na node, namida o nonde kuruma o kau no o akirameta.*

   As much as I hate to, I've given up the idea of buying a car because I have no money.

4. *Sore wa namida o shiboru yō na kanashii eiga datta.*

   That movie was a real tear-jerker.

naminami de wa nai

並並ではない

unusual, exceptional

BUKA:

Taishoku shite, kaisha o tsukurō to omoun' desu ga.

JŌSHI:

Hitori de kaisha o keiei suru no wa naminami de wa nai yo.

SUBORDINATE:

I plan to retire and start a business of my own.

SUPERVISOR:

It's really difficult to manage a business by yourself.

Naminami, which means normal or regular, is usually used with negative verbs, such as *naminami naranu doryoku* (exceptional effort), and *naminami naranu shinsetsu* (exceptionally kind). *Nami hazureta,* meaning uncommon or abnormal, is used in expressions like *nami hazureta nōryoku* (exceptional intelligence), and *nami hazureta chikara* (extraordinary strength).

EXAMPLES

1. *Daigaku mo denaide sōri ni naru no wa, naminami de wa nai deshō.*
   It would be amazing if a person without a college degree became prime minister.
2. *Shachō ni hantai suru no wa naminami de wa nai.*
   It's unusual to go against the president.
3. *Orinpikku senshu ni naru ni wa naminami naranu doryoku ga iru.*
   It takes extraordinary effort to become an Olympic athlete.
4. *Kanojo wa naminami naranu shinsetsu na hito de, gonin mo koji o sodateta.*
   Out of her exceptional kindness, she raised five orphans.
5. *Mōtsuaruto wa kodomo no koro kara, nami hazureta sainō ga atta.*
   From childhood, Mozart had extraordinary talent.

nan kuse o tsukeru

難癖をつける

criticize, find fault with something

KYAKU:

Kono kuruma, kata ga furui shi iro mo warui shi, kono nedan, taka-sugirun' ja nai?

CHŪKOSHA HANBAI NO HITO:

(kokoro no naka) Nan kuse o tsukete, nebiki saseru ki da na.

CUSTOMER:

This car's style is out-of-date and the color isn't very good. Don't you think you're asking too much for it?

USED CAR DEALER:

(to himself) What's he crabbing about? He's just trying to get me to lower the price.

Nan kuse o tsukeru means to go out of one's way to find fault in something or to criticize it. When put together, *nan* (weak point) and *kuse* (kink or curl) refer to points one wants to criticize. Related expressions include *nan kuse o tsuketagaru* (want to find fault with others) and *kuse o tsukerareru* (be criticized).

EXAMPLES

1. *Kare wa nani goto ni mo, sugu nan kuse o tsuketagaru.*
   No matter what happens, he is always so quick to criticize.
2. *Nan kuse o tsukereba yoi to iu mono de wa arimasen yo.*
   It is certainly not appropriate to carp on about things.
3. *Amerika wa Nihon no nōgyō seisaku ni nan kuse o tsukete kita.*
   America has been criticizing Japan's agricultural policy.
4. *Torihikisaki ga, seihin ni nan kuse o tsukete, kakaku o negitte kita.*
   The client found fault with the product and haggled about the price.
5. *Sō nan kuse o tsukerarete wa, damatte iraremasen.*
   I'm not going to sit back and let you criticize me like that.

naraku no soko

奈落の底

hit rock bottom

TOMODACHI 1:

Dō shitan' desu ka? Genki ga arimasen ne.

TOMODACHI 2:

Kaisha ga tōsan shite, shitsugyō desu. Naraku no soko ni ochimashita yo.

FRIEND 1:

What's the problem? You're not your normal self.

FRIEND 2:

My company's gone bankrupt and I'm out of a job. I'm done for.

Naraku no soko, which combines *naraku* (a Buddhist term for hell) and *soko* (bottom or depth) refers to either a place of inestimable depth or a situation from which one is unable to extricate oneself. *Naraku* can also refer to the trap cellar located beneath a theater stage where props and equipment are stored.

EXAMPLES

1. *Anata to nara, naraku no soko made de mo tsuite ikimasu.*

   I would follow you to the ends of the earth.

2. *Ichido naraku no soko ni ochitara, hai-agaru no wa taihen da.*

   Once you've hit rock bottom, it's very difficult to work your way up again.

3. *Aitsu, itsuka naraku no soko ni otoshite yaru.*

   I'll see to that bastard's downfall someday!

4. *Anna naraku no soko no yō na basho ni, nido to modoritakunai.*

   I don't want to return to that hellish place.

5. *Ukkari shite iru to, naraku no soko ni otosaresō da.*

   Unless I keep my wits about me, I may be led to ruin.

nari-furi kamawanai

形振りかまわない

apathy toward appearance or attitude

MUSUME:

Okāsan, kare no koto, dō omotta?

HAHAOYA:

Atama wa yosasō dakedo, nari-furi kamawanai hito ne.

DAUGHTER:

What did you think of him?

MOTHER:

He seems intelligent but doesn't seem to care about his appearance.

Nari-furi kamawanai, which combines *nari* (appearance), *furi* (attitude), and *kamawanai* (not care) refers to not caring about how one dresses or acts. Some examples of *nari* and *furi* used individually are *yoi nari o shite iru* (wear nice clothes), *kitanai nari o shite iru* (wear filthy clothes), and *hito no furi mite waga furi naose* (improve one's actions and attitudes by watching others).

EXAMPLES

1. *Kare wa nari-furi kamawazu, hataraite iru.*

   He's so absorbed in his work that he doesn't pay any attention to his appearance.

2. *Amari nari-furi kamawanai to, seken no hito ni kirawaremasu yo.*

   If you don't watch your attitude, you could make some enemies.

3. *Itsumo wa nari-furi o kamawanai hito ga, kyō wa kirei ni shitemasu ne.*

   For a person who usually doesn't care about appearances, you look nice today.

4. *Sukoshi nari-furi o kamatta dake de, betsujin no yō da.*

   With a small change in your appearance, you look like a new person.

nawa-bari

縄張り

one's own territory, one's turf

CHIHŌ NO SHISHA NO SHAIN:
Tōkyō-honsha de hatarakeru yō ni, tanonde kuremasen ka?
HONSHA NO SHAIN:
Zan'nen dakedo, jinji wa watashi no nawa-bari de wa nai node . . .

LOCAL BRANCH OFFICE CLERK:
Would you mind asking if I could work at the main Tokyo branch?
HEAD OFFICE CLERK:
Sorry, but personnel placement is not my area.

Nawa-bari refers to someone's particular field of knowledge or area of influence. This expression came from the fact that the boundaries of property used to be marked with rope *(nawa)*. As a result, *nawa* was later used to indicate an area under one's power. *Nawa-bari ga chigau* is a similar expression meaning something is no one's business or that something has nothing to do with others.

EXAMPLES

1. *Gaimushō to monbushō wa otagai ni nawa-bari ishiki ga tsuyoi desu ne.*
   The Ministry of Foreign Affairs and the Ministry of Education are always quarreling over their respective areas of administration.
2. *Kaigai no shijō-chōsa wa boku no nawa-bari de wa arimasen yo.*
   Research on markets overseas is not my area.
3. *Anata-gata no nawa-bari o okasu tsumori wa arimasen.*
   I have no intention of intruding on your ground.
4. *Watashi-tachi no nawa-bari ni kubi o tsukkomanaide kudasai.*
   Mind your own business.
5. *Mukashi kara kono hen wa, aru bōryokudan no nawa-bari desu.*
   This area has always been under the control of a group of gangsters.

ne mo ha mo nai

根も葉もない

totally unfounded, completely untrue

KŌHAI:

Senpai, konyaku shita sō desu ne.

SENPAI:

Sonna, ne mo ha mo nai uwasa, shinjiru na yo.

JUNIOR:

I heard you got engaged.

SENIOR:

There's not a shred of truth to that rumor, so don't believe it.

Ne mo ha mo nai, literally "having neither leaves nor root," means having no basis of truth. For instance, *ne mo ha mo nai uwasa* refers to a rumor without any basis of truth. Other expressions using *ne* include *ne hori ha hori,* literally "from the roots to the end of the leaves" and meaning limitless, thorough, and persistent, and *ne ni motsu,* which means to hold a grudge against someone.

EXAMPLES

1. *Kare wa, ne mo ha mo nai uwasa o taterarete, komatte imasu.*

   He's having problems because people are spreading unfounded rumors about him.

2. *Keisatsu no tori-shirabe de, jiko o mokugeki shita toki no koto o, ne hori ha hori kikarete shimatta.*

   During the police investigation I was thoroughly questioned about the accident I had witnessed.

3. *Tomodachi wa boku ni kanojo no koto o ne hori ha hori tazuneta.*

   My friend asked all sorts of questions about my girlfriend.

4. *Musuko wa, o-taku no o-jōsan ni ijiwaru sareta no o, ne ni motte iru yō da.*

   My son holds a grudge from when your daughter was mean to him.

neko mo shakushi mo

猫も杓子も

anybody and everybody

KYŌJU:

Gakusei no repōto, neko mo shakushi mo onaji koto o kaite, komatta mono da.

GAKUSEI:

Betsu ni, minna de sōdan shita wake de wa arimasen yo.

PROFESSOR:

This is a real problem, because all of the students reports are the same.

STUDENT:

It's not as if we got together to decide what to write about.

The meaning of *neko mo shakushi mo* comes from the fact that the paw of a cat *(neko)* is similar to the shape of a spoon *(shakushi)*. Since every house has spoons and most also have cats, this phrase came to mean everyone in general.

EXAMPLES

1. *Wakamono wa neko mo shakushi mo asa-shan suru yō ni natta.*

   All young people have started to wash their hair in the mornings.

2. *Neko mo shakushi mo kuruma ni noru node, michi ga konde shikata nai.*

   There's so much traffic because everybody drives.

3. *Shinkon-ryokō to iu to, neko mo shakushi mo gaikoku-ryokō ni ikitagaru.*

   Everyone wants to have a honeymoon overseas.

4. *Saikin, neko mo shakushi mo, yofukashi suru yō ni natta.*

   It seems as if everyone stays up late at night these days.

5. *Watashi, neko mo shakushi mo suru yō na koto, shitakunai.*

   I don't want to do what everybody else does.

neko o kaburu

猫を被る

play the hypocrite

ONNA JIMUIN 1:

Anna yasashisō na kao o shite iru kedo, ano hito, hontō wa kowai hito yo.

ONNA JIMUIN 2:

Mā, jā, neko o kabutte iru no ne.

FEMALE OFFICE WORKER 1:

Though she might look kind, she's actually a horrible person.

FEMALE OFFICE WORKER 2:

Really? So she's only pretending to be nice.

Neko o kaburu can mean either to present oneself as reserved and thus not show one's real self, or to feign ignorance. This expression is made up of *neko* (cat) and *kaburu* (put on, wear). The meaning arises from the fact that cats can appear to be gentle when in fact they may be very strong and sometimes cruel. *Neko-kaburi,* as a nominal, means hypocrisy and false modesty.

EXAMPLES

1. *Itsumo kappatsu na kanojo mo, kare no mae de wa neko o kabutte iru.*
   Though she's usually so vivacious, in front of him, she too is feigning an air of modesty.

2. *Tabako mo sake mo hontō wa suki datta nante, kimi wa ima made neko o kabutte itan' da ne.*
   You were just pretending to be innocent. You actually like smoking and drinking, don't you?

3. *Satsujinhan ga neko o kabutte senpuku shite ita.*
   The murderer avoided discovery by feigning innocence.

4. *Itsu made mo neko-kaburi ga tsūyō suru wake wa arimasen.*
   You won't get by forever by playing the hypocrite.

186

nemawashi o suru

根回しをする

negotiate behind the scenes

BUCHŌ:

Kondo no kikaku ni tsuite wa, kaigi de hantai ga ōi ja nai ka ne.

BUKA:

Shinpai nai to omoimasu. Nemawashi wa shite okimashita kara.

DEPARTMENT CHIEF:

There may be a lot of people at the meeting who are opposed to our next project.

SUBORDINATE:

There's no need to worry. I've been doing some maneuvering behind the scenes.

Nemawashi o suru, which is made up of *nemawashi,* literally "around the roots," and *suru* (to do or make), means to hold a preparatory discussion before a task is to be undertaken. One or two years before certain plants are transplanted, a large hole is dug around each in order to cut off some of the roots. This causes the growth of small roots, which, when the plant is finally transplanted, helps improve the plant's ability to take in water and nutrients.

EXAMPLES

1. *Kaigi no nemawashi ga totemo umaku itta.*

   The spadework for the conference was very well done.

2. *Tsuyoi hantai ga aru node, nemawashi ga yarinikui.*

   Since there's strong opposition, it's difficult to get people's support.

3. *Kondo no ken wa, dōshite mo nemawashi ga hitsuyō desu.*

   When it comes to this matter, it's absolutely vital that we sound people out in advance.

4. *Nemawashi o suru hodo de wa arimasen yo.*

   You don't need to go to the extent of negotiating beforehand.

nemimi ni mizu
寝耳に水
a bolt out of the blue

TOMODACHI 1:

Konpyūtā no gamen kara hatsugansei no busshitsu ga dete iru rashii ne.

TOMODACHI 2:

Sore wa nemimi ni mizu desu. Dōshitara fusegerun' deshō?

FRIEND 1:

It seems that cancer-producing forces can come out of computer monitor screens.

FRIENDS 2:

That's certainly news to me. I wonder how you can protect yourself.

Nemimi ni mizu, literally "water in ears when asleep," refers to being surprised by something that happened suddenly or unexpectedly. One theory claims this refers to the surprise someone who is sleeping would experience if water were poured in his ears. Another theory states that the expression derived from the reaction of someone who is woken up with news of a big fire.

EXAMPLES

1. *Raigetsu kara Amerika ni ten'nin to wa, nemimi ni mizu no hanashi desu.*

   My new posting to America next month came as a bolt out of the blue.

2. *Kare ga imōto ni kekkon o mōshikomu nante, nemimi ni mizu desu.*

   He asked my little sister to marry him? What a surprise!

3. *Kare ga gan datta nante, nemimi ni mizu desu.*

   It is a complete shock for me to find out that he, of all people, had cancer.

4. *Nemimi ni mizu nado to tobokenaide kudasai.*

   Please don't pretend that this is news to you.

ni no mai o fumu

二の舞を踏む

repeat another's folly, make the same mistake

MUSUKO:

Raigetsu wa daigaku-juken da. Shinpai da na.

HAHAOYA:

Shippai shite, oniisan no ni no mai o fumanaide ne.

SON:

The university entrance examination is next month. I'm a bit nervous.

MOTHER:

Don't blow it like your older brother did, all right?

Ni no mai o fumu, literally "step on a second dance," means to repeat another's folly, mistake, or failure. This expression originally referred to a comical dance that centered on the inability of the dancers to imitate the original dance.

EXAMPLES

1. *Mata shippai, kyonen no ni no mai o funde shimatta.*

   I failed again, like last year.

2. *Kaisha o kubi ni natta kare no ni no mai wa fumitakunai.*

   I don't want to be fired from the company like he was.

3. *Sonna koto o suru to, kare no ni no mai ni narimasu yo.*

   Doing that would result in repeating his mistake.

4. *O-negai da kara, inshu-unten de tsukamattari shite, otōsan no ni no mai wa fumanaide ne.*

   Please, don't get caught drinking and driving like your father did.

5. *Hoteru ni pasupōto o wasureru yō na kare no ni no mai o fumu koto dake wa sakeyō.*

   Let's just try not to repeat his mistakes, like when he forgot his passport at the hotel.

niban senji

二番煎じ

a repeat performance

TOMODACHI 1:

Kondo no sōsaku barē, deki wa dō desu ka?

TOMODACHI 2:

*Zan'nen nagara, sakunen no niban senji de, shinsensa ga arimasen
ne.*

FRIEND 1:

How did this year's modern ballet turn out?

FRIEND 2:

Unfortunately, it was really just a redoing of last year's performance; there wasn't anything new.

Niban senji refers to either an imitation of a certain plan, program,
or idea, or a lack of freshness and originality. *Niban* means second
and *senji* comes from the verb *senjiru,* meaning to boil or brew. The
first time tea or herbal medicine is brewed, the flavor and effect is
best, but both are diminished the second time hot water is added.

EXAMPLES

1. *Sekkaku share o itte mo, niban senji de wa omoshirokunai.*
   It's no use telling that joke; the second time around it's not funny.
2. *Anata no hanashi wa kare no hanashi no niban senji desu ne.*
   Your story smacks quite a bit of his.
3. *Ano shukō wa, dare ka no niban senji desu ne.*
   That plan was copied from someone else's, wasn't it?
4. *Kono eiga ga ataranai no wa, yūmei na eiga no niban senji dakara da.*
   The reason no one likes this movie is because it's merely an imitation of
   that famous film.

nisoku-sanmon

二束三文

dirt cheap, a giveaway

KYŌJU:

Shosai no hon, sukoshi seiri shite, uritain' da ga.

FURU-HON'YA NO TENSHU:

Sensei, kau toki wa takakute mo, uru toki wa nisoku-sanmon desu yo.

PROFESSOR:

I want to sell the books in the study after I tidy them up a bit.

SECONDHAND BOOK STORE OWNER:

Professor, even if the books were expensive when you bought them, you must sell them cheaply.

Nisoku-sanmon refers to something that is extremely inexpensive. *Soku* is the counter for stalk, and *mon* was a coin of low value used during the Edo period. The expression literally means "two bundles for three *mon*" and is often used to describe products sold in bulk at an inexpensive price.

EXAMPLES

1. *Nisoku-sanmon de shika urenai no nara, uritakunai.*

   If I can only sell them very cheaply, I don't want to sell.

2. *Senzo-daidai no kabin o nisoku-sanmon de uru ki nado arimasen.*

   I didn't intend to sell the family heirloom vase at a giveaway price.

3. *Mukashi no furui dōgu wa, nisoku-sanmon de uru yori mo, kyōdo shiryō-kan ni kifu shita hō ga yoi.*

   It's better to donate very old objects to a local museum than to sell them cheaply.

4. *Furui konpyūtā wa utte mo nisoku-sanmon ni shika naranai.*

   An old computer won't sell for very much.

nitchi mo satchi mo ikanai

二進も三進もいかない

be in a predicament

KISHA:

Kore kara no Nihon no keizai wa, dō naru deshō ne?

SEIJIKA:

Bōeki-masatsu ga akka suru to, nitchi mo satchi mo ikanaku natte shimaimasu ne.

REPORTER:

What might the future hold for the Japanese economy?

POLITICIAN:

If trade friction worsens, we're going to find ourselves in a serious predicament.

Nitchi mo satchi mo refers to a situation when matters become stalemated, creating a dilemma. With the abacus, the *nishin* scale refers to numbers divisible by two, while the *sanshin* scale refers to those divisible by three. When neither the *nishin* nor the *sanshin* scale can be used, it is impossible to make any calculations,i.e., *nishin mo sanshin mo ikanai.* Over time, *nishin* changed to *nitchi* and *sanshin* changed to *satchi.*

EXAMPLES

1. *Dōro ga jūtai shite ite, nitchi mo satchi mo ikanaku natta.*
   The roads were congested and I was stuck in the traffic.
2. *Fuwatari tegata o tsukamasarete, nitchi mo satchi mo ikanaku natta.*
   Somebody palmed off an unpaid bill, leaving me in a real fix.
3. *Kaigi de iken ga awazu, nitchi mo satchi mo ikanaku natta.*
   They couldn't agree, so the meeting became deadlocked.
4. *Kokkai no tōben de ikizumari, nitchi mo satchi mo ikanaku natta.*
   During the reply session in the Diet, discussion stalemated and the situation became completely bogged down.

nobetsu maku-nashi

のべつ幕なし

perpetually, constantly

TSUMA:

Yachin, kodomo no gakuhi, denki-dai ni gasu-dai made ne-agari shite, sorekara anata no shūnyū wa, agarisō mo nai shi . . .

OTTO:

Sō, nobetsu maku-nashi ni monku o iu na yo.

WIFE:

The prices of everything are going up—the rent, school expenses for the children, the electricity and gas rates—and there's just no sign of your income increasing.

HUSBAND:

Stop your perpetual whining!

Maku in this expression refers to a stage curtain in a theater. Usually the curtain is drawn for a scene change, but with a revolving stage, scenes are switched without the use of a curtain. Thus the new setting is revealed without keeping the audience waiting. This is called *maku-nashi,* literally "without a curtain," and combined with *nobetsu* (continuous), it means perpetually and continually.

EXAMPLES

1. *Kanojo wa nobetsu maku-nashi ni monku o itte iru.*
   She complains continually.
2. *Kare wa nobetsu maku-nashi ni tabako o sū.*
   He's a chain smoker.
3. *Kafun-shō de, kare wa nobetsu maku-nashi ni kushami o shita.*
   He sneezed incessantly because of his hay fever.
4. *Haha no kogoto wa, nobetsu maku-nashi da.*
   My mother is always nagging me.

nukamiso-kusai

糠みそ臭い

a homebody

TOMODACHI 1:

Okusan to wa shibaraku o-me ni kakatte imasen ga . . .

TOMODACHI 2:

Kekkon shite san'nen, kan'nai mo sukkari nukamiso-kusaku narimashita.

FRIEND 1:

I haven't seen your wife for some time . . .

FRIEND 2:

Since we've been married for three years, she's really become a homebody.

Nukamiso-kusai refers to a woman who has become a homebody. *Nukamiso,* salted rice-bran paste, is used to pickle vegetables and to season soups and other dishes. A good wife was expected to become good at making it. Since *nukamiso* is smelly *(kusai),* a new wife would find that she smelled of the paste.

EXAMPLES

1. *Watashi wa kekkon shite mo, nukamiso-kusaku wa naritakunai.*
   Even if I get married, I don't want to become a homebody.
2. *Kanojo, dokushin no koro wa miryoku-teki datta kedo, kekkon shite, zuibun nukamiso-kusaku narimashita ne.*
   When she was single, she was captivating, but once she got married, she really became a homebody.
3. *Watashi, nukamiso-kusaku natta deshō?*
   I've really become a homebody, haven't I?
4. *Nukamiso-kusaku natta kanojo nado, sōzō dekimasen. Datte kanojo wa puro gorufu no senshu datta noni.*
   I can't imagine her at home all day. After all, she was a pro golfer.

194

nuki-sashi naranai

抜き差しならない

be in a dilemma

TOMODACHI 1:

Konna ni, jūtai shite iru no dattara, chigau michi o ikeba yokatta.

TOMODACHI 2:

Kore de wa iku no mo modoru no mo nuki-sashi narimasen ne.

FRIEND 1:

With this much traffic, we should have taken a different road.

FRIEND 2:

In this traffic, we'll be in a fix whether we keep going or turn back.

Nuki-sashi naranai refers to a situation in which one cannot control the course of events. If a samurai were confronted by enemies and was not able to pull out *(nuku)* or stab *(sasu)* with his sword, he would be rendered almost completely helpless. In short, he would be in a dilemma, or *nuki-sashi naranai*.

EXAMPLES

1. *Kaisha wa tōsan chokuzen de, nuki-sashi naranai yō da.*

   The company seems to be in a fix since it is on the verge of bankruptcy.

2. *Murabito-tachi wa, kazan no funka de shima kara derarezu ni, nuki-sashi naranai jōtai ni aru.*

   The villagers are in a pinch because they can't leave the island due to a volcanic eruption.

3. *Dōshite, konna ni nuki-sashi naranaku natta no darō?*

   I wonder how we got into such a dilemma.

4. *Kono kuni wa Nihon no enjo ga nakereba, nuki-sashi naranaku naru.*

   If this country loses Japanese aid, it will be in a real fix.

5. *Kare no shitsugen ga, mina o nuki-sashi naranai tachiba ni oikonda.*

   His improper comment put everyone in a difficult situation.

nuki-uchi

抜き打ち

surprise

TOMODACHI 1:

Zeimusho ga nuki-uchi de shirabe ni kimashite ne.

TOMODACHI 2:

Sore de, dō narimashita?

TOMODACHI 1:

Nihyakuman'en no tsuichōkin desu yo.

FRIEND 1:

The tax office made a surprise inspection.

FRIEND 2:

And so what happened?

FRIEND 1:

We've got to pay an additional two million yen.

Nuki-uchi refers to a surprise, and stems from sword fighting. When two samurai dueled, they would draw their long swords and wait for the appropriate instant to attack. In some cases, however, a samurai would launch a surprise attack, suddenly drawing *(nuku)* his sword and striking *(utsu)* his unwary opponent.

EXAMPLES

1. *Nuki-uchi no chōbo kensa ni wa, odorokimashita.*

   We were surprised by the unexpected audit.

2. *Kesa, nuki-uchi no tesuto ga atta.*

   We had a snap quiz this morning.

3. *Isha ni nuki-uchi de gan o senkoku sareta.*

   Without warning, the doctor told her that she had cancer.

nure-ginu o kiserareru

濡れ衣を着せられる

be falsely accused

SENSEI:

Kimura-kun, kimi ga kyōshitsu no garasu o wattasō da ne.

GAKUSEI:

Sensei, boku wa nure-ginu o kiseraretan' desu. Boku ja arimasen.

TEACHER:

Kimura, I hear it was you who broke the window in the classroom.

STUDENT:

It wasn't me, sir. Someone's just trying to lay the blame on me.

Nure-ginu o kiserareru means to be accused of or blamed for something that one is innocent. Literally, *nure-ginu* means "wet clothes," but it also can mean a false charge. This latter use comes from a story about a stepmother who hid a pile of wet fisherman's clothes in her stepdaughter's bedroom so that she could falsely accuse her of adultery. In its causative form, *nure-ginu o kiseru* means to falsely accuse someone.

EXAMPLES

1. *Kare wa kigyō supai no nure-ginu o kiserarete iru.*
   He has been falsely accused of being an industrial spy.
2. *Kare wa dōryō kara kōkin ōryō no nure-ginu o kiserarete, nayande iru.*
   He has been tormented with false accusations from his colleague that he embezzled public funds.
3. *Kare ni nure-ginu o kiseta no wa dare darō?*
   I wonder who it was that tried to frame him?
4. *Watashi ga satsujinhan de wa arimasen. Roku na shōko mo nai noni, nure-ginu o kisenaide kudasai.*
   I'm not the murderer. With so little evidence, don't try to lay the blame on me.

nure-te de awa

濡れ手で粟

make easy money

TOMODACHI 1:

Kinjo no nōka wa tochi o utte, daibu mōketa rashii yo.

TOMODACHI 2:

Mattaku, nure-te de awa to wa, sono koto da ne.

FRIEND 1:

I hear a local farmer sold his land and made a whole lot of money.

FRIEND 2:

Indeed. It's what's called making easy money.

Nure-te de awa means to make money without having to work very hard. If one puts a wet hand *(nure-te)* into a box of millet seed *(awa)*, one's hand will come out covered with the seed. Since it doesn't take much effort to get the seeds, the phrase has become associated with making easy money.

EXAMPLES

1. *Kare wa oya no isan no tochi o utte, nure-te de awa no ōmōke o shita.*
   He struck it rich by selling some land he inherited from his parents.

2. *Nure-te de awa no shōbai, nanika arimasen ka?*
   Do you happen to know a job that will allow me to make some easy money?

3. *Tarento no hōgai na kōenryō wa nure-te de awa da.*
   TV personalities make easy money by charging extravagant fees to give talks.

4. *Kabu de nure-te de awa o nerau no wa kiken desu.*
   It's dangerous to try and strike it rich by playing the stock market.

5. *Anata no shōbai wa nure-te de awa desu ne.*
   You really hit the jackpot with your business.

ōburoshiki o hirogeru

大風呂敷を広げる

exaggerate, brag

CHICHIOYA:

Musume no kekkon-shiki ni wa sen'nin o shōtai suru yo.

HAHAOYA:

Anata, sonna ni ōburoshiki o hirogete, daijōbu desu ka?

FATHER:

I'm going to invite one thousand people to our daughter's wedding.

MOTHER:

Do you really think you can get away with exaggerating that much?

Ōburoshiki o hirogeru literally means "to spread a large *furoshiki* (a cloth used to wrap things in)." Legend has it that *furoshiki* first appeared when a shogun invited many daimyo to bathe with him in a tub. Cloths were spread out *(hirogeru)* for each daimyo to place his kimono on while he bathed. These cloths were called *furoshiki,* literally "bath cloths." Since each daimyo would wear an extravagantly decorated kimono as a way to demonstrate his wealth and power, the phrase *ōburoshiki o hirogeru* came to mean to exaggerate.

EXAMPLES

1. *Kare wa itsumo ōburoshiki o hirogete, watashi-tachi o odorokaseru.*
   He's always making exaggerations and surprising us.
2. *Sonna ni ōburoshiki o hirogete mo iin' desu ka?*
   Do you think it's all right to brag that much?
3. *Kore wa ōburoshiki de wa nai. Jitsugen dekiru hanashi da.*
   I'm not just making this up. It's really going to happen.
4. *Kanojo no ōburoshiki ni wa, minna, akirete imasu.*
   Everyone's gotten tired of listening to her brag.

o-hachi ga mawaru

お鉢が回る

one's turn comes around

ANI:

Kotoshi no shin'nenkai, omae no tokoro de suru ban da yo.

OTŌTO:

Boku no tokoro ni mo o-hachi ga yatto mawatte kita ka? Donna ryōri o dasō ka na?

OLDER BROTHER:

This year it's your turn to have the New Year's party at your place.

YOUNGER BROTHER:

So, my turn's come around? What kind of food shall I serve?

O-hachi ga mawaru indicates that one's turn to do something has come around. In the past, cooked rice was put in a rice tub *(hachi)*, which was passed around *(mawaru)* the table. Each person would then serve himself or herself. Although having one's turn to help oneself to the rice was something to look forward to, this phrase now often has a negative connotation.

EXAMPLES

1. *Kondo wa anata ni o-hachi ga mawatte ikimasu yo.*
   Your turn will be coming up next.
2. *Watashi no tokoro ni o-hachi ga mawatte konai to ii na.*
   I wish my turn would come quickly so I can get this over with.
3. *Kare ni o-hachi ga mawattara, dō surun' darō?*
   What are we going to do when his turn comes around?
4. *Konna ni hayaku o-hachi ga mawatte kuru to wa omowanakatta.*
   I didn't think that my turn would come around so quickly.
5. *Tōtō watashi ni o-hachi ga mawatte kitan' desu ne.*
   Finally my turn has come!

oharai-bako ni suru

おはらい箱にする

throw away, fire someone, be fired

ARUBAITO NO GAKUSEI:

Sumimasen, okurete.

TENSHU:

Kondo okurete kitara, oharai-bako ni suru kara ne.

PART-TIME EMPLOYEE:

Sorry I'm late.

STORE OWNER:

Next time you turn up late, you're fired.

Oharai-bako ni suru can mean to either throw away something that you no longer need, or to fire one of your employees. Originally, an *oharai-bako* was a box *(hako)* in which lucky charms *(oharai)* from Ise Shrine, the main Shinto shrine in Japan, were transported. These *oharai-bako* were then distributed to smaller regional shrines across the country where people could buy them. The expression's present meaning arises from the fact that *oharai-bako* are thrown out at New Year's.

EXAMPLES

1. *Sentakki ga furuku natta node, oharai-bako ni shita.*
   The washing machine had gotten so old I decided to throw it out.
2. *Mō sonna furui mono, oharai-bako ni shinasai.*
   For goodness' sake, just throw that old thing out.
3. *Kimi wa mō oharai-bako da.*
   That's it, you're fired.
4. *Sonna koto o suru to, oharai-bako ni narimasu yo.*
   You'll get yourself fired if you carry on like that.

ohire o tsukeru

尾ひれを付ける

stretch the facts

DŌRYŌ 1:

Kimi, kinō gōtō ni hairarete, korosaresō ni nattan' datte?

DŌRYŌ 2:

Dare ga sonna koto itta no? Dareka ga hanashi ni ohire o tsuketa yō da ne.

COLLEAGUE 1:

Hey, I heard you got robbed and nearly killed yesterday.

COLLEAGUE 2:

Who on earth told you that? It looks like somebody's been stretching the facts.

Ohire o tsukeru, literally "attaching fins and tail of a fish," means to exaggerate, to stretch the facts. To add both a tail and some fins to a story is the same as embellishing it. The intransitive *hanashi ni ohire ga tsuku* means that a story has been exaggerated.

EXAMPLES

1. *Kare wa, hanashi ni ohire o tsukete hanasu kuse ga aru.*

   He has a habit of exaggerating when he tells stories.

2. *Hanashi ni ohire ga tsuite, taihen na koto ni natta.*

   Things became very difficult because the facts had been so exaggerated.

3. *Dare ga, watashi no hanashi ni ohire o tsuketan' desu ka?*

   Who's responsible for stretching the facts in that story?

4. *Nihon ga nanmin kyūsai no tame ni jūokuen no kifu nado, hanashi ni ohire ga tsuita dake desu.*

   Japan donated one billion yen for the refugees? The story has been blown all out of proportion.

ojan ni naru

おじゃんになる

be spoiled, be ruined

GAKUSEI 1:

Ā, kyō wa ame ka?

GAKUSEI 2:

Kore de, undōkai mo ojan ni natte shimatta ne.

STUDENT 1:

Ah, so it's raining today!

STUDENT 2:

That means that the athletic meet has been ruined.

Ojan ni naru indicates that something is spoiled or ruined. In the past, an alarm bell was rung to warn people of a fire. Then, when the fire was extinguished, the alarm bell was rung twice—*jan jan.* Consequently, *jan jan,* abbreviated to *jan,* meant end or finish, and then came to mean spoiled or ruined.

EXAMPLES

1. *Shigoto ga isogashikute, ryokō ga ojan ni natta.*

   Work is busy, so my travel plans have gone up in smoke.

2. *Okane o nusumarete, kuruma o kau no ga ojan ni natta.*

   Having my money stolen destroyed any hope of me purchasing a car.

3. *Rakudai shite, shōgaku-kin ga ojan ni natta.*

   I failed an examination and forfeited the scholarship.

4. *Kare to kenka shite, dēto ga ojan ni natta.*

   I had a fight with my boyfriend and so our date fell through.

5. *Kōhiï o koboshite, sūtsu ga ojan ni natta.*

   My suit was ruined when I spilled some coffee on it.

omou-tsubo ni hamaru

思う壷にはまる

one's wishes, expectations

KAISHAIN 1:

Gorufu konpe, buchō wa korarenai sō da yo.

KAISHAIN 2:

Sore wa, kochira no omou- tsubo da. Kare ga kuru to, guriin ni ana o akerarete komarun' da.

EMPLOYEE 1:

I hear that the director won't be able to make it to the golf tournament.

EMPLOYEE 2:

That's what I was hoping for. When he comes, he makes things difficult for us by chopping holes in the green.

Omou-tsubo ni hamaru combines *omou* (think), *tsubo* (pot), and *hamaru* (fit, suit) to mean things turn out as one has anticipated or hoped. This expression comes from the world of gambling where dice are placed in a pot, shaken, and thrown. *Omou-tsubo* can also be used on its own it which case it describes one's plans or desires.

EXAMPLES

1. *Aite no omou-tsubo ni hamatte shimatta.*

   He played into his opponent's hands.

2. *Anata no omou-tsubo ni wa hamarimasen yo.*

   I won't fall into your trap!

3. *Kanojo ni wa, sore ga kare no omou-tsubo da to wakaranai no darō ka?*

   Perhaps she doesn't realize that she's doing exactly what he wants her to.

4. *Teki no omou-tsubo ni hamaranai yō ni shinakereba ne.*

   You mustn't fall into the clutches of your enemy, right?

on o uru

恩を売る

expect the gratitude of another

TOMODACHI 1:

Senjitsu wa kare ni awasete kudasatte, dōmo arigatō. On ni kimasu yo.

TOMODACHI 2:

On o uru tsumori de wa arimasen deshita kara, go-shinpai naku.

FRIEND 1:

Thanks for your help in arranging for me to meet him the other day. I'm in your debt.

FRIEND 2:

Don't worry about it. I didn't do it because I wanted you to feel obligated to me.

On refers to a moral indebtedness that one has toward a person who has been kind or generous. *On o uru* refers to the expectation that a person should feel a sense of obligation. Related expressions include *on ni kiru* (feel thankful that one has received kindness), *on o kiseru* (making another person feel thankful for a kindness bestowed), and *on shirazu* (not recognizing one's obligation to another for a favor received).

EXAMPLES

1. *Izen, kare ni on o utte oita node, kondo wa tasukete kureru darō.*

   He still feels a sense of indebtedness to me for the favor I did him, so he'll probably help me out this time.

2. *Kare ni tasukete moratta koto o, watashi wa issho on ni kimasu.*

   After saving me like that, I will feel a sense of indebtedness to him for the rest of my life.

3. *Kare ga are hodo on shirazu to wa omowanakatta.*

   I had no idea he was such a thankless person.

ondo o toru

音頭を取る

take the lead

SEIJIKA 1:

Sekai ni wa uete iru kodomo ga takusan iru.

SEIJIKA 2:

Nihon no seifu ga ondo o totte, kō iu kodomo-tachi o sukuitai mono desu.

POLITICIAN 1:

There are many starving children in the world.

POLITICIAN 2:

The Japanese government should take the initiative and help these children.

Ondo o toru means taking the initiative or lead. *Ondo* refers to a song or chorus leader; in imperial court music, the leader would begin singing alone, and then from the second stanza, other singers would join in. *Ondo o toru,* literally "taking the position of chorus leader," has its origin in this style of singing.

EXAMPLES

1. *Kare ga ondo o totte kifu-kin o atsumeru koto ni shita.*
   He took the initiative and decided to collect donations.
2. *Orinpikku chiimu no ketsudan-shiki de kanojo ni kanpai no ondo o totte moraimashō.*
   Let's have her lead the toast at the inaugural ceremony for the Olympic team.
3. *Kare ga ondo o toru to, subete ga umaku iku.*
   When he is in charge, everything goes smoothly.
4. *Suimasen ga, kanpai no ondo o totte itadakemasu ka?*
   Excuse me, would you mind leading a toast?

oni no inu ma ni sentaku

鬼の居ぬ間に洗濯

when the cat's away the mice will play, relax while the heat's off

---

DŌRYŌ 1:

Buchō wa isshūkan, kaigai shutchō datte.

DŌRYŌ 2:

Sore wa ii ne. Oni no inu ma ni sentaku, minna de nonbiri shiyō yo.

COLLEAGUE 1:

The boss says he's going overseas on business for a week.

COLLEAGUE 2:

That's great. We'll all be able to relax while the heat's off.

Oni no inu ma ni sentaku literally means "to do the wash while the devil's away." Other expressions with *oni* include *oni ni kanabō* (someone who is as strong or successful as he could possibly want to be) and *oni no me ni namida* (surprise at the display of emotion in a person who is usually very stoic and unemotional).

EXAMPLES

1. *Kimi-tachi, oni no inu ma ni sentaku desu ka?*

   You guys aren't taking it easy because the boss isn't around, are you?

2. *Go-shujin ga shutchō de, oni no inu ma ni sentaku deshō.*

   It must be so nice for you to relax while your husband's away on a business trip.

3. *Oni no inu ma ni sentaku nado, tondemo arimasen.*

   It's really not right for you to loaf about just because there's no one pressing you to work.

4. *Kono chiimu ni anata ga ireba, oni ni kanabō desu.*

   This team would be invincible if you were to play for us.

5. *Otōsan, naite iru no? Oni no me ni namida ne.*

   Father, are you crying? It's not like you to get so emotional.

o-rekireki

お歴歴

distinguished persons, VIPs

TOMODACHI 1:

Kūkō no keikai ga genjū desu ne.

TOMODACHI 2:

Samitto-shusseki no tame ni, kakkoku no o-rekireki ga kuru kara da to omoimasu yo.

FRIEND 1:

Security at the airport is tight, isn't it?

FRIEND 2:

I think it's because dignitaries from many countries are coming to attend the summit.

O-rekireki refers to influential people in society—those who enjoy high social standing. *Reki* means clear and distinct, and when doubled, it means those with high status and reputation.

EXAMPLES

1. *Kare no musuko no kekkon-shiki ni wa kaisha no o-rekireki ga shusseki shita.*

   Prominent figures from the company attended his son's wedding.

2. *Kōkō no sōritsu kinenbi no shikiten de danjō ni wa, o-rekireki ga sei-zoroi shita.*

   At the high school's founding anniversary ceremony, distinguished persons assembled in full force on the platform.

3. *Yā, o-rekireki ga o-soroi desu ne.*

   Gee, all the big shots are here, aren't they?

4. *Ano kaisha de wa, o-rekireki ga mensetsu-shiken o suru sō desu yo.*

   They say that in that company, the executives do the interviews.

5. *Kare wa kaisha no o-rekireki no uke ga yoi.*

   He is in favor with the bigwigs in the company.

origami-tsuki

折り紙付き

guaranteed, acknowledged

CHICHIOYA:

Musume no o-miai no aite ni, Kimura-kun wa dō darō? Ii hito rashii yo. Jinbutsu ni tsuite wa shachō no origami-tsuki da shi ne.

FATHER:

What do you think of the idea of arranging a marriage meeting between Kimura and our daughter? He seems like a fine fellow. What's more, he has the company president's seal of approval.

Origami-tsuki refers to something or someone that has an established reputation in the public's eye. From the end of the Heian period, a piece of folded paper *(origami)* was attached *(tsuku)* to works of art, calligraphy, and swords. This paper contained a written statement from an expert or authority guaranteeing that the work was authentic. During the Muromachi period, origami was affixed to all forms of official documents, and from this custom came the present meaning of *origami-tsuki*.

EXAMPLES

1. *Kono e wa gashō no origami-tsuki desu.*
   This painting comes with the art-dealer's certification.
2. *Kanojo no bunshō no umasa wa origami-tsuki desu.*
   She has a reputation as a good writer.
3. *Kare wa origami-tsuki no furyō desu.*
   He is a notorious delinquent.
4. *Kono resutoran no dezāto wa origami-tsuki desu.*
   This restaurant has a fine reputation for its desserts.

209

orime-tadashii

折り目正しい

well-mannered

SENSEI:

Kanojo wa yoku dekiru gakusei desu ne.

SEITO:

Atama ga yoi ue ni, orime-tadashii kotoba-zukai o shimasu ne.

TEACHER:

She's quite a capable student.

STUDENT:

On top of being bright, she also has such a well-mannered way of speaking.

Orime-tadashii, which combines *orime* (creases) and *tadashii* (correct), refers to being well-mannered, polite, courteous, or formal. Neatly folding one's clothes produces sharp, clean creases— a sign of good social manners and appearances.

EXAMPLES

1. *Kare wa totemo orime-tadashii hito da.*
   He is very polite and courteous.
2. *Kanojo wa orime-tadashi-sugite, kyūkutsu na kanji desu.*
   She's a bit too formal and stuffy.
3. *Ano hito wa itsumo orime-tadashii aisatsu o suru.*
   She always greets people politely.
4. *Kare wa orime-tadashii seiji shisei de, mina no shinrai o ete iru.*
   His clean approach to politics means he has gained everyone's trust.
5. *Kodomo ni mo, orime-tadashii taido o shitsuketai mono desu.*
   I want to teach my children to be well-mannered and courteous to others.

210

oya no nana hikari

親の七光

riding on one's father's coattails

TOMODACHI 1:

Jimintō no A giin, konkai mo tōsen shita ne.

TOMODACHI 2:

Ano hito wa otōsan no jiban ga aru kara ne. Oya no nana hikari sa.

FRIEND 1:

So, LDP representative A got elected again.

FRIEND 2:

That's because he can rely on his father's constituency. He's just riding on his father's coattails.

Oya no nana hikari comes from *oya no hikari wa nana hikari,* literally "a father's influence is sevenfold." The phrase refers to a father's influence used to help his children. Seven is considered a large and propitious number in Asian cultures.

EXAMPLES

1. *Oya no nana hikari de tarento ni naru hito mo ōi.*

   There are also many people who become TV personalities because of their parent's fame.

2. *Oya no nana hikari nado de shūshoku shitakunai.*

   I don't want to get a job by just riding on my parent's coattails.

3. *Oya no nana hikari no aru hito ga urayamashii na.*

   I'm jealous of people who can rely on the influence of their parents.

4. *Itsu made mo oya no nana hikari ni tayotte ite wa ikemasen.*

   You mustn't expect to always be able to shelter yourself under your parents' wing.

5. *Hajime wa oya no nana hikari de mo, ato wa jibun no doryoku desu.*

   Though at first you might profit from your father's fame, later on you'll have to depend on your own efforts.

o-zendate

お膳立て

making arrangements, paving the way for

BUCHŌ:

Kondo no kaigi no o-zendate, kimi ni o-negai shite ii ka na?

BUKA:

Watashi de yoroshikereba, dekiru dake no koto wa itashimasu.

DEPARTMENT CHIEF:

About the arrangements for the up-and-coming party—is it alright to ask you to take care of that?

SUBORDINATE:

If it's OK with you, I'd be happy to do it.

O-zendate means planning or doing the preparations for something. *O-zen* is a small, low table or tray used to serve food, and with *date,* refers to a table that is fully set. Though originally an expression concerning dining arrangements, it can now be used for any undertaking.

EXAMPLES

1. *Kōshō no o-zendate wa, sukkari totonotta.*

   All arrangements for the negotiations were completely finished.

2. *O-zendate ga totonotte, anshin shimashita.*

   With the arrangements all in order, I could relax.

3. *Bōnenkai no o-zendate wa, anata ni o-makase shimasu.*

   I'm going to put you in charge of making all the arrangements for the end-of-the-year party.

4. *Kare no o-zendate no okage de, torihiki ga seikō shita.*

   Thanks to his paving the way, the negotiations were a success.

5. *Kaisha sōritsu no o-zendate wa kore de jūbun da.*

   With these preparations, I think we are now sufficiently prepared to begin the company.

rachi ga akanai

埒が明かない

remain unsettled

OTTO:

Boku wa zettai ni rikon shinai kara na.

TSUMA:

Koko de giron shite mo rachi ga akanai wa. Saibansho de hanashi-aimashō.

HUSBAND:

I absolutely will not divorce you.

WIFE:

There's no sense in arguing with you. We'll settle this in court.

Rachi ga akanai refers to a situation in which an issue remains unsettled. *Rachi* is a fence usually used at horse stables. At the Nara Kasuga shrine, people are not allowed to enter inside the fence surrounding the *omikoshi* (portable shrine) until all of the prayers are read. From this tradition, *rachi ga akanai,* literally "the fence won't open" refers to a situation where a problem cannot be solved.

EXAMPLES

1. *Anata to hanashite ite mo, rachi ga akimasen.*

   Talking to you won't get me anywhere.

2. *Kono aida no hanashi, mada rachi ga akanain' desu ka?*

   Have you settled the problem you were talking about last time?

3. *Kome no yunyū-kanzei no mondai ni tsuite wa, nakanaka rachi ga akisō ni nai.*

   It seems as if the tariff on rice will remain an unsettled issue.

4. *Ikura buchō to hanashite mo rachi ga akanai node, kono kikaku wa akirameru koto ni shimashita.*

   No matter how much I talk to the department chief about this plan it doesn't make any difference. So, I've given up.

rakuin o osareru

烙印を押される

be branded

SENSEI:

Sonna ni sabotte bakari iru to, ochi-kobore ni natte shimau zo.

SEITO:

Sensei wa, sugu ni sō shita rakuin o oshitagarun' desu ne.

TEACHER:

If you skip so many classes, you know you're going to end up being a dropout.

STUDENT:

You're always so quick to brand someone a dropout.

Rakuin o osareru means to brand or stigmatize someone. *Rakuin* refers to a branding iron. Though primarily used to mark cows and sheep, criminals in Japan were sometimes punished by being branded on the head with one of the irons.

EXAMPLES

1. *Kare wa uragiri-mono no rakuin o osareta.*

   He was branded a traitor.

2. *Ittan rakuin o osareru to, nakanaka kesenai.*

   It's hard to get rid of a stigma once it's attached itself to one's name.

3. *Kantan ni hito ni warumono no rakuin o oshite wa ikemasen.*

   One shouldn't be quick to call someone a name, or to brand him as a bad person.

4. *Kanojo ni uwakimono to iu yō na rakuin o oshite wa, kawaisō da yo.*

   It's unfair to brand her a loose woman.

5. *Nihonjin wa, ekonomikku animaru to iu rakuin o osarete iru.*

   Japanese have been branded economic animals.

saba o yomu

鯖を読む

falsify numbers

MUSUME:

Otōsan, kotoshi de nansai ni natta no?

CHICHIOYA:

E, mada gojussai da yo.

HAHAOYA:

Musume ni saba o yomu koto wa nai deshō?

DAUGHTER:

Dad, how old are you this year?

FATHER:

I'm still only fifty years old.

MOTHER:

There's no need to deceive your daughter, is there?

Saba o yomu means to give a number that is higher or lower than the actual figure. *Saba* (mackerel) are counted at great speed as they are thrown into boxes at the fish markets, and when the same fish are recounted, the numbers often do not match the original count.

EXAMPLES

1. *Josei ga nenrei no saba o yomu no wa jōshiki desu.*
   It's normal for a woman to misrepresent her age.
2. *Zeimusho ni saba o yonda uriage o shinkoku shita.*
   I reported inaccurate sales figures to the tax office.
3. *Saba o yonde wa imasen yo.*
   I'm not falsifying the numbers.
4. *Kare ga kyūryō saba yonde iu no mo, muri wa nai.*
   It's reasonable that he should misrepresent the amount of his pay.

saji o nageru

匙を投げる

give up in despair

ISHA:

Shujutsu o shite mo, teokure da to omoimasu yo.

KANJA:

Sensei, sonna koto itte, saji o nagenaide kudasai.

DOCTOR:

Even if we operate, I think you're past treatment.

PATIENT:

Doctor, please don't say that and give up.

Saji o nageru can specifically describe when a doctor loses hope for a patient's recovery, or more generally when one gives up in despair because success cannot be achieved. Doctors, long ago, used a spoon *(saji)* to make medicine. When a patient had an incurable ailment, the spoon was thrown away *(nageru)*.

EXAMPLES

1. *Isha wa saigo made saji o nagezu ni chiryō shita.*

   The doctor continued the medical treatment until the end without giving up hope.

2. *Kanji o oboeru koto nanka, tokku ni saji o nagemashita.*

   I gave up on learning kanji a long time ago.

3. *Kare ni ofisu-konpyūtā no sōsa o oshieru no wa, tokidoki saji o nagetaku naru.*

   Sometimes I feel like giving up on trying to teach him how to operate the office computer.

4. *Muzukashii hōteishiki de mo, sonna ni kantan ni saji o nagete wa ikemasen.*

   Even if it is a difficult equation, you shouldn't lose hope so easily.

sasen suru

左遷する

degrade, demote, humiliate

DŌRYŌ 1:

Buchō, shisha ni sasen sareru sō desu ne.

DŌRYŌ 2:

Ē, o-ki no doku ni, kono aida no shippai ga gen'in da sō desu.

COLLEAGUE 1:

I hear that the department chief is going to be sent off to a branch company.

COLLEAGUE 2:

It's quite unfortunate. I hear it's because of his recent mistakes.

Sasen suru means to demote someone to a lower position or status. *Sa* means left and *sen* means to transfer or move. In Imperial China, if a government official was "moved to the left" it was symbolic of demotion and resulted in his being sent to a province in the country. This phrase is usually used in the passive form, *sasen sareru*. *Eiten suru*, to promote, is an antonym of *sasen suru*.

EXAMPLES

1. *Uwayaku no aida de, kare o sasen suru ugoki ga aru.*
   There is a movement among the top officials to demote him.
2. *Sasen sareru kare wa, hontō ni ki no doku da.*
   I feel sorry for the guy who will be demoted.
3. *Sasen sareru kare ni wa, sore-nari no riyū ga aru hazu desu.*
   There has to be a good reason for him to have been demoted.
4. *Dōshite, sasen sareru no ka, watashi ni wa wakarimasen.*
   I don't know why I'm being demoted.
5. *Sasen sareru to, kyūryō ga sagatte shimau.*
   When demoted, your pay will go down.

sashi-gane

差し金

instigation, suggestion

HISHO:

Kyō no yakusoku desu ga, tori-keshita hō ga yoroshii no de wa?

BUCHŌ:

Sore wa, dare no sashi-gane ni yoru mono ka ne?

SECRETARY:

Don't you think it would be better to cancel today's appointment?

DEPARTMENT CHIEF:

I wonder who put you up to this suggestion.

Sashi-gane means to work behind the scenes so as to influence a person's decision. *Sashi-gane* are the rods that control the arms of puppets used in marionette theater. Thus, *sashi-gane* has come to mean manipulating a person from behind the scenes.

EXAMPLES

1. *Kore, dare no sashi-gane de mo arimasen.*
   I'm not doing this at anyone else's instruction.
2. *Kare no sashi-gane de kabu o kai-shimeta.*
   At his suggestion, I bought up some stocks.
3. *Nanshii no sashi-gane de, Donarudo wa kare o kubi ni shita.*
   Donald fired him at Nancy's instigation.
4. *Kore wa, Nanshii no sashi-gane nanka de wa arimasen.*
   Nancy did not influence me in this.
5. *Kare no sashi-gane dōri ni kōdō shinasai.*
   Act along the lines of his suggestion.

seki no yama

関の山

the best one can do, the best one can expect

KYAKU:

*Mō chotto hayaku hashiremasen ka? Hikōki ni nori-okuresō nan'
desu ga.*

TAKUSHII NO UNTENSHU:

*Kore ga seki no yama desu. Kore ijō da to supiido ihan ni natte
shimau.*

PASSENGER:

Can't you go a bit faster? I think I'm going to miss my plane.

TAXI DRIVER:

This is the best I can do. If I go any faster I'll be speeding.

Seki no yama refers to a limit beyond which one can do or expect no
more. *Yama* in this expression was originally used to describe a kind
of decorated float that appears in religious festivals. Seki is a town
in Mie Prefecture where the *yama* of a particular shrine became
known for its outstandingly sumptuous decoration.

EXAMPLES

1. *Kimi ni motto okane o kashite agetai ga, kore ga seki no yama da.*
   I'd like to lend you more money, but this is the best I can do.
2. *Watashi ni wa, apāto o kariru no ga seki no yama desu.*
   The best I can afford is a rented apartment.
3. *Okane ni komatte iru kare o tasuketai ga, issho ni nomi ni itte
   nagusameru no ga seki no yama da.*
   I'd like to help him with his financial problems, but all I can do is to take
   him drinking and try to console him.
4. *Kanojo ni totte wa hisho ni naru no ga seki no yama desu.*
   In her situation, the best she can hope for is to get a job as a secretary.

shibire o kirasu

しびれを切らす

lose one's patience

SAKKA:

Warui kedo, genkō, mō sukoshi matte moraemasen ka?

HENSHŪSHA:

Sensei no genkō o, minna shibire o kirashite, matte irun' desu ga.

WRITER:

I hate to ask, but could you wait a little longer for the manuscript?

EDITOR:

But everyone's just about run out of patience waiting.

The phrase *shibire o kirasu* refers to being forced to wait so long that one runs out of patience or grows impatient. The phrase arises from the fact that if one is made to use the Japanese method of kneeling for a long time, one's legs will fall asleep *(ashi ga shibirete kuru)*. *Shibire ga kireru* also describes one's legs going numb after one has been sitting on them for a long time.

EXAMPLES

1. *Kare ga nakanaka konai node, shibire o kirashite shimatta.*

   I grew impatient waiting for him to come.

2. *Kanojo ga puropōzu ni kotaezu, shibire ga kireta.*

   I grew impatient because she took so long to respond to my marriage proposal.

3. *Nihon no bōeki kuroji kajō ni taisuru taiō no ososa ni, Amerika wa shibire o kirashita yō da.*

   America grew impatient with Japan's tardy response to the trade imbalance.

shikii ga takai

敷居が高い

hesitating to visit someone

DŌRYŌ 1:

Kimi, saikin, buchō no o-taku ni ikanai yō da ne.

DŌRYŌ 2:

Buchō no susumete kureta endan o kotowatta node, shikii ga takakute ne.

COLLEAGUE 1:

Recently you haven't visited the chief's house.

COLLEAGUE 2:

Since I turned down the girl the boss recommended I marry, I just don't feel up to visiting his house.

Shikii ga takai refers to not wanting to visit someone's house because one has failed to perform some social duty or because one is ashamed of something one has done. It can also be used about one's own house. *Shikii* is a threshold and *takai* means high.

EXAMPLES

1. *Anna shippai o shita ato de wa, buchō no ie no shikii ga takaku, ukagaenai.*

   Since I made that mistake, I have felt self-conscious about visiting the department chief's house and so I have not been back yet.

2. *Koibito no ie no shikii o takaku shita no wa, hoka no hito to bakari dekakete ita jibun no sekinin da.*

   You're the one to blame if you feel hesitant about visiting your lover's place since you are always going out with other people.

3. *Seiseki ga waruku, sensei no ie no shikii ga takai.*

   Since his grades were so bad, the student didn't feel up to visiting the teacher's house.

shiku hakku suru

四苦八苦する

have difficulties, be in dire straits

SHIMIN:

Eki-mae no dōro, motto seibi dekimasen ka?

KŌMUIN:

Kochira mo yosan ga nakute, shiku hakku shite irun' desu yo.

CITY RESIDENT:

Can't you repair the road in front of the station?

GOVERNMENT OFFICE WORKER:

With an insufficient budget, we're having difficulties.

Shiku hakku suru refers to being in a difficult situation because things aren't going well. This phrase comes from Buddhism where it is believed that people must experience the four sufferings *(shiku)*: birth, old age, sickness, and death. Four other sufferings were added to this list, for a total of eight sufferings *(hakku).*

EXAMPLES

1. *Seifu wa, kankyō mondai no kaizen ni shiku hakku shite iru.*

   The government is having difficulties dealing with environmental issues.

2. *Kare ga kondo no kikaku de shiku hakku shite iru no wa, yoku shitte imasu ga . . .*

   I know very well that he is having a hard time with this year's plan, but . . .

3. *Kare no josei mondai ni, kanojo wa itsumo shiku hakku shite iru.*

   She is always having difficulties dealing with his philandering.

4. *Dōshite, konna ni shiku hakku saserareru no deshō?*

   Why are people always making things difficult for me?

5. *Sensei o shiku hakku saseru tsumori wa nakatta no desu.*

   I didn't mean to cause you any trouble, professor.

shimen-soka

四面楚歌

completely surrounded by foes

DŌRYŌ 1:

Dōshite, kaisha no warukuchi, soto de itta no desu ka?

DŌRYŌ 2:

Hansei shite imasu. Are kara shanai de, shimen-soka desu yo.

COLLEAGUE 1:

Why did you speak ill of the company in public?

COLLEAGUE 2:

I regret saying that. Since that time I've been shunned by everyone in the company.

Shimen-soka means to be completely surrounded by adversaries and hence isolated. According to Chinese folklore, the military commander of the Chu forces was surrounded by the Han army. The commander of the Han forces had his soldiers sing a Chu song. When the commander of the Chu army heard this, he mistakenly thought that the entire population of Chu had surrendered to the Han forces. *Shimen* means the four directions and *soka* refers to the Chu song.

EXAMPLES

1. *Dōshite, shimen-soka no yō na koto ni natta no desu ka?*
   Why is it that you seem to have the whole world against you?
2. *Watashi no fuchūi na hitokoto de, ima wa shimen-soka desu.*
   Due to a careless oversight on my part, I now find myself spurned by everyone.
3. *Seiji ni taisuru iken no chigai de, tomodachi no gurūpu de wa shimen-soka desu.*
   Because of a difference in political opinion, I find myself without a friend among my cohorts.

shinmai

新米

a beginner, new hand

KYAKU:
Byōin e itte kudasai.

TAKUSHII NO UNTENSHU:
Sumimasen. Shinmai na mono de, michi ga yoku wakaranain' desu ga.

PASSENGER:
Hospital, please.

TAXI DRIVER:
I'm sorry. I'm new at this job and so I'm not very sure of the way.

Shinmai refers to either a person who has just begun a new job and has not become accustomed to it, or a person who has only just started to learn about something and thus lacks skill. This expression is said to have derived from the word *shinmae,* which referred to new *(shin)* aprons *(mae,* from *maekake*) worn by servants. *Shinmai* is frequently coupled with nouns describing professions such as *shinmai-junsa* (new policeman, rookie) and *shinmai-kisha* (new journalist, cub reporter).

EXAMPLES

1. *Shinmai na mono desu kara, yoroshiku o-negai shimasu.*
   Since I am young and inexperienced, please be patient with me.
2. *Shinmai-doraibā no kuruma ni wa, ki o tsukete ne.*
   Take care when riding in cars with inexperienced drivers.
3. *Kare wa shinmai-kyōshi da.*
   He is a new hand at teaching.
4. *Shinmai nan' dakara, senpai no iu koto o kikinasai.*
   You're a newcomer, so listen to what your superiors say.

shinogi o kezuru

鎬を削る

compete fiercely

KAISHAIN 1:

B-sha no kabu ga agatte kimashita ne.

KAISHAIN 2:

Saikin, B-sha wa A-sha to uriage de shinogi o kezutte imasu kara ne.

EMPLOYEE 1:

The stocks of company B have gone up, haven't they?

EMPLOYEE 2:

It's because recently company A and company B have been competing fiercely in sales.

Shinogi o kezuru refers to a situation in which two competitors fight furiously. *Shinogi* is the ridge on a sword between the sharp end of the blade and the back of the blade. When samurai fought furiously with their swords, that area would be damaged. Therefore, *shinogi o kezuru*, literally "chip or scrape the ridge of a sword," has come to mean fighting or competing furiously.

EXAMPLES

1. *Uchi no kaisha mo, A-sha to shinogi o kezuru made ni seichō shimashita.*

   Our company has grown to the point where it can compete with company A.

2. *Shinogi o kezuri-au aite ga iru no wa yoi koto desu.*

   It's good to have someone to compete against.

3. *Shinogi o kezuri-au koto de, o-tagai ni seichō suru deshō.*

   Fierce competition will help us both grow stronger.

4. *Kare to wa gakkō no seiseki de shinogi o kezutte iru.*

   I am competing with him for better grades at school.

shinshō bōdai

針小棒大

making a mountain out of a molehill

KŌHAI:

Sukii gasshuku de, nadare ni atte, shinu tokoro datta sō desu ne.

SENPAI:

Sono hanashi wa shinshō bōdai sugiru yo. Dare ga, sonna koto itta no?

JUNIOR:

I heard that you got caught in an avalanche during the ski training camp and almost died.

SENIOR:

Is that ever an exaggeration. Who told you that?

Shinshō bōdai, literally "to magnify a needle to the proportions of a stick," means to exaggerate. *Shinshō bōdai* can also be replaced with *ōgesa* without a significant change in meaning.

EXAMPLES

1. *Uwasa wa shinshō bōdai ni nariyasui.*

   It's easy for a rumor to get blown out of proportion.

2. *Kare no hanashi wa shinshō bōdai no keikō ga aru.*

   He tends to make mountains out of molehills.

3. *Dōmo hanashi ga shinshō bōdai ni tsutawatte iru rashii.*

   It seems that the story has been passed on in quite an exaggerated form.

4. *Jittai o shinshō bōdai ni uketori-sugite imasen ka?*

   Don't you think your interpretation of the facts is too exaggerated?

5. *Kanojo ga shinshō bōdai ni hanashi shita tame ni, ōsawagi ni natta.*

   Because she exaggerated the facts, everyone has become quite alarmed.

shira o kiru

白を切る

play innocent, feign ignorance

ONNA JIMUIN 1:

Kono aida, watashi no warukuchi o itta deshō?

ONNA JIMUIN 2:

E, warukuchi nanka, zettai ni ittemasen yo.

ONNA JIMUIN 1:

Chanto kiitan' dakara, shira o kiranaide yo.

FEMALE OFFICE WORKER 1:

The other day you said something bad about me, didn't you?

FEMALE OFFICE WORKER 2:

What? I absolutely did not say bad things about you.

FEMALE OFFICE WORKER 1:

I heard all about it so don't play innocent.

Shira o kiru means to pretend that one is unaware or ignorant. In Japan, being innocent or without fault is associated with the color white, while black is associated with guilt. *Shira* is a derivation of *shiro* (white) and *kiru* means to cut.

EXAMPLES

1. *Kare ni ikura naze garasu o watta no ka o kiite mo, shira o kitte hanasanai.*

   No matter how often I ask him why he broke the window, he feigns ignorance and doesn't talk.

2. *Dōshite, shira o kitte bakari iru no desu ka?*

   Why do you always pretend not to know?

3. *Shakkin no koto de, kare ga anna ni shira o kiru to wa omowanakatta.*

   I never thought he would feign ignorance about the borrowed money.

4. *Koibito no koto o kikarete, shira o kiri-tōshita.*

   When I was asked about my lover, I feigned ignorance.

shiraha no ya ga tatsu

白羽の矢が立つ

be chosen

BUCHŌ:

Kondo no kokusai-kaigi no shikai, kimi ni shiraha no ya ga tatte ne.

BUKA:

Sore wa taihen kōei desu. Zehi sasete kudasai.

DEPARTMENT CHIEF:

You've been singled out to be the chairperson for the upcoming international conference.

SUBORDINATE:

It would be a great honor. I would be very pleased to do it.

Shiraha no ya ga tatsu means to be specially selected from among many. According to legend, when the god of the mountains or the god of the waters wanted to have a young girl as a human sacrifice, he would shoot a white arrow *(shiraha no ya)* at the house she lived in. From the specific meaning of being selected to be a sacrifice, this phrase now has the more general meaning of being chosen.

EXAMPLES

1. *Tsugi no Amerika-taishi wa kare ni shiraha no ya ga tatta.*

   He has been chosen to be the next ambassador to the United States.

2. *Dare ga, kare ni shiraha no ya o tatete ita no deshō ne?*

   I wonder who selected him for that post?

3. *Kare wa majime dakara, iinkai no menbā to shite shiraha no ya ga tatte mo, fushigi de wa nai.*

   It wouldn't be surprising if he were nominated to be a committee member since he is so conscientious.

4. *Anata wa, watashi-tachi ni shiraha no ya ga tatsu to omoimashita ka?*

   Did you think that we would be chosen?

shiranu ga hotoke

知らぬが仏

ignorance is bliss

OTTO:

Ano kuruma, sugoi supiido da ne.

TSUMA:

Kono saki de, supiido ihan no torishimari o shite iru noni, shiranu ga hotoke ne.

HUSBAND:

That car certainly is going fast.

WIFE:

Ignorance is bliss. There's a speed trap up ahead.

Shiranu ga hotoke refers to being calm, cool, and indifferent because one is ignorant of the real state of affairs. If one doesn't know something one is like the Buddha *(hotoke)*—calm, compassionate, and pure of heart. Another phrase which uses *hotoke* is *hotoke no kao mo sando,* meaning that no matter how good-tempered a person might be, after being wronged repeatedly, he or she too will get angry.

EXAMPLES

1. *Shiranu ga hotoke, sagishi ni shinsetsu ni shite shimatta.*

   Totally ignorant of who the man was, he was kind to the swindler.

2. *Okusan ni totte, goshujin no uwaki wa shiranu ga hotoke desu.*

   The wife is blissfully ignorant of her husband's fooling around.

3. *Uchi no kodomo ga tonari no inu o itsumo ijimete iru koto o shitte wa ita ga, shiranu ga hotoke o kime-konda.*

   Even though I knew my son had been tormenting the neighbors' dog, I pretended that I knew nothing about it.

4. *Shiranu ga hotoke, kare ni wa damatte imashō.*

   Ignorance is bliss. So let's not tell him about it.

shita o maku

舌を巻く

be amazed at

TOMODACHI 1:

Kare no tenisu no sābu, hontō ni hayai desu ne.

TOMODACHI 2:

Hontō ni, daremo ga shita o maku hodo desu yo.

FRIEND 1:

He really has a fast serve, doesn't he?

FRIEND 2:

You said it. It would amaze anyone.

Shita o maku means to be overwhelmed by and thus come to admire a person's superior performance or technique. The expression refers to how people open their mouth and curl *(maku)* their tongue *(shita)* when surprised. Other expressions that use *shita* include *shita ga mawaru* (speak fluently, without a single break or pause) and *shita o dasu* (stick one's tongue out at people to ridicule them).

EXAMPLES

1. *Kanojo no tōan wa sensei ga shita o maku hodo no deki datta.*
   Her answers were so good that even the professor was amazed.
2. *Kare no ensō, shinsain mo shita o maku dekibae da ne.*
   Even the judges were amazed by her performance.
3. *Kare no saiki ni wa, daremo ga odoroite shita o maku darō.*
   I'm sure anyone would be amazed by his talent.
4. *Ano ko no yūki ni wa, oya no watashi sae shita o makimasu.*
   Even I, his parent, was overwhelmed by his courageousness.
5. *Kare no yūkan na tatakai buri ni, teki wa shita o maite taisan shita.*
   His gallant display of fighting so amazed the enemy that they withdrew.

shita tarazu

舌足らず

incomplete and unclear expression or pronunciation

BUCHŌ:

Mō ichido setsumei shite kurenai ka? Kimi no hyōgen wa shita tarazu de, yoku wakaranai yo.

KAISHAIN:

Hai, dōmo sumimasen.

DEPARTMENT CHIEF:

Would you mind explaining that again? The way you express yourself is so vague I can't make out what you're saying.

EMPLOYEE:

Yes, sir. I'm sorry about that.

Shita tarazu means either to lisp, to be unable to pronounce words clearly, or to not express oneself clearly. As a side note, *tarazu* (to be short of or lacking) is used as a suffix with numbers to stress how small they are.

EXAMPLES

1. *Ano ko, shita tarazu na hanashikata ga kawaii ne.*

   It's cute the way that child speaks with a lisp, isn't it?

2. *Kare no kinō no setsumei wa shita tarazu ja nakatta deshō ka?*

   Didn't you think the explanation he gave yesterday was a bit unclear?

3. *Nihon seifu no kotae wa shita tarazu de, gaikokujin ni wa rikai sarenai.*

   The Japanese government's response is so vague that foreigners can't understand it.

4. *Kono setsumeisho wa shita tarazu de, fakkusu no okurikata ga wakaranai.*

   This instruction manual is so vague that I can't understand how to use the fax.

shita tsuzumi o utsu

舌鼓をうつ

smack one's lips

ANI:

Kinō, otōsan to osushiya-san ni itta sō da ne.

IMŌTO:

Otōsan, oishii'tte, shita tsuzumi o utte irashita wa.

OLDER BROTHER:

I hear you went out for sushi with dad yesterday.

YOUNGER SISTER:

Dad thought it was great. He really enjoyed himself.

Shita tsuzumi o utsu refers to smacking one's lips when eating or drinking something really tasty or delicious. *Tsuzumi* is a general term for Japanese percussion instruments. *Shita tsuzumi o utsu* means to smack one's tongue *(shita)* as if hitting *(utsu)* a drum. *Narasu* (beat) can be used instead of *utsu*.

EXAMPLES

1. *Haha no tezukuri no ryōri ni, omowazu shita tsuzumi o utta.*
   My mother's home cooking was so good, I couldn't help smacking my lips.
2. *Kyō no ryōri no amari no oishisa ni, shita tsuzumi o uchimashita.*
   Today's meal was so good I smacked my lips as I ate.
3. *Anata ni shita tsuzumi o utte morau no ga ureshiin' desu.*
   For you to eat with such gusto makes me so happy.
4. *Donna ryōri dattara, kare ni shita tsuzumi o utaseru koto ga dekiru ka na?*
   I wonder what kind of food I can cook that he would really like?
5. *Otto wa watashi no ryōri ni itsumo shita tsuzumi o utsu.*
   My husband always really enjoys my cooking.

shubi yoku

首尾良く

successfully, with success

KISHA:

Nichibei kaigi wa donna guai ni susunde imasu ka?

SEIJIKA:

Shubi yoku itte iru yo. Shinpai suru na.

REPORTER:

How are the meetings between the U.S. and Japan progressing?

POLITICIAN:

Very successfully. There is no need to worry.

Shubi yoku, which combines *shu* (animal's neck), *bi* (animal's tail), and *yoku* (good), means to succeed in doing something. It is often used to describe a process from beginning to end. By itself *shubi* means a result or outcome. *Jōshubi* has the same meaning as *shubi yoku,* but *fushubi* means to fail. *Shubi ikkan* refers to something that is consistent from beginning to end; for example, *shubi ikkan shita shisō* means a consistent set of ideas or way of thinking.

EXAMPLES

1. *Kondo no kaigi wa shubi yoku itte, hotto shita.*
   The meeting went really well. What a relief.
2. *Sakujitsu no torihiki wa shubi yoku ikimashita.*
   Yesterday's transactions went successfully.
3. *Gorufu no seiseki ga jōshubi da to, shachō mo go-kigen desu yo.*
   When his golf score is good, even the president is in a good mood.
4. *Shubi ga dōmo umaku ikazu shinpai desu.*
   For some reason, the results have not turned out well and I'm concerned.
5. *Kōenkai, shubi yoku itte yokatta desu ne.*
   You must be happy everything went so well with your lecture.

shuraba

修羅場

violent scene, scene of carnage

TOMODACHI 1:

Kinō, kono hen de, kaji ga atta sō da ne.

TOMODACHI 2:

Un, nige-madou hito-tachi de, marude shuraba datta yo.

FRIEND 1:

I hear there was a fire somewhere near here yesterday.

FRIEND 2:

Yeah, it was absolute chaos with people running this way and that trying to escape.

Shuraba describes a violent, tragic fighting scene. *Shura* comes from Ashura, an evil god who constantly does battle with benevolent gods. *Shuraba* is where this combat takes place. This expression is used when likening a situation to that of a battlefield.

EXAMPLES

1. *Kare wa nando mo shuraba o kuguri-nukete kita hito da.*
   He is a person who has survived many difficult situations.
2. *Fūfu-genka no shuraba o mise-tsukerareta.*
   I saw a violent argument between a husband and wife.
3. *Hito no mae de shuraba o sarashite shimatte, hazukashii.*
   I'm ashamed of myself for having made a scene in public.
4. *Hikōki no tsuiraku genba wa masa ni shuraba datta.*
   The airplane crash site was a scene of complete carnage.
5. *Isha wa shuraba de mo reiseisa o ushinatte wa naranai.*
   Doctors must maintain their composure even when faced with a scene of great bloodshed.

sode no shita

袖の下

bribe

BUCHŌ:

Torihikisaki no aite ni, sukoshi kōshō shite hoshii tokoro da ne.

BUKA:

Sode no shita de mo tsukamasemasu ka?

DEPARTMENT CHIEF:

I'd like you to make, you know, a deal with our client.

SUBORDINATE:

Shall I pass him a little money under the table?

Sode no shita refers to bribery. To influence a government official, people used to slip the official a gift from under *(shita)* their sleeve *(sode)*. In the Edo period, people wore kimono with long sleeves, which made it easy for them to hide a gift. Another expression with *sode* is *sode ni suru,* to give someone the cold shoulder.

EXAMPLES

1. *Ano yakunin wa, sode no shita o moratte iru to iu uwasa da.*

   It's rumored that the government official is getting money under the table.

2. *Kare ni wa sode no shita wa tsūyō shinai.*

   It's no use trying to give him money under the table. He won't accept it.

3. *Satō-san wa sode no shita o tsukatte, uraguchi nyūgaku shita.*

   Mr. Sato got into the university through the backdoor—he bribed someone.

4. *Kare ni wa, sode no shita o tsukamaseru no ga ichiban da.*

   He's the best at greasing someone's palm.

sora de oboeru

空で覚える

commit to memory

TOMODACHI 1:

Kanojo wa Shopan no Poronēzu, wa zenbu fumen mo minaide hikerun' desu yo.

TOMODACHI 2:

Kitto, sora de oboete iru no deshō ne.

FRIEND 1:

She can play all of Chopin's Polonaises without even reading the scores.

FRIEND 2:

I'm sure she has them memorized.

Sora de oboeru refers to having something memorized. *Sora de* can be used with other verbs such as *sora de utau* (sing extemporaneously), *sora de kaku* (write extemporaneously), *sora de iu* (recite extemporaneously), and *sora de hanasu* (talk extemporaneously). Other phrases using *sora* are *sora namida* (crying even though one is not sad), *sora ni* (two people who look alike but are not related by blood), and *sora mimi* (one who hears things even though there is no sound).

EXAMPLES

1. *Amerika no daitōryō no namae nara, zenbu sora de oboete imasu.*

   I have memorized all the names of the American presidents.

2. *Zenbu sora de oboeru no wa taihen datta deshō?*

   I'm sure it was difficult to memorize everything.

3. *Anata no denwa bangō nara, sora de iemasu yo.*

   If it's your telephone number, I can recite it from memory.

4. *Haine no shi o sora de kakemasu yo.*

   I can write Heine's poem by heart.

sori ga awanai

反りが合わない

not see eye to eye

KANKŌ BASU NO UNTENSHU:

Kore kara yoroshiku o-negai shimasu.

GAIDO:

Watashi no hō koso. Untenshu-san to sori ga awanakattara, taihen desu mono.

TOUR BUS DRIVER:

Let me know if there's anything I can do to help things go smoothly.

GUIDE:

Same here. It wouldn't do to not get along with the driver.

Sori ga awanai describes two people not getting along well, not seeing eye to eye, or being on bad terms with each other. Originally, *sori* was used to refer to the curved part of a sword. Samurai always carried their swords in a sheath at their side, and if the shape of the sheath didn't match *(awanai)* the curve of the sword, it could not be used. *Sori ga au* means that two people get along well.

EXAMPLES

1. *Ano shinbun-kisha to kameraman wa sori ga awanai yō da.*
   That journalist and his cameraman don't seem to get along very well.
2. *Futari wa sori ga awazu ni, kenka bakari shite iru.*
   Those two don't see eye to eye at all; they're always arguing.
3. *Karera wa saisho kara sori ga awanakattan' desu yo.*
   They didn't get along from the start.
4. *Fūfu de sori ga awanakute wa, rikon suru shika nai.*
   The best thing for a couple who don't get along is to get a divorce.
5. *Kimi, minna to sori ga au yō de yokatta ne.*
   You're so lucky; you seem to get along with everyone.

suikō suru

推敲する

polish, improve

HENSHŪSHA:

Sensei, genkō ga kakemashita deshō ka?

SAKKA:

Mada nan' desu yo. Mō chotto, bunshō o suikō shite, kaki-naoshitai node . . .

EDITOR:

Have you completed your manuscript, professor?

WRITER:

Not yet. I'd like to do a little more rewriting and polish up what I've written.

Suikō suru refers to the numerous reworkings when composing poetry or writing prose. It originates from a story about a Tang dynasty poet who once wrote a poem while riding on a donkey. He had composed the phrase *Sō wa osu, gekka no mon* (A priest pushes a moonlit gate) but had had difficulty deciding whether to use the word *tataku* (knock at) or *osu* (push). The Chinese reading for *osu* and *tataku* are *sui* and *kō* respectively, hence *suikō suru*.

EXAMPLES

1. *Kare no bunshō wa suikō ni suikō ga kasanerarete iru.*

   He has worked his writing over and over again to polish it.

2. *Kono bun ni wa, mada suikō no yochi ga aru.*

   There's still room for improvement in this text.

3. *Kanojo no repōto ni wa suikō no ato ga ukagaeru.*

   You can see she has taken great pains in writing her research paper.

4. *Suikō suru yori, kaki-naoshita hō ga hayai.*

   Rather than trying to revise it, it would be quicker to rewrite.

suzushii kao

涼しい顔

assuming a nonchalant air, looking unconcerned

KAISHAIN 1:

Kono kaisha, tōtō fuwatari tegata o dashite, tōsan rashii yo.

KAISHAIN 2:

Sore ni shite wa, shachō mo buchō mo suzushii kao o shite imasu ne.

EMPLOYEE 1:

I hear the company bounced a check and is going bankrupt.

EMPLOYEE 2:

In spite of that, the boss and his department chief certainly look pretty unconcerned.

Suzushii kao means to appear unconcerned and unruffled though one ought to appear worried. *Suzushii* (cool) is primarily used to describe the weather, but it can also be used when referring to a cool attitude. From this has come the meaning of not being influenced by others, and remaining calm, cool, and collected.

EXAMPLES

1. *Kare wa suzushii kao de uso o tsuku.*

   He tells lies with such nonchalance.

2. *Minna ga ōdishon ni buji ukaru ka dō ka shinpai shite iru noni, tōnin wa suzushii kao da.*

   Though everyone else was worried about whether or not she would get the role, the girl herself looked completely unconcerned.

3. *Suzushii kao o shite iru bāi de wa arimasen yo.*

   This is no time to be acting unconcerned.

4. *Ima ni kitto shōtai ga barete, sonna suzushii kao o shite irarenaku naru.*

   Sooner or later your true self will be revealed and you won't be able to look so composed.

tachi-ōjō suru

立ち往生する

be stranded, be nonplussed

KACHŌ:

Buchō no kaeri ga osoi na. Dō shitan' darō?

BUKA:

Kōsoku-dōro no jūtai de, kuruma ga tachi-ōjō shite irun' ja nai desu ka?

SECTION CHIEF:

The director is late in getting back. I wonder what could have happened?

SUBORDINATE:

He's probably stuck in a traffic jam on the freeway.

Tachi-ōjō suru means that in the midst of something, things come to a standstill and one becomes unable to proceed. This phrase literally means "to die on one's feet"—*tachi* means standing, and *ōjō* means death. This phrase describes the death of the well-known priest Benkei, who, despite having had his body shot full of arrows, refused to fall and died on his feet. From this, the expression has come to mean to be stranded or nonplussed.

EXAMPLES

1. *Kyūkyūsha ga jūtai no dōro de tachi-ōjō shite iru.*

   The ambulance is being held up by a traffic jam on the highway.

2. *Sutā ga fan ni tori-kakomarete konsāto hōru no gakuya de tachi-ōjō shite ita.*

   The celebrity was stranded backstage when he was surrounded by fans.

3. *Supiichi de kotoba ni tsumari, tachi-ōjō shite shimatta.*

   I became lost for words in my speech and got myself in a real fix.

4. *Ōyuki de shinkansen wa tachi-ōjō shite shimatta.*

   The heavy snowfall caused the bullet train to become snowbound.

takabisha na taido
高飛車な態度
having an overbearing attitude

DANSHI GAKUSEI:
Jimushitsu ni ittara, jimuin ga takabisha na taido de ne.
JOSHI GAKUSEI:
Watashi mo keiken ga aru wa. Hontō ni kanji ga warui wa ne.

MALE STUDENT:
When I went to the office, the clerks were putting on a high and mighty act.
FEMALE STUDENT:
I've had a similar experience. It's really disgusting, isn't it?

Takabisha na taido means that from the very outset, the person about whom one is talking has taken a high-handed attitude. In Japanese chess, one of the pieces is called *hisha* (castle, rook). *Takabisha* refers to the increased pressure one can apply to one's opponent when the piece advances.

EXAMPLES

1. *Kare wa, dōshite itsumo ā takabisha na taido o toru no darō?*
   Why does he always adopt such an overbearing attitude?
2. *Kokusai mondai de wa, taikoku ga takabisha na taido o toru koto ga ōi.*
   When there are international problems, there are many times when major powers assume a domineering stance.
3. *Kare no takabisha na taido ni wa, hontō ni hara ga tatsu.*
   His high-handed manner makes me angry.
4. *Aite-gawa wa, kyū ni takabisha na taido ni natta.*
   The opposite party suddenly adopted an overbearing attitude.
5. *Kaisha-gawa wa, takabisha na taido o tori-tsuzuketa.*
   The company continued to act with a high-handed attitude.

tama no koshi ni noru

玉の輿にのる

do well for oneself by marrying into a wealthy family

TOMODACHI 1:

Keiko-san, shachō no musuko-san to kon'yaku shita yo.

TOMODACHI 2:

Mā, urayamashii. Tama no koshi ni noru'tte kono koto ne.

FRIEND 1:

Keiko has gotten engaged to the boss's son.

FRIEND 2:

Lucky thing. She's really done well for herself, hasn't she?

The *koshi,* or palanquin, was a form of transportation used many years ago by nobles. *Tama no koshi* was a highly decorated kind of *koshi*—one studded with *tama* (precious stones)—that was sent to pick up the bride of a noble person on her wedding day. Nowadays, *tama no koshi ni noru* is used to describe the way in which a woman of relatively low social status suddenly becomes rich or noble by marrying into a family of higher status.

EXAMPLES

1. *Anata ga ano hito to kekkon dekitara, tama no koshi nan' dakedo.*

   You'd do very well for yourself by marrying him.

2. *Tama no koshi ni notta kara to itte, shiawase ni nareru to wa omoimasen.*

   There's no reason to think that you'll be happy just because you've married into a good family.

3. *Yo no naka ni wa, tama no koshi ni noreru hito wa sonna ni imasen.*

   There aren't many people in this world who have the opportunity to improve their lives by marrying into a wealthy family.

4. *Watashi mo kanojo no yō ni, tama no koshi ni noretara yoi noni.*

   If only I had the chance to marry someone rich like she did.

tana ni ageru

棚に上げる

not acknowledge one's own faults

NIHON NO SEIJIKA:

Kankyo hogo no tame ni wa, shinrin shigen o mamorō.

GAIKOKU NO SEIJIKA:

Jibun no kuni no koto o tana ni agete, yoku sonna koto ga ieru na.

JAPANESE POLITICIAN:

In order to protect our environment we must preserve our forests.

FOREIGN POLITICIAN:

You should talk! I'm surprised that you can disregard your own country's environment like that.

Tana ni ageru, literally "to put something away on a shelf and not use it," refers to intentionally refusing to take up or discuss some subject. Other expressions using *tana* include *tana-age ni suru* (shelve or suspend something) and *tana kara botamochi* (a piece of good luck, a godsend, or a windfall).

EXAMPLES

1. *Buchō wa jibun no shippai wa tana ni agete, buka o semeta.*
   The department chief, ignoring his own faults, reproached the workers.
2. *Sugu jibun no koto o tana ni agete, hito no sekinin ni surun' dakara.*
   You always just ignore your own faults and lay the responsibility on someone else.
3. *Jibun o tana ni agete, hito no koto o hihan suru no wa kantan da.*
   It's easy to ignore one's faults and criticize others.
4. *Shūkyū futsukasei wa, ichibu no hantai de tana-age ni sareta.*
   Because some of the people were opposed, the plan for a five-day workweek was shelved.
5. *Ano mondai o itsu made tana-age ni shite oku no desu ka?*
   Just exactly how long are you going to ignore that problem?

tantō-chokunyū

単刀直入

a direct or frank way of speaking

CHICHIOYA:

Tokoro de, musuko no seiseki wa dō nan' deshō ka?

SENSEI:

Tantō-chokunyū ni mōshi-agete, hijō ni warui desu ne.

FATHER:

Now then, how are my son's grades?

TEACHER:

Well, to be perfectly frank with you, they're extremely bad.

Tantō-chokunyū refers to a way of speaking that launches straight into a subject and leaves out introductory remarks, roundabout expressions, and euphemisms. The origin of this phrase is found in the combination of the word's characters: *tan* means alone, *tō* (also read *katana*) means sword, and *chokunyū* means entering directly. In other words, it suggests charging single-handedly into the enemy ranks carrying a sword.

EXAMPLES

1. *Ikura sensei kara de mo, seiseki furyō de rakudai nado to tantō-chokunyū ni iwareru no wa, iya na mono da.*

   Even if it comes from a teacher, being told too directly that one has failed a test isn't very nice.

2. *Sukoshi wa aite no tachiba mo kangaete, kono kettei wa tantō-chokunyū ni tsutaenai hō ga ii.*

   Looking at it from his point of view, it would be better not to be too blunt when we tell him about our decision.

3. *Dōshite tantō-chokunyū ni itte wa ikenai no desu ka?*

   What's wrong with getting straight to the point?

tanuki-neiri

狸寝入り

pretending to be asleep

TSUMA:

Nē, anata, watashi no hanashi, kiite iru no?

OTTO:

Gū gū . . .

TSUMA:

Mata tanuki-neiri shite iru no ne.

WIFE:

Are you listening to what I'm saying?

HUSBAND:

Zzz . . .

WIFE:

You're just pretending to be asleep again, aren't you?

In Japanese mythology, the *tanuki* (badger) was a mischievous animal that enjoyed deceiving humans. Consequently, *tanuki* is used to refer to sly or crafty people, and *tanuki-neiri* has the same meaning as "to play possum." *Tanuki-oyaji* means crafty old man.

EXAMPLES

1. *Ano hito ni wa ki o tsukenasai. Tanuki nan' dakara.*

   You want to watch him—he's a crafty old thing.

2. *Otōsan wa jibun ni tsugō ga waruku naru to, tanuki-neiri o hajimeru.*

   Whenever my father doesn't want to listen to someone, he just pretends to be asleep.

3. *Okinasai. Tanuki-neiri da to wakatte imasu yo.*

   Wake up. I know you're just pretending to be asleep.

4. *A, mata ano tanuki-oyaji ni gomakasarete shimatta.*

   Oh, no. I've been ripped off again by that damned old swindler.

tarai-mawashi ni suru

たらい回しにする

pass on responsibility from one person to the next

KAISHAIN 1:

Kondo no senkyo de, nanika kawaru to omoimasu ka?

KAISHAIN 2:

Iya, seiken ga tarai-mawashi ni sareru dake de, nanimo kawaranai deshō ne.

EMPLOYEE 1:

Do you think anything is going to change with the next election?

EMPLOYEE 2:

Not with the way they hand over power to members of their own party.

A *tarai* is a small, shallow tub used for washing one's face, hands, or feet. *Tarai-mawashi* referred originally to a form of entertainment in which acrobats balanced a spinning tub on their feet. Today, it is used to describe the way in which something is passed from one place to the next without ever being properly dealt with.

EXAMPLES

1. *Kono shorui ga buchō kara tarai-mawashi sarete kita.*

    I ended up with these documents because the department chief didn't want to deal with them himself.

2. *Byōki no gen'in ga wakaranakute, byōin o achikochi tarai-mawashi saremashita.*

    No one could tell me what was wrong, so I just ended up being sent from one hospital to the next.

3. *Kono mondai wa tsugitsugi ni tarai-mawashi sarete iru.*

    This problem is being passed from one person to the next without being dealt with.

tazuna o shimeru

たずなを締める

tighten the reins

TSUMA:

Anata, kodomo ni sukoshi kibishi-sugirun' ja arimasen ka? Mō sukoshi, tazuna o yurumetara dō kashira?

OTTO:

Iya, shitsuke wa kibishii hō ga ii. Tazuna wa kore kara mo shimete iku yo.

WIFE:

Honey, aren't you a bit strict with the children? What about loosening the reins a bit?

HUSBAND:

No. It's better to be strict. I'm going to continue to be as tough on discipline as ever.

Tazuna o shimeru means to maintain a tight rein over someone and keep them from doing whatever they please. The antonym is *tazuna o yurumeru* (loosen the reins).

EXAMPLES

1. *Juken ga chikai node, seito no tazuna o shimeru hitsuyō ga arimasu ne.*
   With the exams coming up, it's important to tighten the reins on the students.

2. *Fukyō ni sonaete, keiei no tazuna o shimete kakarō.*
   In response to the recession, let's tighten up our management policies.

3. *Kōsaihi no tsukaikata ni tsuite, tazuna o shimeta hō ga ii desu yo.*
   I think you should tighten the reins over how people are using the entertainment expense account.

4. *Toki ni wa, tazuna o yurumeru koto mo hitsuyō desu.*
   It's sometimes necessary to loosen the reins a bit.

te ga todoku

手が届く

be able to do, be careful and thorough, be nearing

TSUMA:

Nē, anata, umibe ni bessō ga hoshii wa.

OTTO:

Boku no kyūryō ja, te ga todokanai yo.

WIFE:

Darling, I'd love to have a summer house by the sea.

HUSBAND:

There's no way we can afford that with my salary.

Te ga todoku has various meanings, including being within one's capability, being careful, considerate, or thorough, or being close to reaching a certain age. The negative form, *te ga todokanai,* is frequently used.

EXAMPLES

1. *Kimi wa itsumo te no todokanai mono o hoshigaru.*

   You always want things you can't get.

2. *Kono byōin wa yoku te ga todoite kanja mo manzoku shite iru.*

   Patients are always satisfied with the thorough treatment and attention they get at this hospital.

3. *(kanja ni) Itsumo te ga todokanakute sumimasen.*

   (to a patient) I'm sorry we can't always help you as much as we'd like to.

4. *Watashi wa sorosoro gojū ni te ga todoku.*

   I'll soon be getting on fifty.

5. *Gojussai ni te ga todoku made ni wa, mada sūnen arimasu.*

   You still have a good many years to go before you reach fifty.

te o dasu

手を出す

get involved in, hit, make advances, steal

TOMODACHI 1:
Dō shimashita ka?
TOMODACHI 2:
Kabu ni te o dashite, ōzon o shite shimaimashita.

FRIEND 1:
What's the matter?
FRIEND 2:
I got involved with the stock market and now I've lost a lot of money.

Te o dasu means to get involved in something or with somebody: for instance, to hit or punch someone in a fight, to make advances on a woman, or to steal something. *Te o hiku* means to cut off an involvement with something or somebody.

EXAMPLES

1. *Tobaku ni wa te o dasanai hō ga ii.*
   It's not a good idea to get involved with gambling.
2. *Itsu kara kabu ni te o dashi-hajimetan' desu ka?*
   When did you first get involved in the stock market?
3. *Kono kenka wa dochira ga saki ni te o dashitan' da?*
   Who started this fight?
4. *Boku no gārufurendo ni te o dasu na yo!*
   Keep your hands off my girlfriend!
5. *Kanojo wa tsui kaisha no o-kane ni te o dashita.*
   Without really thinking about what she was doing, she stole some money from the company.

te o nuku

手を抜く

cut corners, do things in a slipshod fashion

MUSUKO:

Okāsan, kyō no yūshoku amari oishikunai ne.

OTTO:

Hontō da. Te o nuitan' ja nai no ka?

SON:

Dinner doesn't taste very good today, mom.

HUSBAND:

He's right. You haven't spent as much time as usual on this, have you?

Te o nuku means to not do something that one should—for example, to cover up one's mistake, to cut corners in one's work, or do things in a slipshod fashion. In this expression, *te* means a method or way of doing something, and *nuku* means to cut down, reduce, or economize. *Te-nuki* has the same meaning as *te o nuku. Te o kakeru* means to spend time doing a job properly.

EXAMPLES

1. *Kare wa itsumo shigoto no te o nuite, jōshi o komarasete iru.*
   His slipshod work is always causing problems for his bosses.
2. *(jishin de kowareta ie o mite) Kore wa te-nuki kōji desu ne.*
   (looking at a house destroyed in an earthquake) That must have been a shoddy construction job, don't you think?
3. *Kimi, chōsa no te o nuite wa komarimasu ne.*
   You shouldn't cut corners in doing your research.
4. *Kare wa te o nuita ni chigai arimasen.*
   I'm sure he must have put a minimum of time and effort into this.

te o utsu

手を打つ

close a deal

HOKEN-GAISHA NO HITO:
Jidōsha jiko no jidan-kin desu ga, hyakuman'en de dō desu ka?
JIKO NI ATTA HITO:
Sō desu ne. Sono hen de, te o utte okimashō ka?

PERSON FROM THE INSURANCE COMPANY:
As for the money to be paid as compensation for the car accident, how about a million yen?
PERSON WHO HAD AN ACCIDENT:
Yes, let's settle the matter with that amount.

Te o utsu, literally "clap hands," means to come to some kind of compromise in order to close a business transaction or to settle a domestic dispute. It can also mean to devise some means to reach a compromise.

EXAMPLES

1. *Kono kōshō wa, kono hen de te o utte okimashō.*
   This is a good time to conclude our negotiations. Let's shake on it.
2. *Hayaku te o utanai to, mondai no kaiketsu ga okuremasu yo.*
   Unless you make a deal quickly, it's going to take longer to find a solution to the problems.
3. *Yamu o ezu, sono jōken de te o utsu koto ni shita.*
   Out of necessity, we settled with those conditions.
4. *Jitai ga akka shinai uchi ni, te o utsu hitsuyō ga aru.*
   It's necessary to close the deal before conditions worsen.
5. *Shūshoku ni kanshite wa, hayame ni te o utte oita hō ga ii desu yo.*
   As far as getting a job goes, it's a good idea to settle the matter sooner than later.

tedama ni toru

手玉に取る

wrap around one's finger, have a person well in hand

TOMODACHI 1:

Kanojo, saikin atte kurenain' da. Boku no koto, kirai ni natta no ka na?

TOMODACHI 2:

Kanojo, kimi no kimochi o tedama ni totterun' da yo.

FRIEND 1:

Recently, my girlfriend won't see me. I wonder if she dislikes me.

FRIEND 2:

She's playing with your feelings.

Tedama ni toru means to control someone as one would control a puppet. *Tedama,* small cloth sacks filled with red beans, are often used by magicians who are very good at manipulating them during their performances. As a result, *tedama ni toru* refers to having a person well in hand or under control.

EXAMPLES

1. *Kare wa kanojo ni tedama ni torarete iru yō da.*
   He seems to be wrapped around her finger.
2. *Itsu kara kanojo wa kare o tedama ni toru yō ni natta no desu ka?*
   Since when has she had him wrapped around her finger?
3. *Seijika-tachi wa, masukomi o tedama ni totte iru.*
   Politicians have the press well in hand.
4. *Jānarisuto-tachi wa, yoron o tedama ni totte iru.*
   Journalists control public opinion.
5. *Sō kantan ni kaisha-gawa no tedama ni wa toraremasen yo.*
   I'm not going to let the company control me that easily.

teishu kanpaku

亭主関白

wearing the pants in the family

TOMODACHI 1:

Anata no goshujin, yasashisō na kata desu ne.

TOMODACHI 2:

Sore ga, taihen na teishu kanpaku de, nan de mo shujin ga kimenai to, ki ga sumanai no.

FRIEND 1:

Your husband appears to be such a sweet kind of guy.

FRIEND 2:

In fact, he's an absolute dictator around the house. He never feels satisfied unless he makes all the decisions.

Teishu kanpaku refers to a man who is the absolute leader of his family, a man especially haughty with his wife. *Teishu* means lord or master of a house and *kanpaku* refers to the counselor who was the most important and powerful of the ancient Japanese emperor's retainers. When a husband is haughty and proud he is like this counselor.

EXAMPLES

1. *Asoko no ie wa teishu kanpaku na no yo.*

   The husband wears the pants in the family in that home.

2. *Wagaya wa teishu kanpaku ni miete, jitsu wa kakaa-denka desu.*

   Though it might appear that my husband wears the pants in our family, he's in fact quite henpecked.

3. *Teishu kanpaku na kare to wa mō wakaretai.*

   I want a separation. He's such a dictator around the house.

4. *Teishu kanpaku datta otto mo, toshi totte, yasashiku natta.*

   My husband, once quite the dictator at home, has become much more gentle and kind as he has gotten older.

tekagen

手加減

estimate, making allowances, taking into consideration

SEITO:

Sensei, kono aida no shiken, shippai shitan' desu. Seiseki o sukoshi tekagen shite itadakemasen ka?

SENSEI:

Zan'nen da ga, seiseki ni tekagen wa dekinai yo. Kondo, ganbaritamae.

STUDENT:

I didn't do as well as usual in the last test. Could you take that into consideration when you give our grades, please?

TEACHER:

Sorry, I can't do that. Better luck next time.

Tekagen refers to addition and subtraction, and when used with *suru,* suggests adjusting or making allowances for something. *Tekagen suru* can also mean to roughly estimate the weight, amount, or level of something, or it can mean to adjust the way in which one deals with a person or thing according to that particular situation.

EXAMPLES

1. *Kono sūtsukēsu, tekagen desu ga, nijukkiro ijō arisō desu yo.*

   I'm only judging by the feel of it, but I think this suitcase weighs over twenty kilograms.

2. *(massaji no hito ni) Itai node, sukoshi tekagen shite kudasai.*

   (to a masseur) That hurts. Please go a bit easy there.

3. *(tenisu de) Watashi ga heta datta kara, aite ni tekagen saremashita.*

   (after playing tennis) My opponent took it easy on me because I wasn't a very good player.

4. *Kare ni renshū o sukoshi tekagen sasemashō.*

   Let's get him to take it easy on the training.

teki-paki shite iru

テキパキしている

get things done quickly and efficiently

KAISHAIN 1:
Kondo no buchō, shigoto ga dekisō desu ne.
KAISHAIN 2:
Teki-paki shite ite, jitsu ni kimochi ga ii desu yo.

EMPLOYEE 1:
The new department chief seems like a capable person, doesn't he?
EMPLOYEE 2:
Yes, I really like the way he gets on with things so quickly and efficiently.

Teki-paki imitates through its own sound the way in which someone works quickly and efficiently, getting things sorted out in a systematic fashion. Other similar expressions include *hakihaki shite iru* (speak clearly and confidently), *guzuguzu shite iru* (do things in a sluggish way).

EXAMPLES

1. *Kare no taido wa jitsu ni teki-paki shite iru.*
   He has a very good attitude about getting things done quickly and efficiently.
2. *Kanojo wa teki-paki to shiji o konashita.*
   She gave very clear, concise instructions.
3. *Motto, teki-paki to kōdō dekinain' desu ka?*
   Can't you work a bit more efficiently?
4. *Kare ga teki-paki to hanashi o matomete kurete, tasukatta.*
   He really helped us by speaking so clearly and concisely.
5. *Kanojo no yō ni teki-paki shita hito wa hajimete da.*
   I've never met anyone as fast and efficient as her.

teko de mo ugokanai

てこでも動かない

be obstinate, not yield an inch

MUSUKO:

Otōsan, kono aida shōkai shita hito to kekkon shiyō to omoun' da.

CHICHIOYA:

Boku wa ki ni iranai ne. Zettai ni hantai da.

MUSUKO:

Komatta na. Otōsan, ii-dashitara teko de mo ugokanai kara.

SON:

I'm thinking of marrying the girl I introduced you to the other day.

FATHER:

I'm not happy about it. In fact, I'm completely opposed to it.

SON:

This is going to make things difficult. Once you've had your say on something, you won't give an inch.

Teko de mo ugokani, literally "won't move even with a lever," means that someone is stubborn and won't yield an inch. *Ganko* is another word used to describe stubbornness.

EXAMPLES

1. *Kare ga ittan kō to kimetara, teko de mo ugokanai.*

   Once he decides to do it a certain way, he won't budge an inch.

2. *Kare no jinin no ishi wa kataku, teko de mo ugokisō mo nai.*

   He is adamant in his intention to resign from office and there is no likelihood of him backing down.

3. *Kanojo wa ii-dashitara, teko de mo ugokimasen yo.*

   When she speaks her mind, she stands firm in her opinion.

4. *Otto wa, dame da to ii-dashitara, teko de mo ugokanai.*

   Once my husband says that something won't do, he won't budge at all.

tekozuru

てこずる

---

be difficult to solve, afford, manage, or take care of

BUCHŌ:

Dō da ne. Kondo no torihiki wa?

KAISHAIN:

Aite no yōkyū ga ōkii node, tekozurisō desu yo.

DEPARTMENT CHIEF:

How's the latest deal going?

EMPLOYEE:

Well, they're asking a lot, so it looks as if we'll have problems.

Tekozuru can mean to have trouble solving a problem, to be unable to afford something, to be more than one can manage, or to have trouble dealing with a person or thing. This expression comes from a combination of the words *teko*, meaning lever, and *zureru,* meaning to slip out of place. If a lever slips out of place, it makes the task difficult to accomplish.

EXAMPLES

1. *Kono mondai o kaiketsu suru noni, totemo tekozutta.*

   I went to a lot of trouble to solve this problem.

2. *Kanojo no wagamama ni wa minna tekozurasarete imasu.*

   She's so selfish that other people are always having to go out of their way for her.

3. *O-negai desu kara, sonna ni watashi o tekozurasenaide kudasai.*

   Please don't make things so difficult for me.

4. *Kono kikai o kumi-tateru noni, sonna ni tekozuru to wa omowanakatta.*

   I didn't imagine assembling this machine would be such a tough job.

5. *Kono ko ni wa sukoshi tekozuru kamo shiremasen ga, kinaga ni o-negai shimasu.*

   This child might be difficult to handle, but please be patient with him.

tenbin ni kakeru

天秤に掛ける

weigh one's options

MUSUME:

Futari no dansei kara puropōzu sarete iru no. Hitori wa atama wa yosasō dakedo, sensu ga nakute, mō hitori wa yasashiin' dakedo, shusse shisō mo nai no.

HAHAOYA:

Oya oya, futari wa jibun-tachi ga tenbin ni kakerarete iru koto o shitte iru no kashira?

DAUGHTER:

I've been proposed to by two men. One seems intelligent but lacks sophistication; the other is sweet but his future prospects don't appear very promising.

MOTHER:

Good heavens. I wonder if they realize that they are being weighed one against the other?

Tenbin ni kakeru is used when choosing between two things—when comparing their merits and demerits or their advantages and disadvantages. A *tenbin* is a hanging scale that uses counterweights to estimate the weight of things.

EXAMPLES

1. *Futatsu no kaisha o tenbin ni kake, yoi hō ni shūshoku shitai.*

   I'm weighing the advantages and disadvantages of the two companies and I'd like to work for the better one.

2. *Gōkaku shita futatsu no daigaku o tenbin ni kakete mita.*

   I passed the entrance examinations for two universities and tried to choose between them.

todo no tsumari

とどのつまり

ultimate result, final consequence

BUKA:

Izen kara, yūjin no kaisha ni konai ka to iwarete imashite . . .

JŌSHI:

Todo no tsumari, taishoku shitai to iu koto da ne.

SUBORDINATE:

For a long time, I've been asked to join my friend's company . . .

SUPERVISOR:

In short, you're planning on quitting, right?

Todo no tsumari is used to signify the final outcome of a situation. In Japan, there is a fish, similar to a mullet, that has four different names: *oboko, subashiri, ina,* and *todo.* The name of the fish depends on its age and size. *Todo,* being the name of the fish when it has reached maturity, is used in this idiom with *tsumari,* meaning final.

EXAMPLES

1. *Kare wa shippai o kasane, todo no tsumari wa kaisha o kubi ni natta.*
   After many failures, he was finally fired from the company.
2. *Hantai shite ita ryōshin mo, todo no tsumari wa Furansu e no ryūgaku o yurushite kureta.*
   My parents, who were opposed to my plan to study in France, finally gave their approval.
3. *Minshū no fuman ga, todo no tsumari, kakumei ni made natte shimatta.*
   The populace's dissatisfaction, in the end, led to a revolution.
4. *Tabako o sui-sugi, todo no tsumari, haigan de shinda.*
   His excessive smoking resulted in lung cancer and death.

tōge o kosu

峠を越す

pass the critical point, pass the peak

MUSUKO:

Ojiisan no kitoku-jōtai, mada tsuzuite iru no?

HAHAOYA:

Mō daijōbu. O-ishasama mo tōge o koshita'tte osshatta kara.

SON:

Is grandfather still in critical condition?

MOTHER:

He's going to be all right. The doctor said that he has passed the critical stage.

Tōge o kosu, literally "to go through a pass," indicates the period in which something was most fashionable, critical, or difficult has passed. *Tōge* (pass) refers to the highest point at which a road passes over a mountain.

EXAMPLES

1. *Musuko no byōki mo nantoka tōge o koshite, hito-anshin desu.*

   I feel temporarily relieved now that my son's illness has passed the critical point.

2. *Taifū no seiryoku mo tōge o koshita node, kaze mo osamatte kuru deshō.*

   Since the typhoon has passed its peak, the wind will blow itself out too.

3. *Minisukāto no ryūkō wa, mō tōge o koshita.*

   The mini-skirt fad has had its day.

4. *Tōge o koshita sumōtori wa, intai o matsu bakari da.*

   Sumo wrestlers who have passed their prime just wait around to retire.

5. *Ano senshu wa tōge o koshita ato mo ganbatte iru.*

   Even after reaching his peak, that player still pushes himself.

tōkaku o arawasu

頭角を現す

stand head and shoulders above others

TOMODACHI 1

Jimu-kun, pinchi-hittā to wa omoenai yō na tōkaku o arawashite kimashita ne.

TOMODACHI 2

Shiai wa kore kara omoshiroku narimasu yo.

FRIEND 1:

For just a pinch hitter, Jim has really started to show what he's made of, hasn't he?

FRIEND 2:

Yes, it's going to be an interesting game from now on.

Tōkaku refers to the top of the head or to an animal's horns or antlers, and *arawasu* signifies something that stands out. Thus *tōkaku o arawasu* refers to the way in which a stag's antlers stand out above the other heads in a herd of deer. As an idiom, it is used to express the way a person's particular talent or scholastic achievements distinguish him or her from the crowd.

EXAMPLES

1. *Kare wa shōgakko no koro kara tōkaku o arawashite kita.*

   He's been particularly bright ever since he was at primary school.

2. *Ainshutain wa seinen no toki, tōkaku o arawashita.*

   Einstein showed how brilliant he was while he was still young.

3. *Kare ga tōkaku o arawashi-dashita no wa itsu goro kara desu ka?*

   When did he begin to show signs of being so talented?

4. *Ima ni kono shōnen wa, ichiryū no kenchikuka to shite tōkaku o arawasu deshō.*

   One day this young boy is going to be a first-rate architect.

tokoton made

とことんまで

all the way, to the bitter end, thoroughly

SEITO:

Sensei, daigaku e no shingaku o yamete, shūshoku shiyō to omo-imasu.

SENSEI:

Tokoton made kangaeta kekka desu ka?

STUDENT:

I'm thinking about not going on to university and finding a job instead.

TEACHER:

Have you fully thought this through?

Tokoton is often used with *made* to mean that something is done thoroughly or carried through until the very end. Originally, *tokoton* was a term used in Japanese dance to refer to the sound of the dancers' heels keeping time to the music. It was important in theatrical dances that this rhythm-keeping be carried on through to the end of the performance, and it is from this that the idiom derives its meaning.

EXAMPLES

1. *Kare wa han'nin o tokoton made oi-kaketa.*

   He chased the criminal until he finally caught him.

2. *Minamata mondai wa tokoton made tsuikyū sareru beki da.*

   The Minamata case should be thoroughly investigated.

3. *Konban wa tokoton made anata to hanashi-aimashō.*

   Let's get together tonight and thoroughly talk things out.

4. *Kanojo wa tokoton made gan to tatakai, naku natta.*

   She carried on fighting her cancer until the bitter end.

toppyōshi mo nai

突拍子もない

sudden, unexpected, surprising

MUSUME:

Rainen kara Indo ni itte, komatte iru hito no tame ni hatarakō to omou no.

HAHAOYA:

Kyū ni toppyōshi mo nai koto o itte, bikkuri sasenaide.

DAUGHTER:

I'm thinking of going to work in India next year to help the poor.

MOTHER:

I wish you wouldn't spring these sudden ideas of yours on me.

Toppyōshi mo nai describes something sudden, surprising, or unexpected. Originally, *toppyōshi* was a musical term used to describe the technique of suddenly raising the pitch of one's voice and then lowering it in an otherwise gently moving passage. Today, it refers to anything that takes one by surprise.

EXAMPLES

1. *Musume wa itsumo toppyōshi mo nai koto o ii-dashite, oya o odoro-kaseru.*

   Our daughter is always surprising us by saying impulsive things.

2. *Anata, nan de sonna toppyōshi mo nai kakkō o shite iru no?*

   What on earth are you dressed like that for?

3. *Kimi, sonna toppyōshi mo nai kangae, yametamae.*

   You can forget that outlandish idea right now.

4. *Kare ga daigishi ni naritai nado, toppyōshi mo nai yume da.*

   His hope of becoming a member of parliament is just a wild dream.

tora no ko

とらの子

savings, a nest egg, treasured belongings

TOMODACHI 1:

Ii konpyūtā o kaimashita ne.

TOMODACHI 2:

Ē, tora no ko no hyakuman'en o tsukatte shimaimashita yo.

FRIEND 1:

I see you bought a nice computer.

FRIEND 2:

Yes, and it cost me a million yen of the savings I was keeping aside.

Tora no ko refers to money or a valuable thing that is kept safely protected or hidden. *Tora no ko* literally is "tiger cub," and its meaning in this expression comes from the way that tigers carefully protect their young. An older saying using tiger (here read *ko*) is *koketsu ni irazunba, koji o ezu,* literally "to catch a tiger cub you must enter the tiger's cave," and is used in the same way as the expression "nothing ventured, nothing gained."

EXAMPLES

1. *Okāsan, tora no ko o gaku no ura ni kakushite arun' deshō?*
   You've got savings hidden behind the picture frame, don't you mother?
2. *Watashi wa tora no ko nado, zenzen arimasen.*
   I have no savings at all.
3. *Tora no ko o tamete, kaigai ryoko ni iku tsumori desu.*
   I'm planning to save up my money and then go and travel abroad.
4. *Ojiisan wa taisetsu na tora no ko o nusumarete shimatta.*
   Grandfather had all his treasured valuables stolen.
5. *Tora no ko wa nanika no tame ni motte ita hō ga ii.*
   It's worth keeping a little nest egg in case you need it one day.

torikoshi-gurō

取り越し苦労

worrying unnecessarily

OTTO:

Musume-tachi, kaeri ga osoi ne. Nanika attan' ja nai ka?

TSUMA:

Anata, sore wa torikoshi-gurō desu yo.

HUSBAND:

The girls are late coming home, aren't they? I wonder if something has happened to them?

WIFE:

Oh, you're worrying too much about them.

Torikoshi-gurō is made up of *torikoshi,* which comes from the verb *torikosu*(do something in advance), and *kurō* (suffering or trouble). Thus, the expression means to worry pointlessly about the future.

1. *Kare ni torikoshi-gurō sasete warukatta.*

   I really shouldn't have caused him such a lot of worry.
2. *Chichi ga torikoshi-gurō suru to ikenai node, mō kaerimasu.*

   I don't want my father to worry so I think I'll go home now.
3. *Musume ni wa itsumo torikoshi-gurō saserareru.*

   My daughters are always giving me something to worry about.
4. *Sensō ni naru kamo shirenai nante torikoshi-gurō desu yo.*

   I think it's pessimistic of you to say there's going to be a war.
5. *Hontō ni torikoshi-gurō nara yoi no desu ga . . .*

   I hope I am only worrying.

torimaki

取り巻き

a group of hangers-on

KAISHAIN 1:

Buchō ni iitai koto ga arun' desu ga, nakanaka chansu ga na-kute. . .

KAISHAIN 2:

Kare wa itsumo torimaki ni kakomarete imasu kara ne.

EMPLOYEE 1:

There's something I want to talk to the boss about, but I never seem to get the chance.

EMPLOYEE 2:

Yes, he's always surrounded by his own little group of hangers-on, isn't he?

Torimaki describes people who cling onto a person in a position of power or authority for personal gain. In the dialogue above, the second speaker uses this word to suggest that the boss is followed around wherever he goes by an obsequious entourage of flatterers, which makes it impossible to speak to him individually.

EXAMPLES

1. *Kare no torimaki-renchū, iya na kanji desu ne.*

   That group of parasites that follow him around really annoys me.

2. *Kare no torimaki no iken dake de monogoto o kettei suru.*

   He only makes decisions on the basis of what his followers think.

3. *Gādoman ni torimakarete iru hito wa dare desu ka?*

   Who's that person being followed around by a group of guards?

4. *Buchō wa itsumo no torimaki o tsurete, nomi ni itta.*

   The department chief went out drinking with his usual crowd of hangers-on.

toshiyori no hiyamizu

年寄の冷や水

the indiscretion of old age

SOBO:

Kotoshi no natsu, Fuji-san ni noborō to omotte ne.

MAGO-MUSUME:

Obāchan, toshiyori no hiyamizu wa yamete oita hō ga ii wa.

GRANDMOTHER:

I think I'll climb Mount Fuji this summer.

GRANDDAUGHTER:

Grandma, don't you think you'd better to give up that idea? You're a bit old for it.

Toshiyori no hiyamizu refers to something dangerous and unsuitable for old people. During the Edo Period the quality of water was poor, and in the summer months, water merchants would collect cold water *(hiyamizu)* from the Sumida River and sell it. Although the Sumida River was thought of as clean, the water wasn't pure and elderly people *(toshiyori)* often got sick after drinking it.

EXAMPLES

1. *Toshiyori no hiyamizu to wa shitsurei na!*
   How dare you say that I should know better at my age!
2. *Kesshite toshiyori no hiyamizu nado de wa arimasen.*
   It's definitely not something that an old person should not attempt!
3. *Toshiyori no hiyamizu nado to iwarereba, dare de mo okorimasu.*
   Anyone would get angry if he were accused of being a typical headstrong old fool.
4. *Kanchū-suiei nado, masa ni toshiyori no hiyamizu de wa arimasen ka?*
   Don't you think that swimming outdoors in mid-winter is a perfect example of being indiscreet in one's old age?

tsujitsuma o awaseru

辻褄を合わせる

make something (sound) coherent

HISHO:

Daijin, sakihodo no kokkai tōben desu ga, jijitsu to chigau bubun ga arimasu.

DAIJIN:

Tsujitsuma o awaseru no ga kimi no yakume darō?

SECRETARY:

Minister, in the Diet reply session just now there was a part that is inconsistent with the facts.

MINISTER:

Isn't it your duty to see that we avoid contradicting ourselves?

Tsujitsuma o awaseru, which combines *tsujitsuma* (consistency) and *awaseru* (adjust, put together), means to make something consistent. *Tsuji* are the seams that run lengthwise and breadthwise in a kimono, while *tsuma* refers to the hemline where the seams meet. If the seams don't align front and back, this ruins the shape of the kimono. This has given us the meaning of the phrase as we know it today. *Tsujitsuma ga au* (be coherent) and *tsujitsuma ga awanai* (be inconsistent) are common related expressions.

EXAMPLES

1. *Sakujitsu no kare no hanashi wa dōmo tsujitsuma ga awanai.*
   What he said yesterday was self-contradictory.
2. *Dō shitara tsujitsuma o awaserareru deshō ne.*
   How might we be able to make things sound plausible?
3. *Sono nedan wa, sakujitsu no denwa no hanashi to wa tsujitsuma ga aimasen ne.*
   That isn't the same price that you said on the telephone yesterday.

tsuke-yakiba

付焼刃

veneer, hastily but not thorougly acquired knowledge

DANSHI GAKUSEI:

Bengoshi no shiken o ukete miyō to omoun' da.

JOSHI GAKUSEI:

Tsuke-yakiba no benkyō de wa, totemo muri da to omou wa.

MALE STUDENT:

I think I'll take the bar examination.

FEMALE STUDENT:

I don't think cramming for it will save you.

Tsuke-yakiba refers to a person who, despite having little ability from the outset, hastily tries to acquire knowledge for a particular occasion. In the making of Japanese swords, if the blade is not sufficiently beaten, even though on the surface it may appear to cut well, the blade will lack elasticity and strength. It is from this that the expression has gained its present meaning.

EXAMPLES

1. *Kare wa tsuke-yakiba no chishiki o furi-mawashite komaru.*
   The way he shows off his hastily acquired knowledge is an embarrassment.
2. *Kore wa shosen tsuke-yakiba no chishiki ni sugimasen.*
   After all, this is nothing more than knowledge acquired for affect.
3. *Tsuke-yakiba no Eikaiwa wa yaku ni wa tachimasen.*
   A hastily acquired study of English conversation is useless.
4. *Kanojo no jōhin na manā wa tsuke-yakiba ja nai ka na.*
   Her elegant manners are probably just for show.

tsuki to suppon

月とスッポン

ferent as day and night, totally different, no comparison

TOMODACHI 1:

Furansujin wa natsu ni nikagetsu mo bakansu o toru sō desu yo.

TOMODACHI 2:

Isshūkan shika yasumenai Nihon no seikatsu to wa, tsuki to suppon desu ne.

FRIEND 1:

I hear that the French take up to two months for summer vacation.

FRIEND 2:

It's entirely different from life in Japan where we can only have one week's holiday.

Tsuki to suppon, literally "moon and turtle," refers to two things that are vastly different. Though the moon and a turtle are both round, all similarities end there. The phrase *undei no sa* (a big difference) has a similar meaning.

EXAMPLES

1. *Kare to watashi de wa tsuki to suppon, totemo shiai ni narimasen.*

   He and I are are so far apart in ability that it wouldn't be a good match at all.

2. *Asoko no resutoran to wa tsuki to suppon, danzen kotchi no hō ga oishii.*

   That restaurant over there and this one are worlds apart—the food at this one is definitely better.

3. *Kare wa shachō, watashi wa hira-shain, onaji toshi de mo, shūnyū wa tsuki to suppon da.*

   He is the company president and I am an ordinary employee—we are the same age and yet our incomes are completely different.

tsume no aka o senjite nomu

爪の垢を煎じて飲む

learn to be like someone else

MUSUKO:

Kimura-kun, seiseki ichiban datte.

HAHAOYA:

Mā, anata mo kare no tsume no aka de mo senjite nondara?

SON:

I heard that Kimura got the highest grades.

MOTHER:

Why don't you try to be more like him?

Tsume no aka o senjite suggests boiling the dirt from under the nails of a prominent person. *Nomu* means to drink. The idea was that if this concoction was drunk, some of that person's qualities would be passed on to the drinker. Even if it were something as small as the dirt from under the nails, it would hopefully have some good effect. *Senjiru* is used in reference to boiling a medicinal root or tea leaves. By itself, *tsume no aka* means very little.

EXAMPLES

1. *Buchō no tsume no aka de mo senjite nondara, gorufu umaku naru ka na?*

   I wonder if I can improve my golf if I get a few tips from the department chief?

2. *Kimi nanka wa majime na kare no tsume no aka o senjite nonda hō ga ii desu ne.*

   Why don't you be like him and start taking things more seriously?

3. *Anata o utagau kimochi wa, tsume no aka hodo mo arimasen.*

   I don't doubt you at all.

tsumuji-magari

つむじ曲がり

awkward, difficult, moody

TOMODACHI 1:

Kimura-san mo pātii ni sasoimashō ka?

TOMODACHI 2:

Kare wa tsumuji-magari dakara, sasowanai hō ga ii desu yo.

FRIEND 1:

Shall we invite Mr. Kimura to the party as well?

FRIEND 2:

I don't think it's a good idea—he's really difficult to get along with.

Tsumuji-magari refers to people who are deliberately awkward, difficult to get along with, or prone to bad moods. *Tsumuji* is the hair whorl and *magaru* refers to it being off-center. *Tsumuji ga magaru* is used to describe a permanent characteristic of someone's personality, whereas in contrast, *tsumuji o mageru* describes a temporary state.

EXAMPLES

1. *Ano hito ga anna ni tsumuji-magari da to wa omoimasen deshita.*
   I didn't realize she could be so awkward.

2. *Ato de tsumuji o magenaide kudasai ne.*
   Just don't make a fuss about it later, ok?

3. *Kare ni tsumuji o magerareru to, minna ga komatte shimau.*
   Nobody likes it when he gets moody.

4. *Kanojo wa anata ga kangaeru hodo tsumuji-magari de wa arimasen.*
   She's not as difficult to get along with as you think.

5. *Sonna koto de watashi wa tsumuji o magetari shimasen.*
   I'm not going to get into a bad mood over something like that.

tsunbo-sajiki

つんぼ桟敷

keeping someone in the dark

TOMODACHI 1:

Jibun no kaisha no koto na noni, nanimo shirasarete inain' desu ka?

TOMODACHI 2:

E, dōmo tsunbo-sajiki ni sarete ita rashiin' desu.

FRIEND 1:

You mean they don't even let you know what's going on within your own company?

FRIEND 2:

Yes, I just get the feeling I'm being kept in the dark.

Tsunbo-sajiki refers to when a person who should be kept properly informed about a particular situation or state of affairs is instead told nothing about it. *Tsunbo* means deafness and *sajiki* are seats, such as in a theater or hall. *Tsunbo-sajiki* originates from the Edo period, when it was used to refer to the theater seats at the far back on the second floor, seats so far from the stage that it was difficult to hear what the actors or actresses were saying.

EXAMPLES

1. *Itsu made watashi o tsunbo-sajiki ni shite okun' desu ka?*
   How long are you going to keep me in the dark?

2. *Itsu made mo anata o tsunbo-sajiki ni shite oku tsumori wa arimasen.*
   I intend to tell you about it sooner or later.

3. *Dōmo watashi wa tsunbo-sajiki ni sarete ita yō desu.*
   Somehow it seems as if I wasn't properly informed about this.

4. *Kokumin o tsunbo-sajiki ni oita seiji wa, minshu-seiji to wa ienai.*
   A government that keeps its people in the dark cannot be called democratic.

tsuno o dasu

角を出す

be jealous, get angry

DŌRYŌ 1:

Konban, kaisha no kaeri ni ippai dō?

DŌRYŌ 2:

Warui kedo, osoku kaeru to kanai ga sugu tsuno o dasun' da.

COLLEAGUE 1:

How about a quick drink on the way home this evening?

COLLEAGUE 2:

Sorry, but if I'm late getting home, my wife immediately goes into a fit.

Tsuno o dasu indicates that a woman is jealous or angry. This expression originally referred to a woman's mask in the Noh theater, which depicted a witch with horns in a mad fit of jealousy. At marriage ceremonies the *tsuno-kakushi,* the bride's headpiece (literally "the horn-hider"), consists of a white cloth that is wound around the head to prevent the bride from revealing her horns when she becomes jealous (because of her philandering husband).

EXAMPLES

1. *Kanojo ga tsuno o dasu to kowai desu yo.*
   She's a fearsome sight when she's angry.
2. *Nyōbō ga tsuno o dasanai uchi ni hayaku kaerō.*
   I'm going to hurry home before my wife gets upset.
3. *Hanayome-ishō wa uchi-kake ni tsuno-kakushi ni shimasu.*
   In a bridal costume the headpiece is worn over the long outer garment.
4. *Kanojo wa tsuno nado dashita koto wa arimasen.*
   I've never known her to become jealous.

tsuru no hitokoe

鶴の一声

a voice of authority

KAISHAIN 1:

Kaisha no gappei no hanashi, dō narimashita ka?

KAISHAIN 2:

Shachō no tsuru no hitokoe de toriyame ni narimashita yo.

EMPLOYEE 1:

How did the talks about the merger work out?

EMPLOYEE 2:

The president disagreed with it so it had to be called off.

The *tsuru,* or crane, is traditionally a sign of good luck, and being said to live a thousand years, is seen also as a symbol of long life. In the same way that the crane's voice stands out clearly above the voices of other birds, *tsuru no hitokoe* describes the way in which just one word from a person of authority can override or resolve differences of opinion among large numbers of less powerful people.

EXAMPLES

1. *Kyōshitsu ga kare no tsuru no hitokoe de shizuka ni natta.*
   All he had to do was speak and the whole class fell quiet.
2. *Kare no koe wa masa ni tsuru no hitokoe datta.*
   What he said really decided the matter.
3. *Kanojo no tsuru no hitokoe ga hantaiha o osaeta no desu.*
   She spoke so strongly that the opposition couldn't argue with her.
4. *Anata no tsuru no hitokoe ga nakattara, kitto kimaranakatta deshō.*
   I don't think we'd have reached a decision if you hadn't stepped in.
5. *Kekkyoku, tsuru no hitokoe de kimatte shimatta no desu ne.*
   In the end it was decided by the person of highest rank, wasn't it?

u no me taka no me

鵜の目鷹の目

with one's eyes peeled, looking intensely for

YŪMEI KASHU:

Hito ni mirarenaide, kaijō o deru hōhō, arimasen ka?

HOAN KAKARI:

Kochira desu. Fan ga u no me taka no me de sagashite imasu kara, ki o tsukete.

FAMOUS SINGER:

Is there any way I can leave the hall without being seen?

GUARD:

You can go this way, but be careful. Fans are on the lookout for you.

U no me taka no me describes the look people have on their faces when they avidly search for something; literally it means "searching with the keen eyes of a cormorant or falcon." Cormorant fishing and falconry were once common hunting methods in old Japan, which partially explains why this expression has been in use since the Muromachi period (1333–1573).

EXAMPLES

1. *Minna ga anata o u no me taka no me de sagashite imasu yo.*
   Everyone's been looking for you like crazy.

2. *Watashi no ketten o u no me taka no me de sagasanaide kudasai.*
   Please stop trying to find my failings with such vigor.

3. *Keisatsu ga han'nin o u no me taka no me de sagashite iru.*
   The police are making a full search for the criminal.

4. *Anata o u no me taka no me de sagashita keredo, mitsukaranakatta.*
   I kept my eyes peeled for you, but couldn't see where you were.

5. *Dorobō wa hōseki o u no me taka no me de sagashi-mawatta.*
   The thief looked all over the place for the jewels.

uchi-awaseru

打ち合せる

to make arrangements, plan an activity ahead of time

SEIJIKA 1:

Asu no kokkai no tōben desu ga, ima kara uchi-awaseru hō ga yoi no de wa arimasen ka?

SEIJIKA 2:

Yatō ga donna shitsumon o shite kuru ka, wakarimasen kara ne.

POLITICIAN 1:

About the proceedings at the Diet tomorrow, don't you think we ought to make arrangements ahead of time?

POLITICIAN 2:

Yes, because we don't know what sort of questions the opposition parties might ask us.

In the past, *uchi-awaseru* described the correct coordination of wind and percussion instruments in the performance of imperial court music. It now means to discuss something in advance so as to avoid problems during the actual event. The nominal form *uchi-awase* is also often used.

EXAMPLES

1. *Kyō no kaigi wa uchi-awase dōri ni, o-negai shimasu.*

   I would like to conduct today's meeting along the lines of our previous discussion.

2. *Uchi-awase shinakatta node, kaigi ga nagabiita.*

   The meeting went on so long because we didn't plan it in advance.

3. *Shinpojiumu no uchi-awase ni wa, jikan o kaketa hō ga ii.*

   It's a good idea to take your time when preparing for a symposium.

4. *Kinō uchi-awaseta yō ni susumete ii desu ka?*

   Is it all right to proceed the way we planned yesterday?

uchi-benkei

内弁慶

strong and assertive at home but weak and timid outside

SHUFU 1:

Otaku no botchan, otonashii desu ne.

SHUFU 2:

Uchi-benkei nan' desu yo. Uchi de wa ibatte irun' desu yo.

HOUSEWIFE 1:

Your son's very well-behaved, isn't he?

HOUSEWIFE 2:

Only when we go out. He's terrible at home.

Uchi-benkei consists of *uchi* (inside, referring to the internal affairs of a family) and *benkei,* (from Benkei, the name of a monk). Because Benkei, who served under the samurai lord Minamoto Yoshitsune during the Kamakura period (1185–1336), was famous for his strength and bravery, *uchi-benkei* came to refer to a person who seems to be strong, like Benkei, when at home, but who is weak and timid outside the house.

EXAMPLES

1. *Kare wa totemo uchi-benkei da.*

   He gets really quiet when he goes out.

2. *Uchi-benkei na kodomo na node shinpai desu.*

   My child is so timid outside the house, I'm worried about him.

3. *Ano hito ga anna ni uchi-benkei da to wa omowanakatta.*

   I didn't think he was such a weakling outside the house.

4. *Dōshite anata wa sonna ni uchi-benkei na no?*

   Why are you so opinionated at home and yet so meek everywhere else?

5. *Minna wa boku no koto o uchi-benkei da to omotte iru.*

   Outside the house, everyone thinks I'm a bit of a weakling.

uchiwa no hanashi

内輪の話

a private matter, a family affair

MUSUME:

Okāsan, ima no hanashi hontō na no?

HAHAOYA:

Ii desu ka? Kore wa uchiwa no hanashi dakara, hoka no hito ni iun' ja arimasen yo.

DAUGHTER:

Is that a true story, mother?

MOTHER:

Now listen, it's a private family matter, so I don't want you telling anyone else about it.

Uchiwa refers to the members of a particular group, such as one's family, one's relatives, or one's close friends. *Uchi* stresses the distinction, common in Japanese society, between *uchi* (inside) and *soto* (outside). *Wa* means circle or ring, further stressing the idea of a division between the inside and outside. Thus *uchiwa no hanashi* refers to a matter that should not be discussed outside the particular group concerned.

EXAMPLES

1. *Futari no kekkon-shiki ni wa, uchiwa no hito dake yobimashō.*
   Let's just invite family and close friends to the wedding.
2. *Doko no ie ni mo tanin ni shiraretakunai uchiwa no hanashi ga aru.*
   Every family has certain things it doesn't want other people to know about.
3. *Dōshite uchiwa no hanashi ga soto ni moretan' deshō?*
   I wonder how such a private matter managed to get out into the open.
4. *Ano ie de wa uchiwa-genka ga taenai.*
   They're always fighting about one thing or another in that family.

uchōten ni naru

有頂天になる

be in seventh heaven, be carried away, be overjoyed

GAKA:

Yatto tenrankai ni nyūshō shimashita.

GAKA NO TOMODACHI:

Hontō ni omedetō. De mo, uchōten ni naranaide, mata yoi e o kaite kudasai.

ARTIST:

I've finally won a prize at an exhibition.

ARTIST'S FRIEND:

Congratulations. But, please, don't get too carried away and forget to keep making wonderful paintings.

According to Buddhism, the universe is divided into three worlds: the world of delusions and desires, the world free of desires but constrained by physical reality, and the world of pure spirituality that transcends all physical limitations. *Uchōten* refers to the happiness felt in the highest level of heaven within the world of physical reality. *U* means to have or exist and *chōten* means uppermost place.

EXAMPLES

1. *Kare wa seiseki ga ichiban ni natta to uchōten da.*

   He's in seventh heaven after getting the best grade in the class.

2. *Kare wa daigishi no senkyo ni tōsen shi, kitto uchōten ni natte iru.*

   He must feel on top of the world, having won the election for a Diet seat.

3. *Amari uchōten ni natte iru to, shippai shimasu yo.*

   If you allow yourself to get too excited, you'll end up failing.

4. *Kanojo wa suki na hito ni puropōzu sarete, uchōten desu.*

   She is beside herself with joy because the man she likes proposed to her.

udatsu ga agaranai

うだつが上がらない

cannot get ahead, have no hope of rising in the world

KAISHAIN 1:

Kimura, mada hira-shain datte?

KAISHAIN 2:

Nannen tatte mo udatsu no agaranai hito ne.

EMPLOYEE 1:

So Mr. Kimura still hasn't been promoted then?

EMPLOYEE 2:

He never seems to get anywhere in the world, does he?

Udatsu ga agaranai means to never get ahead in life. An *udatsu* is a vital beam in a traditional Japanese house, without which it is impossible to raise the complete framework of the building. This phrase can mean that one is unable to achieve the position, status, or lifestyle that one desires, or that, like the *udatsu* in the house, one is prevented from moving freely by pressure from above.

EXAMPLES

1. *Uchi no shujin, hataraite mo hataraite mo udatsu ga agaranakute . . .*
   I don't know. No matter how hard my husband works, he never gets promoted.
2. *Nōryoku ga atte mo udatsu no agaranai hito mo imasu yo.*
   Even perfectly capable people find it difficult to get ahead in life sometimes.
3. *Dōshite kimi wa sō nannen tatte mo udatsu ga agaranain' darō ne?*
   I wonder why you never seem to be getting anywhere in life?
4. *Kare wa itsu made tatte mo udatsu ga agaranai.*
   He's never going to get ahead in the world.

ukeuri

受け売り

borrowing someone else's ideas

GAKUSEI 1:

Kimura-kun no iken, subarashii desu ne.

GAKUSEI 2:

Jitsu wa kore, sensei no iken no ukeuri nan' desu yo.

STUDENT 1:

Kimura, that's a brilliant idea.

STUDENT 2:

To tell the truth, it's not actually my idea—I borrowed it from the teacher.

Literally, *ukeuri* refers to the process whereby a consignment of merchandise is received from a manufacturer and sold at retail. Used as an idiom, it describes the way in which someone puts forward another person's opinions or theories as if they were his own. By adding *suru* to *ukeuri,* this expression can be used as a transitive verb.

EXAMPLES

1. *Kare no iu-koto wa itsumo dareka no ukeuri desu ne.*
   He's always copying what other people say.
2. *Sore wa hito no iken no ukeuri de wa arimasen ka?*
   Are you sure you haven't borrowed that idea from someone else?
3. *Boku no iken o ukeuri sarete mo komaru nā.*
   I don't like people stealing my ideas.
4. *Shitsurei desu ga, sore, shinbun no shasetsu no ukeuri desu ne.*
   I hope you don't mind my saying this, but what you've just said is straight from the editorial column in the newspaper, isn't it?

ukiashi-datsu

浮き足立つ

waver or panic, be ready to run away

JŪMIN 1:

Ame de kawa no mizu-kasa ga mashite imasu ne.

JŪMIN 2:

Kawa ga hanran suru no de wa nai ka to, mina ukiashi-datte imasu yo.

RESIDENT 1:

The river certainly is rising with this rain, isn't it?

RESIDENT 2:

People are ready to run because they think the river is going to overflow.

In the stock market, when values begin to fluctuate rapidly and nobody knows whether the market will go high or low, prices are described as *ukiashi-datsu,* literally "stand on wavering legs." From this came the meaning of panic.

EXAMPLES

1. *Sensō ga shinpai de, hitobito wa ukiashi-datte iru.*
   The people are panicking with fears about the war.
2. *Fune ga shizumu kamo shirenai to, jōkyaku wa ukiashi-datta.*
   The passengers panicked, fearing that the ship might sink.
3. *Senchō wa ukiashi-datsu jōkyaku ni itta.*
   The captain spoke to the panicking passengers.
4. *Minasan, fune wa anzen desu. Ukiashi-datsu koto wa arimasen.*
   Everyone, the ship is safe. There is no reason to panic.
5. *Ukiashi-datte iru shain o ochi-tsukaseru no wa muzukashii.*
   It's not easy to calm panicky employees.

uma no mimi ni nenbutsu

馬の耳に念仏

in one ear and out the other

BUCHŌ:

Kimura-kun ni chūkoku shite kureta ka ne.

KACHŌ:

Ē shimashita ga, ikura itte mo uma no mimi ni nenbutsu nan' desu yo.

DEPARTMENT CHIEF:

Did you have a word with Mr. Kimura?

SECTION CHIEF:

Yes, I did, but with him it's just in one ear and out the other.

Uma no mimi ni nenbutsu describes a situation in which someone pays no attention to the advice, opinion, or warning of other people. Literally, this phrase means "a Buddhist prayer *(nenbutsu)* in a horse's ear *(uma no mimi ni)*." However much you make a horse listen to a Buddhist prayer, it will never understand the meaning of what you are saying.

EXAMPLES

1. *Kare ni wa nani o itte mo uma no mimi ni nenbutsu da.*

   It doesn't matter what you say to him, it's just in one ear and out the other.

2. *Uma no mimi ni nenbutsu to wa omotte mo, tsui iitaku naru.*

   I know he never listens to a word you say, but I can't help wanting to say something to him anyway.

3. *Kanojo ni wa uma no mimi ni nenbutsu dakara, yameta hō ga ii desu yo.*

   I shouldn't bother mentioning it to her—it'll just go in one ear and out the other.

4. *Kare e no chūkoku ga uma no mimi ni nenbutsu datta to wa omoenai.*

   I can't believe he didn't take any notice of the warning I gave him.

umi sen yama sen

海千山千

a sly old fox, someone who knows every trick in the book

DŌRYŌ 1:
Kondo no torihiki aite no koto, dō omoimasu ka?
DŌRYŌ 2:
Umi sen yama sen to iu kanji desu. Ki o tsuketa hō ga yosasō desu yo.

COLLEAGUE 1:
What do you think of that guy I'm supposed to do business with?
COLLEAGUE 2:
He looks to me like an old pro. You'd best be careful.

There is a tale of how a clever snake who lived for a thousand years in the sea and a thousand years more in the mountains turned into a dragon. *Umi sen yama sen* comes from this tale, literally meaning "a thousand seas and mountains," and refers to a person who has been around a long time and has consequently become very cunning.

EXAMPLES

1. *Kare wa umi sen yama sen no seijika da.*
   That man is a politician who knows every trick in the book.
2. *Umi sen yama sen no kare ni totte, anata o damasu no wa kantan yo.*
   It's not difficult for an old fox like him to trick you.
3. *Dōshite mo, kare ga umi sen yama sen no hito ni wa miemasen.*
   He really doesn't look like a clever old fox to me.
4. *Umi sen yama sen no sagishi datta kare ga tsui ni tsukamatta.*
   In the end, they caught the sly old crook.
5. *Nihon no sōridaijin wa, umi sen yama sen de nakereba tsutomaranai.*
   A Japanese prime minister who isn't cunning and experienced is not capable of getting the job done.

unagi-nobori

うなぎ昇り

rising rapidly and steadily

SARARIIMAN 1:

Saikin bukka ga unagi-nobori ni agatte ikimasu ne.

SARARIIMAN 2:

O-kage de ikura hataraite mo oi-tsukimasen yo.

BUSINESSMAN 1:

Prices have been skyrocketing recently, haven't they?

BUSINESSMAN 2:

Yes, with the way things are, no matter how hard I work I can't keep up.

Unagi-nobori describes a situation in which the value of something rises rapidly and steadily. This can also apply to prices, the temperature, or a person's rate of promotion. Two theories exist as to the origin of this expression: the first claims that it relates to the way eels *(unagi)* swim upstream *(sakanoboru)* even in shallow water; the second argues that it is based on the way they slip upward and out of your hands if you try to grasp them.

EXAMPLES

1. *Rokugatsu da to iu noni kion ga unagi-nobori ni agatte imasu.*
   Considering it's only June, the temperature's rising very sharply.
2. *Bukka ga kono mama unagi-nobori ni agaru no deshō ka.*
   I wonder if prices are going to keep on going up like this.
3. *Kare no shusse wa unagi-nobori desu ne.*
   He's really shooting up through the ranks, isn't he?
4. *Kuruma ni yoru jikoshi ga unagi-nobori ni fuete iru.*
   The number of people being killed in car-related accidents is increasing all the time.

undei no sa

雲泥の差

a big difference

TOMODACHI 1:

Kinō no shiai, yahari Nihon ga makemashita ne.

TOMODACHI 2:

Aite no chiimu no jitsu-ryoku to wa, undei no sa ga arimashita kara ne.

FRIEND 1:

I see Japan lost the game yesterday—just like we expected, eh?

FRIEND 2:

Yes. Well, the other team was so much stronger, wasn't it?

Undei no sa is made up of *un* (cloud), *dei* (mud), and *sa* (difference) and refers to two things as different as heaven and earth. A similar expression is *tsuki to suppon,* which uses the contrasting images of *tsuki* (moon) and *suppon* (turtle).

EXAMPLES

1. *Tōkyō to Bankoku de wa seikatsu-hi ni undei no sa ga aru.*
   There's no comparison between the cost of living in Tokyo and the cost of living in Bangkok.
2. *Kare to watashi no kyūryō de wa undei no sa da.*
   There's a considerable difference between his salary and mine.
3. *Watashi-tachi no tenisu no jitsu-ryoku ni wa undei no sa ga arimasu.*
   You're much better at tennis than I.
4. *Kare to watashi de wa Eigo-ryoku ni undei no sa ga aru.*
   There's no comparing his English and mine.
5. *Anzen to iu ten de wa, Tōkyō to Nyūyōku wa undei no sa da.*
   In terms of safety, Tokyo and New York are worlds apart.

u-nomi ni suru

鵜呑みにする

believe anything

TOMODACHI 1:

Kabu ga bōraku suru sō da yo.

TOMODACHI 2:

Kimi'tte, hito no uwasa o sugu u-nomi ni surun' da ne.

FRIEND 1:

I hear the stock market is in for a sharp decline.

FRIEND 2:

You believe everything you hear, don't you?

U-nomi, combining *u* (comorant) and *nomi* (swallow), means to believe everything one hears without question or thought. Cormorants are used for catching *ayu* (sweetfish) in rivers. They either guide the fish into nets or swallow them whole; thus the meaning of this expression. After it swallows the fish, the cormorant is forced to regurgitate it, which is usually still alive.

EXAMPLES

1. *Kare no hanashi o u-nomi ni shite wa ikemasen.*
   Don't believe everything he tells you.
2. *Boku no iken o u-nomi ni shinaide, jibun de mo kangaenasai.*
   Don't agree with everything I say. Think for yourself sometimes.
3. *Sērusuman no kotoba o sukkari u-nomi ni shite shimatta.*
   I was taken in by a salesman.
4. *Sensei no hanashi o u-nomi ni suru hitsuyō wa nai.*
   There's no reason to believe everything the teacher says.
5. *Jōdan desu yo. Boku no hanashi o u-nomi ni shinaide kudasai.*
   I'm just kidding. Don't take everything I say seriously.

urame ni deru

裏目に出る

turn out badly, backfire

TSUMA:

Jiko kashira? Sugoi jūtai ne.

OTTO:

Kōsoku-dōro de kita noni, urame ni deta ne. Kore de wa pātii ni okurete shimau.

WIFE:

I wonder if there's been an accident. Look at this traffic jam!

HUSBAND:

It wasn't such a good idea to take the expressway after all, was it? Now we're going to be late for the party.

Urame refers to the face of a die on the opposite side to that of the upward-facing side. It is used, for example, when you hope to roll a six, and instead a one comes up—the direct opposite of what you wanted. *Me* refers to the dots on the die; *ii me ga deta* means that things worked out as you hoped or expected.

EXAMPLES

1. *Kanojo o shōkai shita no ga urame ni deta.*
   It wasn't such a good idea to introduce her to him after all.
2. *Yasashii aite da to omotte, yudan shita no ga urame ni demashita ne.*
   We underestimated how difficult it would be to beat them, didn't we?
3. *Gakusei ni kitai shi-sugiru to urame ni demasu yo.*
   If you expect too much of your students you'll only be disappointed.
4. *Shinsetsu ni shite ageta no ga urame ni deru to wa!*
   So this is all the thanks I get for my kindness!
5. *Urame ni deta to itte, gakkari shinaide kudasai.*
   Don't be disappointed if things don't work out as you expected.

289

uri futatsu

瓜二つ

like two peas in a pod

CHICHIOYA:
Kore ga chōnan no Ichirō desu.
CHICHIOYA NO TOMODACHI:
Otōsan ni uri futatsu desu ne.

FATHER:
This is Ichirō, my eldest boy.
FATHER'S FRIEND:
He looks just like you, doesn't he?

Uri refers to the gourd family, which includes cucumbers, melons, and gourds. When any of these are cut in half lengthwise, two identical parts are produced; hence the expression *uri futatsu,* which is used to describe any two people who look very similar to one another. It is similar to the English expression "like two peas in a pod."

EXAMPLES

1. *Kare wa chichioya ni uri futatsu da.*
   He looks just like his father.
2. *Anata ga onēsan ni uri futatsu de bikkuri shimashita.*
   I was really surprised to see how much you look like your sister.
3. *Yoku hito kara hahaoya ni uri futatsu to iwaremasu.*
   I'm often told that I look just like my mother.
4. *Anna ni uri futatsu no shimai wa mita koto ga nai.*
   I've never seen two sisters who look so much alike.
5. *Ano futari wa shinjirarenai hodo uri futatsu desu ne.*
   I can't believe how alike those two are.

usa-barashi

憂さ晴らし

something to cheer one up, a diversion, a break

TSUMA:

Anata, mata pachinko desu ka?

OTTO:

Shigoto ga taihen de ne. Usa-barashi ga hitsuyō nan' da yo.

WIFE:

You're not going out to play pachinko again, are you?

HUSBAND:

Work is such a grind; I have to have a break sometime.

Usa-barashi combines *usa* (gloom, melancholy) and *barashi* (from *harasu,* to clear away). Thus *usa-barashi* is used to describe something that you do in order to clear your mind, to cheer yourself up, or to relieve tedium. By adding *suru,* it can also be used as a verb.

EXAMPLES

1. *Raigetsu usa-barashi ni tabi ni deyō to omotte iru.*
   We're thinking of going away somewhere next month for a break.
2. *Taikutsu desu ne. Nanika usa-barashi ga hoshii desu ne.*
   This is boring, isn't it? I wish there was something to do for a change.
3. *Kare wa kuruma o unten suru koto de usa-barashi shite iru.*
   When he gets fed up he goes out for a drive to cheer himself up.
4. *Sonna koto ga usa-barashi ni narimasu ka?*
   Does that help to cheer him up?
5. *Gorufu o shita gurai de wa, usa-barashi ni narimasen.*
   A simple game of golf isn't going to make me feel any better.

usan-kusai

うさん臭い

fishy, suspicious-looking

GĀDOMAN:

Mise no mae, usan-kusai otoko ga urouro shite imasu ga.

TENSHU:

Chūi shite yoku mite oite kudasai.

SECURITY GUARD:

There's a suspicious-looking man hanging around in front of the store.

STORE OWNER:

Well, be careful and keep an eye on him for me please.

Usan-kusai describes either a feeling of suspicion one has about somebody else, or a person who seems to be thinking something suspicious. *Usan* itself means suspicious and *kusai* in this case adds the idea that this is the way something appears. Similar examples are *interi-kusai* (looking highbrow) and *byōnin-kusai* (looking like a sick person).

EXAMPLES

1. *Watashi wa kare no koto o hajime kara usan-kusai otoko da to omotta.*
   I thought he looked a bit shady right from the start.

2. *Kare ga sukoshi de mo usan-kusakattara, ie ni yobanai hō ga ii.*
   If you think he looks even a little bit suspicious, you'd better not invite him to your house.

3. *Ano ie ni wa, itsumo usan-kusai hito-tachi ga deiri shite iru.*
   There are always suspicious-looking people going in and out of that house.

4. *Hanashi-kakeru to, kare wa usan-kusasō na kao-tsuki de watashi o mita.*
   He gave me a very dubious look when I started talking to him.

uso mo hōben

うそも方便

a lie is sometimes expedient

TOMODACHI 1:

Konya, kimi no ie ni tomaru'tte, tsuma ni itte aru kara.

TOMODACHI 2:

Wakarimashita. Uso mo hōben desu ne.

FRIEND 1:

I've told my wife that I will be staying at your place tonight.

FRIEND 2:

I see. A lie is sometimes expedient!

Originally *Uso mo hōben* was used in Buddhism to explain that various means are employed in order to elucidate the truth. From this, the meaning has become more general, indicating that even though lying may be wrong, there are occasions when it is necessary to lie so that one's purpose may be accomplished. *Uso kara deta makoto* describes when what was said as a lie becomes true.

EXAMPLES

1. *Ryōshin o anshin saseru tame ni wa, uso mo hōben desu yo.*

   Sometimes it's necessary to tell a white lie to reassure my parents.

2. *Kodomo ni chichi wa mada ikite iru to shinjisaseta. Uso mo hōben desu kara.*

   Because a lie is sometimes expedient, I had the children believe that their father was still alive.

3. *Uso mo hōben. Kodomo o shinpai sasenai hō ga ii.*

   Sometimes it's better to lie, so as not to make the children worry.

4. *Uso kara deta makoto, kimi ni koibito to shōkai shita kanojo wa, boku no tsuma ni natta.*

   As a lie sometimes turns into a truth—you, the girl whom I had conveniently introduced as my girlfriend, became my wife.

utsutsu o nukasu

うつつを抜かす

be engrossed in, be addicted to

BUCHŌ:

Kimi, konogoro, keiba ni utsutsu o nukashite iru sō da ne.

BUKA:

Sonna koto, dare ga iimashita ka? Keiba ni wa ichido shika itta koto ga arimasen kedo.

DEPARTMENT CHIEF:

I hear you're addicted to horse racing these days.

SUBORDINATE:

Who told you that? I've only been to the horse races once.

Utsutsu o nukasu means to be engrossed in something and frequently has a negative connotation. *Utsutsu* derives from the expression *yume ka utsutsu ka* (dream or reality) and has come to describe a situation in which a person does not know whether something is real or imaginary.

EXAMPLES

1. *Itsu kara, kimi wa gyanburu ni utsutsu o nukasu yō ni natta no?*
   When did you become addicted to gambling?
2. *Kare wa konogoro, hisho no josei ni utsutsu o nukashite iru.*
   Lately he's been infatuated with a secretary.
3. *Pachinko ni utsutsu o nukashi-sugite, okane ga naku natta.*
   I went completely overboard playing pachinko and spent all my money.
4. *Uchi no musuko wa, kurabu ni utsutsu o nukashite benkyō shinai.*
   Our son is completely engrossed in after-school activities and doesn't study.
5. *Dōshite, sonna koto ni utsutsu o nukashite bakari iru no?*
   Why did you become so totally engrossed in something like that?

uyamuya ni suru

うやむやにする

be wishy-washy, hedge or obscure the issue

RŌSO-GAWA:

Yūkyū-kyūka no hanashi, dō natta no desu ka?

KAISHA-GAWA:

Uyamuya ni suru tsumori wa arimasen. Yakusoku shimasu.

UNION REPRESENTATIVE:

What happened to the topic of paid holidays?

COMPANY REPRESENTATIVE:

I promise that I have no intention of avoiding the issue.

The two characters that mean to exist and not exist can be read *u* and *mu*; *ya* is an interjection expressing doubt. Used with *suru, uyamuya* expresses a lack of commitment or conclusion. The passive form is *uyamuya ni sareru,* which means to be made obscure. Another form is *uyamuya ni naru,* meaning to become obscure.

EXAMPLES

1. *Anata-gata wa, kono jiken o uyamuya ni suru tsumori desu ka?*
   Do you intend to obscure the issue?
2. *Sensō no sekinin wa uyamuya ni subeki de wa nai.*
   Responsibility for the war is not the kind of issue we can hedge on.
3. *Ano mondai, itsu no ma ni ka uyamuya ni natte shimaimashita ne.*
   The topic ended up becoming obscured somehow, didn't it?
4. *Watakushi wa mondai o uyamuya ni wa shitaku arimasen.*
   I don't want to be wishy-washy on this issue.
5. *Kaji no gen'in wa wakaranai mama, uyamuya ni natte shimatta.*
   No definite conclusion as to the cause of the fire was ever discovered.

warikan ni suru

割り勘にする

split the bill, go Dutch

KURABU NO MENBĀ:

Kyō no shokuji, kōchi no ogori desu ka?

KŌCHI:

Ainiku futokoro ga sabishii kara, warikan ni shite yo.

CLUB MEMBER:

Are you going to treat us to dinner today?

COACH:

I don't have much money on me right now, so let's split the bill.

Warikan ni suru means either to split the total cost of something by dividing it among the number of people who are paying, or to pay for your own part of a bill. This expression is an abbreviated form of *warimae-kanjō*. *Warimae* means one's share and *kanjō* means calculation or bill in a restaurant. *Warikan* can also be used on its own.

EXAMPLES

1. *Takushii-dai, san'nin de warikan ni shimashō.*
   Let's split the taxi fare between the three of us.
2. *Kare to wa itsumo warikan de, ogotte moratta koto wa nai.*
   Whenever I go out with him, we always go halves on everything; he's never once treated me to anything.
3. *Konban no shokuji-dai, warikan ni shimasen ka?*
   Shall we split the bill for this evening's meal?
4. *Kekkon-iwai, minna de warikan de kaimasen ka?*
   Why don't we buy a wedding present collectively?
5. *Warikan de katta jisho na noni, itsumo kare ga tsukatte iru.*
   Even though we shared the cost of the dictionary, he's always using it himself.

yabu-hebi

薮蛇

put one's foot in one's mouth

TOMODACHI 1:

Uchi no kurabu ni mo manējā ga ita hō ga ii desu ne.

TOMODACHI 2:

Sore nara, anata ga tekiyaku desu yo.

TOMODACHI 1:

Jibun de ii-dashite, yabu-hebi ni natta yō desu ne.

FRIEND 1:

We probably need a manager for our club.

FRIEND 2:

In that case, you're just the person. Please, be the manager.

FRIEND 1:

I had to go and speak up. It looks like I've put my foot in my mouth.

Yabu-hebi comes from *yabu o tsutsuite hebi o dasu,* (literally, "to prod a thicket so that a snake comes out") and refers to making unnecessary trouble for oneself. A similar English expression is "don't stir up a hornet's nest." Another expression with *yabu* is *yabu-isha,* which means a quack doctor.

EXAMPLES

1. *Heta na koto o iu to, yabu-hebi ni naru.*

   If you say something odd, you may stir up a hornet's nest.

2. *Kare ni gakkō no seiseki ga sagatte kita koto o chūkoku shitara, uramarete shimai, yabu-hebi datta.*

   When I warned him that his grades were going down, I put my foot in my mouth and he got angry.

3. *Yabu-hebi ni naranai yō ni, ki o tsukeyō.*

   Be careful that you don't put your foot in your mouth.

yaji o tobasu

野次を飛ばす

heckle

TOMODACHI 1:

Kinō no kokkai-chūkei, mimashita ka?

TOMODACHI 2:

Ē, giin ga daibu yaji o tobashite imashita ne.

FRIEND 1:

Did you watch the live broadcast of the Diet session yesterday?

FRIEND 2:

Yes, the Diet members were doing quite a lot of heckling, weren't they?

Yaji o tobasu is made up of *yaji* (cat-calling) and *tobasu* (let fly with/ send out), and means to loudly denounce, jeer, and interrupt another person's speech and action. There are two theories as to the derivation of this expression: one says that *yaji* is a contraction of *oyaji* (one's father), the other says that *yaji* derives from *yancha* (mischievous youngster).

EXAMPLES

1. *Kinō no supiichi de, yaji o tobashita no wa anata desu ka?*
   Are you the person who booed and hissed during my speech yesterday?
2. *Watashi wa yaji nado tobashita koto wa arimasen.*
   I've never given a catcall or anything of the like.
3. *Soko de yaji o tobashite inaide, jibun no iken o iinasai.*
   Instead of just heckling, you should express your opinion.
4. *Hajimete sutēji de karaoke o utattara, yaji o tobasarete agatte shimatta.*
   When I first did karaoke on a stage, I was greeted with hoots and jeers and lost my composure.

yajiuma

野次馬

curiosity seekers, spectators

GARUFURENDO:

A, shōbōsha no sairen yo.

BŌIFURENDO:

Kitto kaji darō. Mi ni ikō.

GARUFURENDO:

Honto anata'tte, yajiuma yo nē.

GIRLFRIEND:

Hey, I hear a fire engine siren.

BOYFRIEND:

Must be a fire. Let's go see.

GIRLFRIEND:

You're just a curiosity seeker!

Yajiuma describes people who are interested in things that do not really concern them, or people who gather to watch the misfortune of others. *Yajiuma* derives from *oyaji uma,* an old horse that follows the younger horses. Hence this phrase suggests something of little use; i.e., one who merely makes a fuss.

EXAMPLES

1. *Kaji ni wa yajiuma ga takusan atsumarimasu.*

   Many spectators gather when there is a fire.

2. *Yajiuma ga shōka no jama ni naru koto mo aru.*

   Curious bystanders may be a hindrance in the extinguishing of a fire.

3. *Watashi wa tada no yajiuma ni sugimasen.*

   I'm just a bystander.

4. *Demo-tai o yajiuma ga tori-kakonde iru.*

   Curious onlookers are gathered around the demonstrators.

yake ni naru

自棄になる

become desperate

SEITO:

Yappari, juken dame deshita.

SENSEI:

Ochita kara to itte, yake ni natte wa ikenai yo.

STUDENT:

I flunked the examinations, just as I feared.

TEACHER:

Just because you've failed, there's no reason to despair.

Yake ni naru is a combination of *yake* (despair, desperation) plus *naru* (become) and is used in a situation where a person does something rash when things haven't turned out as desired. The phrase *yake o okosu* also has the same meaning.

EXAMPLES

1. *Kare wa yake ni natte o-sake bakari nonde iru.*

   He's so desperate, he's drinking constantly.

2. *Kare ga yake ni naru to kowai desu yo.*

   When he becomes desperate he's scary.

3. *Shitsuren shita kara to itte, yake o okoshite wa ikemasen yo.*

   You mustn't despair just because you're feeling broken-hearted.

4. *Buchō wa jibun no kaihatsu puran ga ikizumatta totan, yake o okoshite, buka o shikari-tsukete iru.*

   The department chief is stressed out because the plan he developed has become dead-locked.

yake-ishi ni mizu

焼け石に水

a mere drop in the bucket

TOMODACHI 1:

Tai wa suigai de ōki na songai o uketa yō desu yo.

TOMODACHI 2:

Kore gurai no enjo de wa yake-ishi ni mizu deshō ne.

FRIEND 1:

It seems there was a big flood in Thailand that caused lots of damage.

FRIEND 2:

To give such a small donation is probably just a drop in the bucket.

Yake-ishi ni mizu means that one's effort or support is not enough to provide significant help. Water (*mizu*) thrown on a hot rock (*yake-ishi*) evaporates immediately and won't help cool down the rock.

EXAMPLES

1. *Kazan no funka de ie mo shigoto mo nakushita hito-bito ni wa, tatta sore dake no hoshō de wa yake-ishi ni mizu da.*

   To pay out so little in reparations to the people who lost their homes and their jobs in the volcanic eruption is like throwing water on thirsty soil.

2. *Kami shigen no risaikuru gurai de wa yake-ishi ni mizu de mo, nanimo shinai yori mashi desu.*

   Recycling paper might be a mere drop in the bucket, but it's better than doing nothing.

3. *Saigo ni tokuten o shita ga, sude ni yake-ishi ni mizu datta.*

   Though they got points at the end, it fell far short of what was needed.

4. *Donna benkai o shite mo, yake-ishi ni mizu desu.*

   No matter what your excuse, it won't be enough.

yaki-mochi o yaku
焼きもちを焼く
envy, get jealous

GĀRUFURENDO:
Nē, kinō issho ni aruite ita hito, dare?
BŌIFURENDO:
Are wa imōto da yo. Kimi, sugu yaki-mochi o yakun' da ne.

GIRLFRIEND:
Who was that person you were walking with yesterday?
BOYFRIEND:
That was my little sister. You get jealous so easily, don't you?

Yaki-mochi o yaku, literally "to toast rice cakes," means to be jealous. One theory explaining the origin of this idiom is that it comes from when toasted *mochi* swell up like a pouting girl's face. *Yaki-mochi yaki* refers to a very jealous person.

EXAMPLES

1. *Kanojo wa yaki-mochi o yaku to, damari-komu.*
   Whenever she gets jealous, she gets very quiet.
2. *Kimi ni yaki-mochi o yakareru hodo, boku wa motenai yo.*
   I'm not popular enough for you to have any reason to be jealous.
3. *Amari kirei dakara, minna kara yaki-mochi o yakarerun' desu.*
   Everyone's jealous of you because you're so pretty.
4. *Kanojo wa yaki-mochi yaki dakara, ki o tsuketa hō ga ii.*
   You should be careful, she gets jealous very easily.
5. *Ningen wa shiawasesō na hito o miru to, yaki-mochi o yaite shimau.*
   One can't help feeling envious when one sees happy people.

yama ga ataru

やまが当たる

meet with success

SENSEI:

Nyūgaku shiken, dō datta?

GAKUSEI:

Dekita to omoimasu. Yama ga atarimashita kara.

TEACHER:

How was the entrance examination?

STUDENT:

I think I did well, because the questions I had prepared for came up.

Yama ga ataru, literally "to have success with the mountain," refers to using one's sixth sense to bring success and good fortune. This phrase was originally used when a large deposit was found in a mine. Related expressions include *yama ga hazureru,* which refers to a situation that ends in failure, *yama-kan,* which means to work in the hopes that a speculation will bring success, and *yama o kakeru* which means to take a chance by only studying what one thinks will be on a test.

EXAMPLES

1. *Shiken no yama o kakete mo, atatta koto ga nain' desu.*
   Even though I study what I think might be on the test, I've never had any luck.
2. *Keiba de ōki na yama ga atarimashita yo.*
   I hit the jackpot at the horse races.
3. *Yama wa atattari hazuretari suru mono desu.*
   Speculations sometimes bring success and sometimes failure.
4. *Kare no yama-kan, sugoku yoku atarun' desu.*
   His intuition often pays off well.

yaochō

八百長

a fixed game

TOMODACHI 1:

Yahari, kare ga yūshō shimashita ne.

TOMODACHI 2:

Kinō no sumō wa yaochō da'tte iu uwasa desu yo.

FRIEND 1:

He won the tournament just as I expected.

FRIEND 2:

There's a rumor that yesterday's sumo match was fixed.

Yaochō refers to a match where the outcome has been decided beforehand. At the beginning of the Meiji period, a person named *Yaoya no chōbe-e*, or *Yaochō* for short, was a good sumo wrestler and *go* player. He almost always won his matches. However sometimes he purposely lost his matches. When people found out about it, fixed sumo matches were labeled *yaochō*. *Yaochō-jiai* means a fixed game.

EXAMPLES

1. *Kyō no shiai wa, kitto yaochō desu yo.*
   I'm sure that today's match was fixed.
2. *Ano shiai wa, yaochō ja nai darō ka?*
   I wonder if that game was fixed.
3. *Kare wa, ichido yaochō o shite kara, shin'yō o ushinatte shimatta.*
   Ever since he fixed a match, he lost everyone's trust.
4. *Yaochō o sasenai yō ni, wareware wa yoku kanshi shiyō.*
   We'll have to keep a careful watch to be sure the game is not fixed.
5. *Yaochō-jiai da to mite ite sugu wakarimasu ne.*
   It's easy to tell if a game is fixed.

yoko-guruma o osu

横車を押す

have one's own way

KAISHAIN:

Kachō, torihikisaki ga, juppāsento no waribiki o yokyū shite kimashita.

KACHŌ:

Mata, yoko-guruma o oshite kita ka? Komatta mon da.

EMPLOYEE:

The clients have requested a ten percent price reduction, sir.

SECTION CHIEF:

So, they're being unreasonable again! What are we going to do?

Yoko-guruma o osu means to force through something that is irrational or illogical. *Kuruma* (carriage, car) refers to the rickshaws used in the Edo period. When loaded, the rickshaw could not move sideways (*yoko*), no matter how hard one tried. Trying to do something even though one fully realizes that it is unreasonable or impossible became the basis of *yoko-guruma o osu. Yoko-guruma* can also be used on its own.

EXAMPLES

1. *Dōmo shachō wa yoko-guruma o osu keikō ga aru.*

   I'm sure that the company president tends to force his ideas on people.

2. *Anata no yoko-guruma de, keikaku ga shippai shite shimatta.*

   The plan was ruined because of your willful behavior.

3. *Amari kuchi-dashi suru to, yoko-guruma o oshite iru to omowareru.*

   If you try to interfere too much, people will think that you are trying to force your ideas on them.

4. *Yoko-guruma o osu no mo, ii kagen ni shite kurenai ka?*

   Will you stop trying to steamroll your idea through?

yoko-yari o ireru

横やりを入れる

interfere

KAISHAIN 1:

Natsu-yasumi, Yamanaka-ko de tenisu gasshuku o keikaku shite imasu.

KAISHAIN 2:

Atsui toki ni tenisu nado, yameta hō ga ii yo.

KAISHAIN 3:

Kimi wa itsumo hito no hanashi ni yoko-yari o ireru ne.

EMPLOYEE 1:

We plan to have a tennis camp at Lake Yamanaka this summer.

EMPLOYEE 2:

Tennis? When it'll be so hot? You'd better think of something else.

EMPLOYE 3:

You're always sticking your nose into other people's business.

Yoko-yari o ireru means to interrupt a person by making a bothersome comment and originally referred to a situation on a battlefield where two warriors were fiercely fighting one another. If a third soldier attacked one of the warriors with his lance *(yari)* from the side *(yoko),* he would be interfering with their personal conflict. From this the phrase has come to mean to meddle or to interfere.

EXAMPLES

1. *Kare wa sugu hito no keikaku ni yoko-yari o iretagaru.*

   He seems so eager to interfere with other people's plans.

2. *Watashi no suru koto ni yoko-yari o irenaide kudasai.*

   Please don't interfere with what I'm doing.

3. *Taikoku no yoko-yari de kankyō hozen jōyaku ga seiritsu shinakatta.*

   Owing to the interference of powerful countries, the treaty on environmental conservation failed to materialize.

yonabe o suru

夜なべをする

work at night, do night work

TOMODACHI 1:

Ii tebukuro da ne.

TOMODACHI 2:

Okāsan ga yonabe o shite ande kuretan' da.

FRIEND 1:

Those are nice gloves.

FRIEND 2:

My mother stayed up all night knitting these for me.

Yonabe o suru means to continue working into the night. One theory claims that the phrase derived from *yoru no nabe,* which referred to cooking food at night so as to have something eat while working.

EXAMPLES

1. *Sakuya wa yonabe o shita node, nemukute shikata arimasen.*

   I am so tired from working late last night.

2. *Yonabe made shite, isshōkenmei suru hodo no isogi no shigoto de wa nakatta noni.*

   You didn't have to work on it all night. It's not that much of a rush job.

3. *Ā, kon'ya wa yonabe o suru koto ni narisō da.*

   Unfortunately, I may have to work all night.

4. *Yonabe shite made shite kudasattan' desu ka?*

   You mean you stayed up all night doing this for me?

5. *Wakai uchi wa yonabe nado nan de mo nakatta.*

   When I was young, I had no trouble working all night.

yudan-taiteki

油断大敵

carelessness is the greatest enemy

GAKUSEI 1:

Kyō, jugyō sabotte eiga ni ikanai ka?

GAKUSEI 2:

Yudan-taiteki, sō iu toki ni kagitte, tesuto ga aru no yo.

STUDENT 1:

How about skipping class today to see a movie?

STUDENT 2:

It's times like this that we have tests—just when we least expect them.

Yudan-taiteki refers to carelessness resulting in unexpected loss or injury. In the Buddhist scriptures, there is a story about a king who orders a retainer to hold a jar of oil. The retainer was warned that spilling even a drop of oil (*yu*) from the container would result in his head being cut (*dan*) off. *Taiteki* means large enemy, in this case, referring to carelessness.

EXAMPLES

1. *Hi no yōjin, yudan-taiteki, kaji no moto.*

   Be careful with fire. Carelessness is the cause of fires.

2. *Kinō, jūdō no shiai ga atte, yudan-taiteki, yowai aite ni makete shimatta.*

   In my judo match yesterday, I got careless and lost to a weak opponent.

3. *Kagi o kake-wasuretara, yudan-taiteki, dorobō ni hairareta.*

   I was robbed because I carelessly forgot to lock the door.

4. *Daietto-chū ni kēki nanka tabete, yudan-taiteki desu yo.*

   Eating cake while you are on a diet can be the beginning of the end.

zu ni noru

図に乗る

be puffed up, push one's luck

TOMODACHI 1:

Kare, daigishi ni tōsen shite, sukoshi ii ki ni natteru to omowanai?

TOMODACHI 2:

Hontō da. Zu ni notterun' da yo.

FRIEND 1:

Since he was elected a member of the Diet, don't you find that he seems a bit full of himself?

FRIEND 2:

You're right. It's really gone to his head.

Zu ni noru describes a person who is puffed up after things have gone much as expected. This expression has its origin in Buddhist chanting. *Zu* refers to the chart that indicates how the chanting goes. If the chanting progressed well, people would say *zu ni noru,* literally "things are proceeding well, according to the chart."

EXAMPLES

1. *Anata wa sukoshi zu ni nori-sugite iru no de wa arimasen ka?*

   Don't you think you're pushing your luck a little too far?

2. *Shiken ni gōkaku shita kara to itte, zu ni norun' ja nai yo.*

   Your passing the examination is no reason to get puffed up!

3. *Kare wa saikin rensen renshō de emu-bui-pii mo kakujitsu to iwarete iru mono dakara, zu ni notte iru.*

   Lately, because they had a string of wins and it has been said that the pitcher will be awarded the most valuable player award, things have gone to his head.

4. *Kodomo-tachi ga zu ni notte, iu koto o kikanai.*

   The children are stuck up and don't listen to what they're told.

zuboshi o sasu

図星を指す

hit the bull's eye, hit the nail on the head

DŌRYŌ:

Anata, kare no koto, suki nan' deshō? Hora, zuboshi o sasarete, akaku natta.

COLLEAGUE:

You like him, don't you? See, I was right—you're blushing.

Zuboshi o sasu expresses the idea that what someone has just said is exactly right, or that they have guessed exactly what someone was thinking. *Zuboshi* refers to the black mark in the center of an archery target, and *zuboshi o sasu* originally meant to hit the center mark with one's arrow. The passive form, *zuboshi o sasareru,* is often used.

EXAMPLES

1. *Koibito no koto, kare ni zuboshi o sasarete odoroita.*
   She was shocked when he guessed about her lover.
2. *Taishoku shitai to omotte itara, buchō ni zuboshi o sasarete shimatta.*
   My boss guessed that I was thinking of quitting my job.
3. *Kanojo ni zuboshi o sasarete, awatete shimatta.*
   I panicked when my girlfriend guessed what I was thinking.
4. *Anata wa sensei desu ka? Zuboshi deshō?*
   Are you a teacher? I guessed right, haven't I?
5. *Kare wa zuboshi o sasarete, totemo hazukashikatta.*
   He was really embarrassed when we guessed what he was thinking.

A LIST OF
ADDITIONAL
EXPRESSIONS

abekobe　　あべこべ

topsy-turvy, upside down

abuhachi torazu　　あぶはちとらず

chase two hares and catch neither

abunai hashi o wataru　　危ない橋を渡る

walk on thin ice

ageku no hate　　挙げ句の果て

making matters worse, as the final outcome

aita kuchi ga fusagaranai　　開いた口がふさがらない

be left dumbfounded, be flabbergasted

aka no tanin　　赤の他人

a complete stranger

aka nukeru　　垢抜ける

be urbane and sophisticated

aku ga tsuyoi　　アクが強い

come on too strong or too assertive

ama no jaku　　あまのじゃく

someone who always disagrees

anchū-mosaku　　暗中模索

groping in the dark, left without a clue

ara-sagashi　　あら捜し

faultfinding, nitpicking

arigata-meiwaku　　ありがた迷惑

unwelcome favor or deed, misplaced favor

arikitari　　ありきたり

commonplace, ordinary

ashi ga deru　　足が出る

run over the budget, be faced with a shortage

ashide matoi　　足手まとい

a wet blanket, burden, impediment

ashimoto o miru　　足元をみる

take advantage of someone's misfortune

atama ga sagaru　　頭が下がる

respect or admire someone

atama ni kuru　頭にくる
  blow one's top, get very angry

atama o hineru　頭をひねる
  be puzzled or perplexed

ate ni naranai　当てにならない
  undependable, unreliable

batsugun　抜群
  outstanding

binbō kuji o hiku　貧乏くじを引く
  draw a bad lot

boketsu o horu　墓穴を掘る
  dig one's own grave

boro-mōke suru　ぼろ儲けする
  make money hand over fist

buttsuke honban　ぶっつけ本番
  do something unprepared, without rehearsal

chakkari shita　ちゃっかりした
  shrewd, cunning, deceiving, calculating

chakushu suru　着手する
  start work on

chi mo namida mo nai　血も涙もない
  cold-blooded, stone-hearted

chi no meguri ga warui　血の巡りが悪い
  slow on the uptake, slow-witted

chiyahoya sareru　ちやほやされる
  be much waited upon, lionized

dada o koneru　駄々をこねる
  be unreasonable, ask for the impossible

daiji o toru　大事をとる
  play it safe, act cautiously

dainashi ni suru　台無しにする
  ruin, spoil, make a mess of

daitan futeki na　大胆不敵な
  audacious, fearless

dashi-nuku　出し抜く
  forestall, outwit, outmaneuver

deashi ga ii　出足がいい
  off to a good start

demakase o iu　出任せを言う
  talk at random, talk without thinking

detchi-ageru　でっちあげる
  make up a story, fabricate

do o kosu　度をこす
  go overboard, overstep one's bounds

dokidoki suru　ドキドキする
  be very nervous, have butterflies in one's stomach

doku ni mo kusuri ni mo naranai　毒にも薬にもならない
  good-for-nothing

dokyō ga aru　度胸がある
  bold, brave, courageous

donguri no sei-kurabe　どんぐりの背比べ
  having little to choose from

doro-kusai　泥臭い
  crude, unpolished

doro-nawa　泥縄
  locking the garage after the car has been stolen

dotchi tsukazu no　どっちつかずの
  ambiguous, noncommittal

do-wasure suru　度忘れする
  slip one's mind, forget for the moment

ebi de tai o tsuru　エビでタイをつる
  use small fry to catch a big fish

eko-hiiki suru　　えこひいきする
　　play favorites

eri o tadasu　　襟を正す
　　shape up, straighten oneself, sit up straight

fude ga tatsu　　筆が立つ
　　write well

fude-bushō　　筆無精
　　a poor letter writer, lazy correspondent

fude-mame　　筆まめ
　　copious writer

fukuro-dataki ni suru　　袋叩きにする
　　gang up and beat someone up

fumi-taosu　　踏み倒す
　　bilk on a bill or debt

furi-mawasu　　振り回す
　　throw one's weight around

furu sōgyō suru　　フル操業する
　　be in full operation

gekirin ni fureru　　逆鱗に触れる
　　incur someone's wrath, step on the toes of a powerful person

gen o sayū ni suru　　言を左右にする
　　try to avoid responsibility, be noncommittal

geta o hakaseru　　下駄をはかせる
　　sweeten someone's grade, jack up the test scores

girigiri　　ぎりぎり
　　with no room to spare, the very limit

go-hasan ni suru　　御破算にする
　　start with a clean slate

gyokuseki konkō　　玉石こんこう
　　mixture of wheat and chaff, mixture of good and bad

ha ga tatanai　　歯が立たない
　　be beyond someone's ability

ha ga uku　歯が浮く
feel resentment, displeasure

ha o kui-shibaru　歯をくいしばる
grit one's teeth

haba o kikaseru　幅をきかせる
reign supreme, exercise great influence

hachi no su o tsutsuita yō　蜂の巣をつついたよう
like a madhouse, stir up a honet's nest, be furious

hachi-awase suru　鉢合わせする
bump into each other, meet unexpectedly

ha-gishiri o suru　歯ぎしりをする
grind one's teeth, be mortified

hakuhyō o fumu　薄氷をふむ
walk on thin ice, face a dangerous situation

hakusha o kakeru　拍車をかける
spur on, place a premium upon

han de oshita yō na kotae　判で押したような答え
always having the same old reply

hana de ashirau　鼻であしらう
give a person a cold reception, treat with scorn

hana yori dango　花よりだんご
bread is better than the songs of birds

hanashi ga hazumu　話しがはずむ
have a lively discussion

hanashi no tane　話しの種
topic of conversation

hara-guroi　腹黒い
scheming, blackhearted

hari no mushiro　針のむしろ
bed of nails, harsh situation

hashi o tsukeru　箸をつける
touch one's food

hatake-chigai　畑違い
outside one's field

hatsumimi　初耳
　something heard for the first time

haya-tochiri suru　早とちりする
　jumping to a conclusion leading to a mistake

heso-magari　へそまがり
　someone who contradicts others just for contradiction's sake

hi ni abura o sosogu　火に油を注ぐ
　add fuel to the fire

hi no me o miru　日の目を見る
　see the light of day

hi no nai tokoro ni kemuri wa tatanai　火のないところに煙はたたない
　where there is smoke, there is fire.

hi no uchi-dokoro ga nai　非のうちどころがない
　no faults to criticize, perfect

hikeme o kanjiru　引け目を感じる
　feel inferior; feel small

hikkomi-jian　引っ込み思案
　shy and withdrawn, introverted, unenterprising

hitogoto　人ごと
　affairs of others

hito-hada nugu　一肌脱ぐ
　lend a helping hand

hito-mebore　一目惚れ
　love at first sight

hitori-jime ni suru　独り占めにする
　monopolize, have something all to oneself

hitori-yogari　独りよがり
　smugness, acting without consulting others

hito-tamari mo nai　一溜りもない
　without the least resistance, helplessly

hōgan-biiki　判官贔屓
　root for the underdog

honeorizon no kutabire mōke　骨折り損のくたびれ儲け
　waste of time, gain nothing for all one's efforts

318

hon'ne　　本音
　　one's real intention

hyakubun wa ikken ni shikazu　　百聞は一見にしかず
　　a picture is worth a thousand words

hyōshi-nuke suru　　拍子抜けする
　　have the wind taken out of one's sails, lose momentum

ichidan raku tsukeru　　一段落つける
　　settle a matter for the time being

ichimō-dajin　　一網打尽
　　arresting a group with one sweep

ichinan satte mata ichinan　　一難去ってまた一難
　　out of the frying pan and into the fire

ichinin-mae ni naru　　一人前になる
　　become an adult, become independent, come of age

ichiren takushō　　一蓮托生
　　be in the same boat

ichiya-zuke　　一夜漬け
　　cramming for an exam

ido-bata kaigi　　井戸端会議
　　housewives' gossip

ihyō o tsuku　　意表をつく
　　catch someone off balance, catch someone by surprise

iki o hiki-toru　　息をひきとる
　　breathe one's last breath, die

ikiatari-battari no　　行きあたりばったりの
　　haphazard, happy-go-lucky

iki-jibiki　　生き字引
　　a walking encyclopedia

ikki-ichiyū suru　　一喜一憂する
　　swing from joy to sorrow

ikkoku ichijō no aruji　　一国一城のあるじ
　　head of a family

inochi-biroi suru　命拾いする
  narrowly escape from death

ippiki ōkami　一匹狼
  a lone wolf

ire-jie suru　入れ知恵する
  plant an idea in someone's head

ishi-bashi o tataite wataru　石橋をたたいて渡る
  look before leaping, act with utmost caution

ishin denshin　以心伝心
  telepathy

isogaba-maware　急がば回れ
  haste makes waste

isshin dōtai　一心同体
  one in body and spirit

isshō ni fusu　一笑に付す
  laugh off a problem

issoku-tobi ni　一足飛びに
  in a single bound

ita-basami　板挟み
  dilemma

itchō isseki ni　一朝一夕に
  in a single day, in a brief time period

itten-bari　一点張り
  stubborn insistence, persistence

jidai-okure　時代遅れ
  out of date

jitensha sōgyō　自転車操業
  being on the point of bankruptcy

jo no kuchi　序の口
  the beginning, first stage

jōtō shudan　常套手段
  old ploy, trick

jūbako no sumi o hojikuru　　重箱の隅をほじくる
　split hairs

kabu ga agaru　　株が上がる
　have one's reputation improve

kado ga tatsu　　角が立つ
　create bitter feelings

kaeru no ko wa kaeru　　カエルの子はカエル
　like father like son

kage ga usui　　影がうすい
　look pale and unhealthy

kai-kaburu　　買いかぶる
　give someone too much credit, overestimate

kai-shimeru　　買い占める
　corner the market, buy up all the goods

kakehiki　　駆け引き
　shrewd bargaining

kao o tsunagu　　顔をつなぐ
　network, keep up one's connections

kao o tateru　　顔をたてる
　show deference to

kao-iro o ukagau　　顔色をうかがう
　be sensitive to someone's mood

kara ni tojikomoru　　殻にとじこもる
　build a wall around oneself, retire into one's shell

kasa ni kiru　　笠にきる
　hide behind one's authority

kata ga koru　　肩がこる
　feel strained, feel pressured

kata o motsu　　肩を持つ
　take sides, support, give assistance, stand up for

kata o naraberu　　肩を並べる
　be on par with, compare with

kata o tsukeru　片をつける

  settle a question, bring one's work to a close

kata-bō o katsugu　片棒をかつぐ

  be a partner, take part in

kata-kurushii　堅苦しい

  stiff, formal, stand on ceremony

kata-narashi　肩ならし

  warming up, light training, limbering up

katazu o nomu　固唾を飲む

  hold one's breath, be intensely anxious

kaze-atari ga tsuyoi　風当たりが強い

  come under severe criticism or pressure

kechi o tsukeru　けちをつける

  find fault with, throw cold water on

kejime o tsukeru　けじめをつける

  draw a line, discriminate

ken-en no naka　犬猿の仲

  fighting like cats and dogs

kenkagoshi　喧嘩腰

  chip on one's shoulder, defiant or aggressive attitude

kessō o kaeru　血相を変える

  turn red with anger

ki ga hikeru　気がひける

  feel reserved, hesitate

ki ga ki de nai　気が気でない

  uneasy, anxious and concerned about something

ki ga kiku　気がきく

  considerate

kijō no kūron　机上の空論

  armchair theory

kiki-ippatsu de　危機一髪で

  by the skin of one's teeth, in the nick of time

kimo o hiyasu　肝を冷やす

  be scared to death, be frightened

kirikiri-mai suru   キリキリ舞いする

hustle about due to work pressures

kogun-funtō suru   孤軍奮闘する

fight without support from others

koharu-biyori   小春日和

Indian summer

kōkaisaki ni tatazu   後悔先にたたず

too late to be sorry, no use crying over spilt milk

komimi ni hasamu   小耳にはさむ

happen to hear, hear word of

korigori   コリゴリ

learning by experience what not to do, having had enough of something

koroshi-monku   殺し文句

a telling phrase, a clincher

koshi ga omoi   腰が重い

slow to act, unwilling to work

kōshi-kondō suru   公私混同する

mix business with personal affairs

kōzen no himitsu   公然の秘密

an open secret

kubi ga mawaranai   首がまわらない

be up to one's neck in debt

kubi o hineru   首をひねる

have doubts, think about seriously

kubi o nagaku shite matsu   首を長くして待つ

anxiously await

kubi o tsukkomu   首をつっこむ

deeply involved in

kubittake   首ったけ

head over heels in love

kuchi ga karui   口が軽い

can't keep a secret, glib talker

kuchi-bashi o ireru   くちばしをいれる

put one's nose into other people's business, meddle in

kuchi-gotae suru　口答えする
　talk back, contradict

kuchi yakusoku　口約束
　verbal agreement, verbal promise

kugi-zuke ni naru　釘付けになる
　be riveted to

kui-chigau　食い違う
　hold contrary opinions

kyakkō o abiru　脚光を浴びる
　come into the limelight, be spotlighted

kyōzame　興ざめ
　spoil the fun, dampen enthusiasm

ma ga motanai　間が持たない
　have nothing to fill the time with

ma ga sasu　魔が差す
　be possessed by an uncontrollable urge, be tempted

ma ni ukeru　真に受ける
　take something at face value

magure-atari　まぐれ当たり
　a fluke, lucky hit

makezu-girai　負けず嫌い
　hate to lose, unbending

makka na uso　真っ赤な嘘
　a barefaced lie

maruku osameru　丸く収める
　work out smoothly, settle amiably

mata to nai kikai　又とない機会
　a golden opportunity

mato-hazure　的外れ
　missing the mark, completely off base

mayu o hisomeru　眉をひそめる
　frown

me ga mawaru　目がまわる
  be hectic, have one's head spin

me no hoyō　目の保養
  feast one's eyes on, be delighted by seeing something

me no kataki　目の敵
  regarding a person or thing with enmity, loathing the very sight of

me no kuroi uchi　目の黒いうち
  as long as one is alive

me o maruku suru　目を丸くする
  be astonished at, stare wide-eyed

me o tsumuru　目をつむる
  wink at

meboshi o tsukeru　目星をつける
  make an educated guess, single out something

medama shōhin　目玉商品
  shop item used to entice people to come in

medo ga tsuku　目処がつく
  see the light at the end of the tunnel

mehana o tsukeru　目鼻をつける
  materialize, take shape

menboku o hodokosu　面目を施す
  win honor, get credit for

mi no hodo o shiranai　身の程を知らない
  be conceited, not know one's place

mi o katameru　身を固める
  marry and settle down

mi o musubu　実を結ぶ
  produce a result, bear fruit

migi e narae suru　右へならえする
  follow suit

mikudarihan　三行半
  letter of divorce, rejecting someone

mimi ga itai　耳が痛い

be ashamed to hear something, have something embarrassing pointed out

mimi ni tako ga dekiru　耳にたこができる

get sick and tired of hearing something

mimi o kasanai　耳を貸さない

shut one's ears to, pay no attention to, disregard

miren ga aru　未練がある

feel regret, have a lingering affection for

mitsugo no tamashii hyaku made　三つ子の魂百まで

what is learned in the cradle is carried to the grave

mizu mo morasanu　水も漏らさぬ

airtight, tight security

mizu ni nagasu　水に流す

forgive and forget

mizu-irazu　水入らず

privately, alone, without outsiders

mochitsu-motaretsu　持ちつ持たれつ

two people helping each other out, give and take

monzen-barai　門前払い

refuse to see someone, shut the door on someone

mote amasu　持て余す

not know what to do with, be embarrassed by

muda-bone o oru　無駄骨を折る

waste one's efforts

muda-guchi o kiku　無駄口をきく

say useless things, talk idly

muna-sawagi ga suru　胸騒ぎがする

feel uneasy without a specific reason

mune o nade orosu　胸をなでおろす

feel relieved, be at ease

mura-hachibu　村八分

ostracism

muri nandai　無理難題

a completely unreasonable demand, impossible demand

mushi ga shiraseru　虫が知らせる

have a premonition or hunch

muyō no chōbutsu　無用の長物

useless and obstructive thing, something good for nothing

nagai me de miru　長い目で見る

take a long-term view, think of the future

nagai mono ni wa makarero　長い物には巻かれろ

if you can't beat them, join them, yield to the powerful

naga-mochi suru　長持ちする

last a long time

naijo no kō　内助の功

assistance of one's wife

nai mono nedari　無い物ねだり

asking for the moon

nai sode wa furenu　ない袖はふれぬ

one cannot give what one hasn't got, can't get blood from a stone

naki-neiri suru　泣き寝入りする

cry oneself to sleep, be compelled to accept, resign oneself to

nakittsura ni hachi　泣きっ面に蜂

misfortunes never come alone

nama-nurui　生温い

wishy-washy, lenient

namida-moroi　涙もろい

sentimental, easily moved to tears

nanakorobi-yaoki　七転び八起き

ups and downs of life

negattari-kanattari　願ったり叶ったり

just what one wants

ne ni motsu　根に持つ

hold a grudge

neko ni koban　猫に小判

like casting pearls before swine, waste something by giving it to someone
who doesn't appreciate it

neko no hitai　　猫の額
　　a narrow piece of land, tiny area

neko no te mo karitai hodo isogashii　　猫の手も借りたいほど忙しい
　　be very busy and shorthanded

nekonade-goe　　猫なで声
　　coaxing voice

ni no ashi o fumu　　二の足を踏む
　　hesitate to do, think twice

ni no ku ga tsugenai　　二の句がつげない
　　be struck dumb, be at a loss for a reply

nichijō sahanji　　日常茶飯事
　　an everyday affair, occurrence

nigiri-tsubusu　　握りつぶす
　　pigeonhole, ignore, not do anything about

nijū-dema　　二重手間
　　doing twice what could just as easily be done once

nijū jinkaku　　二重人格
　　split personality

nimai-jita　　二枚舌
　　double dealing

nisoku no waraji o haku　　二足のわらじをはく
　　pursue two objectives, have fingers in two pies

nodo kara te ga deru　　喉から手が出る
　　want something intensely

noren ni ude-oshi　　暖簾に腕押し
　　useless, like beating the air

nukeme ga nai　　抜け目がない
　　shrewd, cunning

ōbune ni notta tsumori　　大船に乗ったつもり
　　being completely free of worry and concern

ōde o furu　　大手を振る
　　walk with one's head held high, act with impunity

328

ōgesa　大げさ
　　exaggeration

o-kabu o torareru　お株を取られる
　　be outdone in one's own field

o-kabu o ubau　お株を奪う
　　beat someone at their own game

okado-chigai　お門違い
　　barking up the wrong tree

ōki na kao o suru　大きな顔をする
　　be arrogant

oku no te　奥の手
　　secrets, one's best cards

okuba ni mono ga hasamatta　奥歯に物が挟まった
　　talk as if one were concealing something

ōme ni miru　大目に見る
　　overlook someone's fault

omoi-chigai　思い違い
　　misunderstanding

omoi-yari no aru　思いやりのある
　　sympathetic, considerate

on ni kiseru　恩に着せる
　　expect something in return, demand gratitude

on o ada de kaesu　恩を仇で返す
　　bite the hand that feeds you

oni ni kanabō　鬼に金棒
　　immensely powerful

on-shirazu　恩知らず
　　ingratitude

oshidori fūfu　おしどり夫婦
　　a couple of lovebirds

o-takaku tomaru　お高くとまる
　　be stuck up, be supercilious, put on airs

o-tenkiya　　お天気屋

person whose temperament frequently changes

pekopeko suru　　ペコペコする

cringe to, kowtow

rinki ōhen　　臨機応変

adapting to particular circumstances

ryōte ni hana　　両手に花

having two beautiful persons or things

saishoku-kenbi　　才色兼備

having both brains and beauty

saki o yomu　　先を読む

plan ahead

sanbyōshi sorou　　三拍子そろう

be consummate, be ideal, be all-round

sandome no shōjiki　　三度目の正直

third time lucky, three's the charm

san'nin yoreba monju no chie　　三人寄れば文珠の知恵

two heads are better than one

sayū suru　　左右する

have something completely under one's control

seiten no hekireki　　青天の霹靂

a bolt out of the blue

sen'nyū kan　　先入観

preconceived ideas

sesuji ga samuku naru　　背筋が寒くなる

send chills up and down one's spine

shachihokobaru　　しゃちほこばる

be stiff and formal, assume a dignified air

shakushi jōgi de yaru　　杓子定規でやる

go by the book, stick fast to the rules

shibui kao　渋い顔
wry face, perplexed look

shidoro-modoro ni naru　しどろもどろになる
be thrown into confusion due to a lack of preparation

shifuku o koyasu　私腹をこやす
line one's own pocket, feather one's own nest

shikō sakugo　試行錯誤
trial and error

shina sadame suru　品定めする
size up, judge the merits

shinki itten　心機一転
turning over a new leaf, completely changing one's mind

shiran-puri　知らんぷり
feigned ignorance

shiri ni shikareru　尻に敷かれる
be tied to one's wife's apron strings, dominated by one's wife

shiroi me de miru　白い目で見る
look askance at, frown upon

shitta-kaburi o suru　知ったかぶりをする
pretend to know all the answers

shōgi-daoshi ni naru　将棋倒しになる
fall like dominoes, fall down one upon another

soroban ga awanai　ソロバンが合わない
not pay, not be financially worthwhile

soroban-dakai　ソロバン高い
think only of profits or one's own interests

suji o tōsu　筋を通す
act according to one's principles

sumi ni okenai　隅におけない
be sly, know a trick or two

sune-kajiri　脛かじり
a sponge, hanger-on

sushi-zume　すし詰め
　　packed like a can of sardines, jam-packed

tachi-uchi dekinai　太刀打ちできない
　　be so weak as to not provide any competition

taiki-bansei　大器晩成
　　great talents mature late, soon ripe soon rotten

taikoban o osu　太鼓判を押す
　　vouch for something or somebody

taka o kukuru　高をくくる
　　underestimate, take something lightly

takami no kenbutsu　高みの見物
　　standing by idly, unconcerned spectator

takane no hana　高嶺の花
　　beyond one's reach

takara no mochigusare　宝の持ち腐れ
　　a waste of talent, failing to use something useful

tama ni kizu　玉にきず
　　fly in the ointment

tanin gyōgi　他人行儀
　　standing on ceremony, acting distant and reserved

tanomi no tsuna　頼みの綱
　　one's only hope, one's last resort

tate ni toru　楯にとる
　　use something as an excuse, use on the strength of

te ga aku　手があく
　　be free, have time on one's hands

te mo ashi mo denai　手も足も出ない
　　fail inspite of giving one's best efforts

te ni amaru　手に余る
　　be beyond one's powers, be too much, be uncontrollable

te o ireru　手を入れる
　　retouch, rework

temochi-busata　手持ち無沙汰
  having time on one's hands and not knowing what to do with it

te-hodoki suru　手解きする
  teach the rudiments of a subject to someone

tōdai motokurashi　灯台もと暗し
  not seeing what is right in front of one's eyes

tohō ni kureru　途方に暮れる
  be puzzled as to what to do, be stumped

tōhon seisō　東奔西走
  be on the move, make oneself busy

tonbo-gaeri　とんぼ返り
  a quick trip

toriko ni naru　虜になる
  be enslaved, be enthralled with

udo no taiboku　ウドの大木
  clumsy fellow, big oaf

ukanu-kao　浮かぬ顔
  glum expression

ura-zukeru　裏付ける
  back up, support

uwa no sora　上の空
  be preoccupied, be absent-minded

uwasa o sureba kage　噂をすれば影
  speak of the devil

wara ni mo sugaru　ワラにもすがる
  be so desperate as to use any means, grab at straws

wari ga awanai　ワリが合わない
  not be worth the trouble

warikiru　割り切る
  have a positive and clear-cut solution to an issue

ya mo tate mo tamaranai　矢も楯もたまらない

　　be unable to contain oneself

ya no saisoku o suru　矢の催促をする

　　make an urgent request

yabure-kabure　破れかぶれ

　　feeling that one has nothing more to lose, self-abandonment

yakume o hatasu　役目を果たす

　　do one's job

yaridama ni ageru　槍玉にあげる

　　victimize, single out for criticism

yase-gaman　やせがまん

　　grin and bear it, endure for pride's sake

yasu-ukeai suru　安請け合いする

　　be too ready to make promises

yatsu-atari suru　八当たりする

　　snarl at the wrong person, take it out on an innocent person

yatsugi-baya ni　矢継ぎ早に

　　in rapid succession

yoko-michi e soreru　横道へそれる

　　deviate from, digress

yowa-ne o haku　弱音を吐く

　　feel sorry for oneself, give up easily, complain, whine

yowari-me ni tatari-me　弱り目にたたり目

　　things go from bad to worse

yūzū ga kikanai　融通がきかない

　　inflexible, rigid, inelastic

zakku-baran na　ざっくばらんな

　　straightforward, frank

zara ni aru　ザラにある

　　be very common and ordinary

zen wa isoge　善は急げ

　　don't delay in doing what is good